Ethnic Groups in Canada: Adaptations and Transitions

Ethnic Groups in Canada: Adaptations and Transitions

Edward N. Herberg,
University of Toronto

NELSON CANADA

©Nelson Canada,
A Division of International Thomson Limited,
1989

Published in 1989 by
Nelson Canada,
A Division of International Thomson Limited
1120 Birchmount Road
Scarborough, Ontario M1K 5G4

Canadian Cataloguing in Publication Data
Herberg, Edward N. (Edward Norman), 1934–
    Ethnic groups in Canada

Bibliography: p.
Includes index.
ISBN 0-17-603418-8

1. Minorities - Canada. 2. Canada - Foreign
population. 3. Ethnicity - Canada. I. Title.

FC104.H47 1989   305.8'00971   C88-0940919-0
F1035.A1H47 1989

Printed and bound in Canada

1   2   3   4   89   93   92   91   90

Contents

Preface

This book has been a long time in the making—a dozen years now. So many have contributed so much to it over the years that it is impossible to recall, let alone recognize each one. Even so, I must emphasize the importance of the writings of four of my colleagues in the University of Toronto's Department of Sociology: Raymond Breton, W.W. Isajiw, Warren Kalbach and Jeffrey Reitz. Their works have combined insightful, lucid theoretical innovations with empirical assessments that have proven to be exceptionally informative of ethnic community processes. Perhaps more than any others, their works illuminate the path of scholarship for others, like myself. I must also gratefully acknowledge the significant contribution by Leo Driedger in his prolific statistical and conceptual production. I have freely borrowed from his works for this book; one could ask for no better source for academic stimulation and satisfaction.

Over and above these traditional sources of colleagues in the discipline, I must recognize the constant and substantial debt I owe my spouse, Dorothy Chave Herberg, a renowned academic theorizer and researcher in complementary aspects of Canadian ethnicity and multiculturalism. The significance of my benefit from her daily insights and creativity in this field is great; she has helped to invigorate and inform my work. It is rare that both spousal and professional enrichments are combined in the same relationship.

The manuscript for this book would not have existed without the conscientiously intricate and extended efforts of Kerstin Aivasian; I am truly thankful for her careful industriousness. Finally, I stress the helpfulness of my students in ethnicity and race relations courses at Erindale College for their suggestions, critiques and, contributions to this work. It is in large measure both from and for them that this book is due.

Introduction

SURVEY OF THE TEXT

This is a book about Canada's ethnic, racial, and religious groups—their history in Canada; their adaptations to the changing Canadian society at large as well as altered conditions within their own communities; their past and present social organization and their advances. The book also looks at Canada itself, today, as an ethnically mixed society and what it might be like tomorrow. Scarcely anyone in Canada doubts that "ethnicity" is one of the major dimensions of our social organization. Some—myself included—believe that the significance of diverse cultural, racial, and religious characteristics and groups for Canadian social life has been increasing dramatically since the Second World War and will likely continue to gain importance in Canadian social dynamics.

Despite this, relatively little has been published about the history and transitions of Canadian ethnic groups into the 1980s. Reitz (1981) wrote a brief narrative about selected ethnicities, but this served essentially as an introduction to his nation-wide study of the place of four ethno-racial categories in the Canadian economy. Anderson and Frideres' (1981) work had some historical content, but this was, understandably, neither complete nor detailed, since their primary interest was not history, but theory about ethnic groups. And while there have been many histories of various individual ethno-racial-religious groups in Canada, these, of necessity, rarely included comparisons of the individual group with other ethnicities, especially from an historical-developmental perspective. What has long been needed is work that both presents information on multiple ethno-racial-religious groups from as far back as possible and traces their ethnic lives in Canada, in as many dimensions as possible, up to the present. This complex yet essential task is begun here in this text.

The origins of this work are both pragmatic and philosophical.

First, teaching about Canadian ethnicities, races, and religions over the years, I despaired at the lack of any text that systematically traced change in ethnic-group characteristics and social organization—a major handicap to understanding ethnicity in Canada. Second, to appreciate the present and to foresee the future, we must become familiar with the past—as much in the subject of ethnic studies as in any other. The absence of comparable historical information on the variety of Canadian ethnic groups, therefore, was a serious defect that I finally determined to rectify.

Where does one begin?

The major and best source for long-range historical ethnic data in Canada are the censuses taken every ten years from 1871 on. In this, we are fortunate, because ethnic "origin" and religion have been consistent (if not always strictly comparable) foci for the 12 decennial censuses since 1871. For at least the last 50 years, information beyond mere ethnic- or religious-group numbers has also been collected. What the present book provides are data and their interpretation on a wide variety of ethnically-related patterns, as reflected in the censuses covering over a century of change. This permits the depiction of three things: (1) how Canada itself has altered ethnically; (2) shifts in the numbers and distributions of specific ethno-racial-religious groups in Canada; and (3) how Canadian ethnicities have adapted to life in Canada, in terms of their social organization and their cultural practices. Certainly, only selected aspects of ethnic life in Canada can be covered, since the censuses themselves have always been selective in what ethnic information was collected. Even so, a remarkably detailed picture of Canadian ethnicities is made available to us via the census data.

The structure of this book blends social theory with statistical depiction of ethnic-group life and transition within the Canadian context and tries to interpret those changes. The conceptual discussion is highly personal; however, the basic data are present, so that readers can decide for themselves both the appropriateness of my conclusions and interpretations, and in what direction each ethno-racial-religious group is going today.

This book has three parts: Ethnic Groups and Canada, Ethnocultural Maintenance in Canada, and The Adaptations of Ethnic Groups in Canada.

Part 1, Chapter 1 examines the different meanings of "ethnicity" in Canada, along with the processes of ethnic adaptation, integration, and assimilation; this is done from a conceptual perspective. The alternative bases of ethnic-group cohesion and identity are sketched out, and the question of why ethnic culture and identity continue to be sustained in Canada is addressed. Chapter 2 surveys the peoples of Canada and the increasing diversity of the Canadian population by virtue of the progressively greater presence of "non-charter" or "minority" groups. The gender distributions in each group and the extents of urban residence are also inspected. Part 1 concludes by focusing on immigration—for Canada as a whole and for each ethnicity in particular (Chapter 3).

Part 2 deals with ethno-cultural maintenance in Canada. It begins with a general theory of ethnic-group cultural maintenance (Chapter 4). Chapter 5 discusses ethnic language retention and use. Chapter 6 continues with a survey of ethnic residential patterns—regionally and within selected cities. Chapter 7 goes on to examine the religious affiliations of each ethno-racial group. Chapter 8 looks at ethnic marriage and families: first, at the institution of intra-ethnicity marriage (endogamy) and second, at fertility and family size within ethnicities over the last half-century or so. Part 2 concludes with a brief and as yet tentative exploration, in Chapter 9, of institutional completeness—the variety and frequency of formal organizations developed by and within the ethnic communities.

In Part 3 the analysis is narrowed to temporal adaptation patterns. Chapter 10 presents some general theories of ethnic-group adaptation, and then, in Chapter 11, we are given a framework for Dorothy Herberg's analysis of the acculturative experiences of individuals and ethnicities. Finally, in Chapter 12, the changes in indicators of ethnic cohesion are charted, noting the comparative status for each of the various ethnicities in the social transition to the present; this is complemented by an inspection of the intra-ethnicity patterns of ethnic cohesion for the various ethnic indicators.

As noted, the data reported here come principally from the censuses of Canada, begun in 1871 and taken every ten years thereafter, supplemented, at some points, by information from earlier censuses conducted in the separate provinces and by information from other studies of census data. For the topic of institutional completeness, on which the censuses do not inform, but which comprises an essential aspect of ethnic social organization, the author has drawn upon a variety of other sources. Conspicuous among these are the reports of original research conducted by my students in their own ethno-racial-religious communities.

In relying so greatly upon one source of information—Canadian census data—we must naturally have concern for the reliability and validity of these data, especially with regard to "ethnic origin." Driedger, Thaker and Currie (1982) summarized the main issues concerning the confidence with which we can accept such data and reviewed the main questions as to their interpretation. These investigators came to the same conclusion as almost everyone else who has dealt with this question: both the reliability and the validity are quite acceptably high, and the data of the last 12 censuses comprise the best source for research on ethnicity with a macroscopic intent.

Even so, the absolute values of the statistics analyzed here should be accepted with a modicum of caution—a caution that can appropriately be directed at all research statistics.

COLLECTING STATISTICS

Any adequate description of the shifting patterns of cultural cohesion among Canadian ethno-racial groups requires the use of statistics. Certainly, it would be possible to analyze these groups without the use of numerical data; but such a work would be an impoverished one—unsatisfying and ineffective as a learning resource. Any work of this kind that lacked statistics entirely would fail to fulfill the requirements of social analysis in two ways.

First, no reader has to accept, without evidence and simply on the writer's authority that something is the way the author says it is. By presenting the statistical data upon which the narrative of social patterns was based, the text gives to each reader the opportunity to ascertain, independently, the fall of a trend, and to make up his or her own mind about what has happened to whom. The author's narrative is a guide, not the sole authority for the reader's own perception and acquisition of knowledge.

Second, it is not unusual for a researcher to be selective, to emphasize only those topics on which he or she wishes particularly to focus. This means that many things implicit in a set of statistics will not be dealt with: facets of a subject the writer did not wish to write about, was unable to cover because of space or time limitations, or did not even perceive as being present. In a work such as this present one in which many subcategories are inspected (multiple ethno-racial-religious groups, for instance), it is not possible to give complete verbal descriptions of the patterns existing for each and every subcategory, despite the fact that some readers may wish just that. Other readers will want to trace in detail the information regarding one or more particular ethnic groups—perhaps their own—that the author did not or could not do in the desired detail. The presence of statistical tables in the text provides for such contingencies.

There are, then, important reasons for including statistical content, especially when it is this kind of information that serves as the source for the author's description and explanation. Readers are enabled to draw their own independent conclusions and to focus on elements of special interest to them. Further, it is not uncommon for readers to use reported statistics for purposes or in ways different from those of the original writer. The inclusion of the statistical material permits this further pursuit of social knowledge independently of the perspective of the writer.

Locating Statistics

One of the most difficult tasks in developing an adequate analysis of a topic is that of locating the statistical base information. With regard to the cultural cohesion of Canadian ethnicities generally, and the specific cohesion mechanisms inspected here, there is one central source of statistics, the *published reports of the Canadian censuses* between 1871 and 1986. "This is the most consistent objective longitudinal ethnic data we can get" (Driedger et al., 1982:). It must be understood, though, that only selected ethnic-group phenomena are covered in the censuses: number of persons in each ethno-racial-religious category in each political jurisdiction of Canada; possession of the ethnic "Mother Tongue" (and, since 1971, use of that language as the usual medium of communication in the home); ethnic identity of spouses; religious memberships within each ethnicity; fertility and related data for selected ethno-racial and religious groups; educational, occupational distributions and income figures for many ethnic categories. For much, even most of these, statistics are available in each census report since 1921 or 1931.

Increasingly varied kinds of information are available in the more recent reports, especially since the 1931 census. An immense amount of base data—the numerical counts of Canadians in different ethno-demographic categories—are contained in the published volumes of the censuses of Canada. These publications are easily accessible in a variety of places: large public libraries or reference rooms have at least the more recent census reports and perhaps all reports since 1871; university libraries and regional offices of Statistics Canada (StatsCan) should have complete series of the published reports. In some of these places, some of the reports (especially those for the earlier censuses) will be on microfilm-microfiche. Data from the pre-Confederation censuses on parts of what is now Canada are reported in Volumes 4 and 5 of the 1870–1871 census. These include information from the censuses of the British colonial regime, and from the many and copious censuses conducted in New France (Quebec) from 1608 to 1765.

There are additional sources of census statistics—counts of people—available in a variety of forms. Certain types of information for some of the census years (especially before 1961), not included in the published volumes, can be had in *special bulletins* issued from time to time and available in booklet form or on microfilm in StatsCan offices. Each office has a listing of the subjects of the bulletins and their contents held in their office files. Some of these cover the special analyses of regional or city populations that were not covered in the published volumes, while others give more detailed analyses than are typical of that years' census analyses published in the reports. Similarly, beginning with the 1971 census, there are many other useful population counts not included in the published census volumes, available as *microfilm or microfiche data reports* at StatsCan offices. Here, too, each office has a list of what they have in this micro-form.

Another source of published statistics is the specialized work of other researchers, using census data, who report their results in *books, monographs, and journal articles.* Among the first two—books and monographs—are some published directly by Statistics Canada or its predecessor the Dominion Bureau of Statistics; these include many monographs published as addenda to the regular census volumes. There are also many commercially-published works based on and reporting census data. (Perhaps the best of these—in terms of presenting a generalized demographic picture of Canada past and recent—was the second edition (1979) of Kalbach and McVey's

The Demographic Bases of Canadian Society.) Prudent social investigators will try to keep current with all of these, perhaps recording author(s), titles, publishers, dates, and summaries of contents on cards to add to their resource files. Many of these academic studies are on specialized ethnic phenomena and can focus on exactly, or close to, a topic of particular interest to a student or non-academic reader.

Other sources for statistics on Canadian ethno-racial-religious groups exist, two of them connected directly to the census. First, many Canadian universities contain a unit that possesses what is termed a *Public Use Sample* of census data on individuals or families, for the use of university people (faculty and students) and sometimes interested members of the general public. Arrangements for access to this sample of the census must be made through the office or person in each university responsible for it. Using the Public Use Sample, special analyses of aspects not contained in the published census volumes can be conducted.

Second, StatsCan, which is responsible for conducting and administering the census and its reports and data, will conduct *specialized analyses tailored to a customer's wants* on any aspect of the census data.* StatsCan officials in Ottawa have also reported that any of these customized analyses from the 1981 or subsequent censuses are now considered public property, and copies of the data output on a specialized part are available for the cost of duplicating the original computer output sheets. Information on whether a particular topic has had a specialized analysis conducted is available at StatsCan's central office in Ottawa, and perhaps through their regional offices as well.

Third, many *provincial ministries* with jurisdiction over ethno-racial-religious groups and multiculturalism also maintain data banks and other informational sources about the ethnic groups in their provinces. Those that maintain a statistical data bank have the raw data from the Canadian Census on the province itself and its groups in addition to any other material the provincial authority may have assembled. Many of these provincial offices can provide localized analyses on ethnically-related content. Contact with the

---

*The Census Information Services Office of StatsCan (Ottawa, Ontario K1A 0T7; phone (613) 996-5254) can provide specifics for this service.

particular provincial ministry department, if it exists in the reader's province, will provide information on the exact services available.

The final source of statistics on Canada's ethnic groups is *original research* conducted largely by academics. Most universities have researchers who have carried out diverse national or regional studies and projects about ethnicity and ethnic groups. These people are sometimes difficult to locate, since few universities (or anyone else) maintain a good register of such original research. Sometimes the only way to discover some of the original research that exists is to inquire directly from a university researcher-professor with recognized expertise in ethnicity/multiculturalism. Hints as to who these persons are may be culled from an examination of pertinent periodicals, such as *Canadian Ethnic Studies*, *The Canadian Review of Sociology and Anthropology*, *The Canadian Journal of Sociology*, and the many regional scholarly and general interest journals that include or specialize in ethnicity/multiculturalism. The research/reference librarian in the reader's public library will be helpful here.

Original research may also be available from *ethnic-group organizations*, who gather certain kinds of statistics for their own internal purposes and/or for use in public representations. The sole way to determine what, if anything of this kind exists, is to initiate direct contact with prominent members of the ethnic group, with the offices/officers of ethnic organizations, and others knowledgeable about that or other groups.

Lastly, one should not forget *university students* as a source of statistical and other information about one or more ethnicities. Having access to more numerous and more specialized sources than people outside post-secondary facilities, students in courses on introductory sociology, ethnicity, race relations, multiculturalism, Canadian mosaic, Canadian society, history, urban geography, anthropology and others frequently write course papers that would be of interest beyond the walls of the school. Communication with professors can initiate searches for such material.

USING STATISTICS

Comparability of Data

There are problems in comparability of definitions of each of these variables and also in which ethnic, racial or religious categories are covered in each particular published population count. In my opinion, the degree of comparability is not so variant that it seriously interferes with the use of census statistics relating to a particular ethnic factor. The first of these several problems in comparability relates to the slightly *differing definitions* of ethnic-group identities and of other factors over the decades. Recourse to the sociological literature about this and to the specification of definitions in the special section of each census report or volume in a particular year's report, compared to definitions in earlier/later years will enable anyone to determine how consistently the variable was defined in different census years. Referring solely to the ethnic-group labels, for instance, the Scandinavian label used in more recent censuses combines under that collective name the groups of early censuses separately identified as the Danish, Icelandic, Norwegian and Swedish. A second similar problem is that slightly *different ethnic categories are referred to for different variables* in the census reports: Pacific Islanders as a label versus the Filipinos, a subgroup identity; Asians versus Chinese (or Chinese and Japanese together); Native Peoples versus Indians (or Indians and Inuit); Indochinese versus Vietnamese, and so on.

A third difficulty is encountered when one is collecting data for a particular community or set of communities—*the level of community can vary across different variables or census years*, between the city unit alone, the metropolitan political unit, the Census Metropolitan Area (CMA) designation of StatsCan including towns and cities adjacent to but not in the metro jurisdiction, and Census Economic Area, bigger still than a CMA. Fourth, using census data over multiple census years, one soon realizes that there has been arbitrarily *irregular coverage of which particular groups are analyzed in different years*. Usually there is a core of the same groups covered in the published reports for different years, but even one or two of these may not have been included in particular population counts for certain subjects. For such irregularities in the 1971 or subsequent censuses, the missing groups may have been included in special complete microfiche statistics located in regional offices of StatsCan.

Finally, with respect to immigration following the Second World War, especially after the Immigration Act of 1968, certain ethno-racial-religious groups acquired many new members, so that by the next census, those groups were deemed to have accumulated sufficient additional membership to then be *newly identified as a separate ethnic category*. Beginning with the 1971 census, there have been perhaps scores of such "new" groups (compared to pre-1971 census listings), including Arabic, Filipino, Indochinese, Islamic, Indo-Pakistani, Korean, Latin American, Portuguese, and Sikh. Unfortunately, there are usually no data on such "new" groups or their ethnic cohesion before 1981 or 1971. True, in the classic analyses in the 1931 census volumes and monographs, some of the "new" ethnicities or religions were listed, but not in the intervening years afterward. And, until StatsCan conducts retrospective counts from the original census data-collection forms, there will be no earlier information available on these groups. The sole source for information on the earlier years for these groups will be the representatives of ethnic groups or academic researchers. These problems in comparability do not necessarily prevent the collection and manipulation of statistics from the Canadian censuses, as long as precautions are taken, and warnings made about any barriers to comparability.

Abstracting Census Data

Most of the Canadian census data is in "raw" counts of Canadians in various categories. Rarely are percentages or other statistical indices already calculated and reported in the published volumes. Collecting statistics from the censuses means, in practice, that the individual must first locate the specific population counts covering the ethnic-group aspect being investigated in the particular census volume in each year in which one is interested. The desired statistic(s) must then be recorded for each census year by the researcher, and whatever calculations desired made, to transform population counts into measures that are more informative about ethnic-group dynamics. This usually means the calculation of percentages, arithmetic means, selected rates/ratios, and the like—a process that can be tedious and time-consuming.* What results, however, can be very informative time series on the group(s) in which one is interested—valuable not only to the individual who conducted the research but to many others with similar interests.

---

*This book required 11 years of data abstraction from the censuses and transformation into more meaningful measures.

This kind of do-it-yourself ethnicity research can be completed by virtually anyone interested in selected aspects of ethno-racial-religious groups in Canada at any level of community. Along with patience and a willingness to be exact and conscientious, one needs time; access to a library or StatsCan office containing census reports; pencil and pads, and a calculator that will add, subtract, multiply, divide, calculate percentages, and store in memory. While sometimes boring, and/or exasperating in maintaining exactitude over long periods, the process of collecting and manipulating statistics can also be satisfying and exciting for even, or especially, the newcomer.

Using Statistics as a Consumer

It is difficult for one person to tell another how to use statistics they are inspecting because each one seeks and derives different things from the same figures, charts, or whatever. The statistics are presented to convey factual information. What the writer seeks to communicate—via a numerical medium—is the state or condition of a people, a group, or a community. What the writer proffers and what the reader receives is usually a pattern of being or of change, the latter obtaining when a time series of statistics is reported, as is the case so frequently in this book.

A reader can first ascertain what the main trend(s) seem to be, by focusing on increases or decreases in the values of the statistics within and between analytical categories. Such analytical categories can be each ethnic group at different dates or between different ethnicities at the same time or over time. Probably, any statistical array has more meaning for a reader if he or she inspects the data as soon as they are referred to in the text, before the writer gives his or her own interpretation of those statistics. The reader can thereby derive an independent understanding of the pattern(s) implicit in the figures, and compare that with what the researcher has to say about the same data.

The reader should aim to obtain (and the writer to report) the central patterns that exist, especially if comparisons are made between different factors or "controls." One dimension of this is to inspect a table or chart for the degree and direction of variation, or change within an ethnic group over time. A second dimension is to ascertain differences attributable to a control variable: e.g., urban versus rural, generation in Canada, gender. A third dimension is to focus on the differences between different ethnic categories, British versus Asian versus Jewish, and so on. Just because these levels of analysis are mentioned separately does not mean that the interpretation of a statistical table or chart must be so detached. The skill to derive a multifaceted, integrated analysis of a statistical array can come fairly soon with experience, so that with opportunity and interested perseverance, anyone can become relatively expert at deriving multiple meanings from even the most complex set of statistics.

When the statistics are percentages, a good rule of thumb for assessing the magnitude of differences is that a variation of at least 5% is worthwhile considering as "significant," as long as the number of people represented by the statistics is at least 50 to 100 individuals. To a certain extent, the larger the number of people represented by the percentages, the greater is one's confidence that a 5% or more difference represents a "real" difference, although when the base number covered gets beyond 1000 one can be sure that, in at least 95% of the comparisons, a 5% or more difference is reflecting a "true" difference. With variation more than 5% between categories (ethnicities, gender, generation in Canada, years, rural-urban, etc.), one can have increased confidence that a significant variation has been revealed by the statistics. In some kinds of reports, the author employs particular formulas that test whether any differences observed can be considered great enough to be non-random variations, that is, to be "statistically significant" differences. Often, though, and in this book, few statistical tests of differences are calculated, because the purpose is more one of describing group patterns than of probing the surety of the degree of difference.

While the analysis of statistical data may require some getting used to for some readers, those who can themselves "read" a table or chart for the patterns of difference and change are considerably ahead of those who must rely solely on the author's perceptions, and research preferences. In a very real sense, then, the readers of a work containing statistics, should not be passive consumers, satisfied with what the author writes and reliant on the author's predilections alone, but active participants through development and use of their own analytical capabilities. Using statistics to derive an understanding about something should be an active process—

almost a proactive one. When the statistics are in a book or journal article, the reader should construct an interactive process of analysis and interpretation with the writer, an alliance of sorts, in which a reader has almost as much responsibility as the author to ascertain the trend and meaning of the figures presented. The ultimate quest here is to establish what the states of being are today, how and why they differ from patterns of the past, and what this bodes for the future. In this, the reader has as active a role to play as the writer: to interpret, to understand and project, to confirm, and especially to dissent, if that is where the reader's ability to analyze statistics leads.

ETHNIC GROUPS AND CANADA

INTRODUCTION

It's a cliché today to observe that, with the exception of the Indians and Inuit, all Canadians are, from one perspective or another, immigrants to this land. The empirical verification of this fact, however, is not on the agenda of this first part of our text. Instead, the following three chapters examine—from different perspectives—the conceptual and empirical social organizational bases of ethno-racial-religious groups in Canada.

In Chapter 1, we look first at the origins of Canadian ethnicity, with emphasis upon the alternative criteria by which an "ethnic group" can be variously defined. Also involved here is the nature of the processes of adapting to life in Canada: cultural adaptation, integration and assimilation. These processes were experienced both by peoples coming from outside Canada at any given time and by Canadian- and foreign-born alike experiencing the alterations in the social structure and social fabric of Canadian society over the last century and more.

Intimately related to ethno-cultural adaptive processes are the relative conditions of Canadian pluralism over the decades—what today is usually called "multiculturalism." We question whether pluralism—even if unrecognized or unlegitimated—is a long-established or a recent phenomenon. We find that it has existed in Canada at least since the permanent presence of the European colonial peoples on Canadian soil, even if it achieved legitimacy only after the Second-World-War, perhaps as late as 1971.

The concept linking the sociological nature of ethnicity and

Canadian pluralism/multiculturalism is a sense of ethnic-group identity. Therefore, we examine just what ethnic-group identity may be, what its sources are, and the different ways of defining ethnic-group identity used by Canadians. This venture of building sociological theory about ethnic groups concludes Chapter 1.

With that as conceptual foundation, Chapter 2 sets out an empirical analysis of the peoples of Canada—their arrival and their increasing variety in culture, race, and religion—from before Confederation through to 1981. To understand the dynamics of ethnic social organization, we must first be aware of the change in the ethnic composition of the Canadian population. We must also appreciate the shift, over time, in urban-rural distribution within each of the ethnicities, along with the relative proportion of the genders in each group (i.e., the Gender Ratio).

Given the importance of immigration for the growth of the Canadian population, immigration patterns comprise another introductory dimension in outlining the nature of ethnic groups in Canada. This theme is taken up in Chapter 3 where we survey the several "waves" of immigration that peopled first the Atlantic areas through to Ontario, then the land from the Prairies to the Pacific Ocean, and subsequently created the urban dominance that emerged from the rural frontiers. What groups dominated the earlier flow of immigrants? When did each group arrive in Canada? Who are the most recent groups to come here? These are among the questions answered and the patterns uncovered in the concluding chapter of Part 1.

## CHAPTER 1

The Nature of Ethnic Groups

INTRODUCTION: DEFINING ETHNICITY

"Ethnicity" and "ethnic group," as terms denoting a particular ascriptive characteristic of a certain aggregate or collectivity of persons, have been, and continue to be, applied in various ways, depending on whether the writer's purpose was taxonomy (as in listing the various "ethnic groups" in Canada) or analyzing the dynamic quality, structure or process of those defined ethnically. This book, uses the term to include people who have been counted, and/or who have counted themselves, as belonging to a particular group, usually by birth and by practices and perceptions. Generally, the underlying criterion used here to place people in one "ethnic group" rather than another was their having recorded themselves as "belonging" to that category, based on their perception of their origins. But, as we shall see, even this simple picking out of one label can be "unpacked" to uncover a variety of bases for determining the social construction of ethnicity in Canada and how it has altered over the decades.

Indeed, in this work, both race and religion are included under the "ethnicity" rubric as per Isajiw, (1979), giving rise to the term, "ethno-racial-religious group" as a more accurate label—more accurate because race or religion as well as national origin are important, even crucial, organizing principles for "ethnic" communities in Canada. For purposes of simplicity, however, the more common "ethnic group" or "ethnicity" is usually employed.

The definitional issue is hardly that simple, however, for there is a variety of factors that enter into the concept of "ethnicity" in the

Canadian context, and a multiplicity of processes that together appear to comprise "ethnicity" here. There are, first of all, the demographic processes that individuals have created as manifestations of their personal or collective sense of belonging to a particular ethnic group. First in mind here are such indices as the perhaps artificial ethnic, religious or racial ways by which Canadians have identified themselves each ten years since 1871 for the Canadian Census. There are, as well, the experiential definitions of ethnicity arising from use of a heritage language as their first language—their "Mother Tongue"—or from marriage within the same ethnic or religious group (endogamy) and so on. The various aspects of ethnicity may bring into question the usual sociological definitions of "ethnicity" in Canada and demonstrate how varied on the individual and collective levels are the behavioural bases of ethnicity.

Underlying all of the analyses to come is the concept of "ethnic differentiation": the process whereby ethnicities have adapted to changes in their demography and to being in Canada, and have, as a consequence, acquired a pattern of characteristics that makes each ethnicity today *unique* in form, process, and practice. Each of these should be perceived as a continuum, theoretically ranging from complete ethnic maintenance to total loss of the ethnic property (e.g., 100% language retention to 0% language retention). The patterns by which specific ethnic properties or processes have been maintained can be considered as reflecting the general pattern of ethnic differentiation within that ethno-racial-religious entity. It will remain an empirical question throughout this work whether there seems to be a general, overarching pattern of ethnic differentiation in Canada—whether the fact of living in Canada has determined for its ethnic groups a characteristic pattern of transition in the strength and/or nature of its "ethnic" character. In any case, differentiation within an ethnic group reflects the process of that particular group's adaptive social organization in Canada, and whatever overall pattern of ethnic differentiation that emerges represents the outcome of all Canadian ethnic-group cultural transitions.

From another perspective, each ethnic group should be considered as but one "actor" in defining the way ethnicity—as a socially "real" phenomenon—affects the social organization of the Canadian society. From this perspective, the essential questions are how

Canada has changed, and how ethnicity/ethnic groups figure in the social organization of Canada. So, the "nature of ethnic groups" in Canada will be inspected from three separate viewpoints: (1) the evolution of the social organization of each particular ethno-racial-religious entity, (2) the evolution of "ethnicity" in Canada and the social organization of "ethnicity" here, and (3) the function "ethnicity" has had in Canadian society. In each of these there is an underlying assumption of social evolution: that what was, differs from what is (and what is differs from what will be). The nature of ethnic groups, then, is assumed to have altered; what the analyses will do is to inform on how the various groups have changed in their "ethnicity."

THE SOCIAL FOUNDATIONS OF ETHNICITY

If one accepts the premise (originally from Durkheim) that a society, or group in a society, comprised of a multitude of unorganized, isolated or alienated individuals constitutes a veritable sociological monstrosity, one is led to the conclusion that structures mediating between individuals and the larger community or society are necessary to prevent isolation, anomie or anarchy. Rubin (1975) has argued that if a given social organization (not necessarily a "formal" organization) is to serve as an effective bonding force, then it must relate to an aggregate of persons at least in ways that unite them within a social boundary for reasons greater than mere personal interest. Further, such a social organization must incorporate a membership sufficient in size (Rubin characterizes this as "intermediate" size) to remain viable. One such form of social organization in Canada is "ethnicity."

Membership in an ethnic group, even—or especially—in urban, post-industrial societies, is a rather pure form of Gemeinschaft: a form of social organization in which individuals relate to one another through interactional intimacy. An ethnic collectivity can also be seen as an example of Hall's "high context" culture in which social transactions are based on (1) the physical context in which the actors find themselves and/or (2) in the internalized social-interactional meanings shared by the actors, rather than in the coded, explicit, "transmitted" words or actions of the parties (Hall, 1976:91). Members of an ethnic group, then, can be viewed as a solidary unit, acting together, and exercising sanctions concerning attitudes and acts. This is because they are endowed with a homogeneous cultural heritage containing shared values and expectations that the members seek to preserve.

Francis (1947) saw the ethnic group ideally as possessing a distinctive "Kultur"—folkways, mores, and arts—in combination with a common language and style of communication, endogamy and awareness of kinship lines, and a common history. Francis recognized, however, that possession of only some of these properties could still enable a collectivity to consider themselves and be considered by others as an "ethnic group." Thus, we cannot define ethnic groups strictly, as Francis observed, because of their dynamic character." Similarly, Delos (1944:93) saw ethnic groups as founded on a sense of cultural coherence with distinct values, sources of solidarity, and loyalties—what he termed a "community of conscience." In more recent work by Francis (1976:382), the same thing was pointed to: ethnicity refers to the fact that a relatively large number of people are socially defined as belonging together because (1) of their belief in a common ancestry, and (2) the consequent sense of their common identity and shared sentiments of being a community.

Thus, similarities to each other in ancestry, values, norms, and cultural practice are essential components of the nature of ethnicity. Isajiw, however, reminded us that it is not only shared characteristics upon which "ethnicity" is based, but also upon differences in attributes from others in the city, province or nation. The nature of ethnicity, therefore, depends, in part, on the extent to which persons possess particular characteristics that are "neither duplicated nor resembled in another group, *even if* some other attributes are the same or similar" to those in other groups (Isajiw, 1980). The similarity of ethnic-group members to each other and their dissimilarity to other people or groups, however, is not dependent upon the maintenance in all their purity of ethnic attributes brought from the country of origin. Even under conditions of partial acculturation to the host society, dissolution of an ethnic collectivity need not occur. In fact, an acculturated condition (or more precisely, an adapted condition) may actually help to maintain the ethnicity, as long as the traits adopted from the host culture are accepted and shared collectively by group members (Francis, 1976:400). Francis' conception of the conditions for ethnic-group maintenance in a host society like Canada included: ensuring communications with the society of origin; an elastic economic and institutional framework in the host society that enables the accommodation of ethnic-group members in one or more localities; and provisions in the host society that permit expression of distinctive cultural forms, values, and patterns of behaviour.

Francis went on to observe that members of ethnic groups in industrialized host nations are not always concerned with cultural maintenance within the group. Immigrant members of the ethnicity, particularly, may tend to emphasize—as one component of their group culture in the host society—the prevention of unequal treatment of group members (discrimination), rather than the preservation and advancement of their ethnic collectivity (protection) (Francis, 1976:392–398). Indeed, provisions for preventing discrimination, in effect, legitimize the ethnically/racially/religiously plural composition of nations, such as Canada, that have experienced important development through immigration.

It is, of course, an empirical question as to the degree of emphasis that members of a group can place on achieving equality with other members of the society at the expense of maintaining ethnic separation and distinctiveness.

In this, it is essential to distinguish the different concepts that describe the processes of cultural transition within a group vis-a-vis other members of the city or society. In this book, the terms "transition" and "adaptation" mean that an ethnic group has experienced, or has purposefully orchestrated a course of change in its cultural attributes and its processes of cultural maintenance, becoming a culturally different entity within the Canadian context. In part, "adaptation" implies "acculturation"—the taking on of some of the traits of the host society/culture—but an ethnicity can also experience a transition to patterns of ethnic culture that are at once different from the original immigrant culture (or that of more recent immigrants of the ethnicity) as well as from the "dominant" culture (British and/or French in Canada).

Theoretically, the outcomes of the adaptive process for each particular ethnicity, can be located on a continuum of cultural transition, ranging from ethnic-group separation at one end to assimilation at the other. Ethnic-group "separation" here means the development and maintenance of cultural boundaries and mechanisms that aim at retaining as much social and/or physical distance as possible between ethnic-group members and others in

Canada: the past condition of the visible minorities in this country (Blacks, Chinese, East Indians, Japanese, Native Peoples, for instance) is a prime example of involuntary separation (segregation) that, at least in part, bears on the nature of these ethnicities today. The well-documented isolation of Mennonites-Hutterites from others is an excellent instance of voluntary ethnic-group separation. Today, it may not be uncommon for certain ethnic groups, or segments of their memberships, to voluntarily seek ethnic separation in selected ethnic functions (e.g., intra-group marriage, or residential exclusiveness). Breton used the term "ethnic enclosure" to denote this state—successfully establishing and maintaining a set of social boundaries around the group and interactions within it to sustain the group's existence (Breton, 1978a).

"Assimilation," at the opposite end of the continuum, means the process whereby members of an ethnicity take on and celebrate the cultural attributes of another group, often the "dominant" group, and, in this, abandon the values, attitudes, expectations, and/or practices of their original heritage. Any or all of the forms of the original ethnic culture may be discontinued, either through the dominant culture's overwhelming the minority, or through a voluntary, even consciously planned substitution of cultures.

Another dimension of the adaptive process for Canadian ethno-racial-religious groups is "integration," which should not, to my way of thinking, be linked with the ethnic-separation/ethnic-assimilation continuum. As it is used here, "integration" involves the time-limited, temporary or irregular participation by members of an ethnicity in the institutions of the entire city or society or other groups, but without any necessary implication that the members' loyalty toward or practice of the group's culture is endangered. What I have in mind here are such things as are either mandated by law or impractical to avoid by most ethnicities in most locales: formal education of ethnic youth in the "public" (including religiously "separate") schools; participation in local, provincial or federal politics; participation in the economy, and so on.

Kallen (1982:147–156) has included what I term "integration" as a form of what she calls "assimilation," lending an unnecessary touch of overlapping ambiguity to concepts that refer to quite different processes and outcomes. Even so, she went on to amplify the different contexts of integration—as others had done previously: those of *structural integration*, *cultural integration*, and *personal integration*. Structural integration refers to ethnic group members' participation in the basic institutional, formal organizational structures of the city, such as education and the economy. Cultural integration involves participation in the cultural activities of other ethnicities, or of the city as a whole (if a city can be considered to possess its own culture, separate from that of its constituent groups). Finally, personal integration is individual participation in the activities of another group, including, Kallen claimed (1981:149), intermarriage (exogamy). While the last aspect presents a conceptual problem, it is useful at least to the extent that the idea of personal integration suggests that individuals can rather intimately integrate their activities into those of groups outside the ethnic community without necessarily forsaking their own cultural heritage.

Certainly, the retention of the group's cultural autonomy is readily evident for Kallen's structural integration, perhaps a little less evident for her cultural integration, and quite questionable for personal integration. For example, if many members of one or more particular ethnicities participate on a regular and frequent basis in the cultural activities of another group, especially that of the "dominant" group in the city, then it becomes a serious issue as to whether that "minority" culture can endure. Even more critically, if one considers exogamy as "integration"—as Kallen does—it becomes impossible to differentiate between the situations of participating without abandoning one's ethnic culture from those of assimilation, since exogamy is as much a collective concern as it is a "personal" act. Beyond this, it would also seem that by including exogamy in "integration" the whole sense of "integration" as a time-limited temporary, or irregular participation outside the ethnic community boundaries is lost. Therefore, it would seem conceptually clearer to distinguish the integrative process from that of the separation/assimilation continuum, at least until further research firmly establishes that *any* "integration" by members of an ethnic group invariably leads to partial assimilation, or whether the outcome might be better characterized as ethnic "retention" in spite of integrative participation.

To sum up this conceptually ambiguous issue, in this work, "integration" is considered to be a phenomenon different from the ethnocultural separation-assimilation dimension, carrying no implications one way or the other regarding cultural retention. Indeed, a theoretical case can be made that, except for certain groups whose separation from other ethnicities is based on their perception that urban industrialism and its value requisites are antithetical to their culture (here the Mennonite-Hutterites and probably the Native Peoples are the best exemplars), integration is likely practised by members of every Canadian ethno-racial-religious group. Indeed, it is all but inevitable in some form or fashion. The issue, then, is to estimate the extent of integration and assess the degree to which integration results in assimilation. While we will have no index of integration, this will be an underlying concern in the consideration of the nature of ethnicity in Canada and how it has changed, and of how the social organization of ethnic groups in Canada has evolved along the dimension of separation/assimilation.

In any case, the social foundations for the nature of ethnicity in Canada can be seen as a tension between maintaining the sense of common identity and heritage (involving the celebrations of each unique "ethnoculture" by its members) on the one side and, on the other, the need to participate in selected arenas of social-role conduct outside the boundaries of the ethno-racial-religious community. Since this is most properly conceptualized as a process unfolding over the last century or more, the investigation of the nature of ethnic groups and their social foundations can be best approached through considering these questions in terms of ethnic transition. Ethnic transition has meant not only the internally induced adaptations of ethnocultural patterns by different ethnic groups—and different patterns, likely, in different locales within the same ethnic groups—but also the alteration of ethnic communities to adjust to the changing conditions in the external social environments of each group.

The statistically accessible conditions internal to an ethnicity that can influence the degree and direction of ethnic adaptation include variation in: the number of members in the group, their concentration in the regions of Canada (and within the cities of Canada), and the extent to which new members entered the ethnicity through immigration. iuantifiable conditions external to the group that can influence the altering nature of the ethnic group include such things as: the shifting ethno-racial-religious diversity in Canada and in its cities; the conversion from a rural, agricultural nation to an urban, post-industrial one; and the attendant alterations in the national social structure and values. These perspectives comprise the loom upon which the Canadian ethnic mosaic and the pattern for each of its ethnic groups have been woven.

THE PLURALISTIC SOCIETY

Any consideration of ethnicity in Canada today hinges on the notion of a culturally-racially-religiously pluralistic society. Today's increasing geographic and social mobility and the consequent ethno-racial interpenetration make ethnicity an important matter for study, especially in the New World. Pluralistic societies, however, are not something new; they have existed in the countries of origin throughout history, usually as a result of conquest. Ethnic minorities have been present as long as sovereign states have existed; but interethnic/racial/religious relations, even in the New World, have usually been dealt with from the standpoint of political struggles for territory or civil/religious rights, rather than concentrating on what happens when ethnic, racial or religious groups are confronted with the necessity of adapting to a different social order, a new language, and the condition of minority status in order to participate in a society unlike that of their nation of origin (deVos,1975). These latter aspects have characterized not only recent Canadian studies of ethnic groups, but also the government programs aimed at them.

As Vallee, Schwartz, and Darknell pointed out (1957), Canada, since at least "The Conquest" (i.e., since 1763), has always been ethnically, racially, and religiously plural. More recently, Morton (1981) and Dahlie (1983) have re-emphasized the de facto pluralism that lies at the heart of whatever Canada has been and is. Moreover, from the technical-empirical point of view, Haug (1968) demonstrated that, even back in the mid-1960s, Canada was more pluralistic (in terms of heterogeneity of language, race and religion, among other criteria) than any of the nations from which immigrants to Canada had come. This was probably because Canada has maintained a more flexible and open immigration policy than the United States, its geographic and historical neighbour, even taking into consideration Canada's exclusionist policies. The 1967 Immigration Act eliminated the long-standing structural discrimination (based on social, racial, religious, and ethnic origin) in immigration legislation and policy, and substituted for this a point system based on more objective criteria, such as education, occupation, and what immigrants and their families would contribute to the nation's economic activity (Jenness, 1971; Kallen, 198a:140–141). This basic "colour-blind" policy was reaffirmed in subsequent changes to the Immigration Act.

Notwithstanding all of this, what Canadian governments and many citizens demanded of immigrants during the nation-building era from the mid-1700s until only a few decades ago was often conformity to the dominant culture and language of the province of residence, even if this was not legislated. Until recently, few, even among the immigrants, had ever publically questioned the morality of Anglo/Franco conformity. One of the few was David Mills, a federal minister at the end of the nineteenth century:

> The state is not an end, the state is a means to an end. Part of the duties of a state is to protect life, liberty and intellectual freedom, not less than the general public welfare. It has not the right to undertake to destroy the mental vision of one section of the population with the design of creating it anew. (Canada House of Commons, 1890)

In a related fashion and only a quarter century later, the American, Horace Kallen* coined the term "cultural pluralism" to describe the multiethnic, multiracial, multireligious condition existing in the United States. His writings and addresses over the following decade focused on the way in which the various American ethnicities were coincident with particular locations, each group trying to preserve its own heritage and institutions—even while adapting to American life linguistically, economically, politically, and socially.

These developments, Kallen argued, were leading to "a co-operation of cultural diversities...a federation or commonwealth of...cultures" (Kallen, 1924:123–124). He fervently espoused the legitimization of cultural pluralism through consciously encouraging American ethnic groups to develop democratically, each emphasizing its particular cultural forms. In 1915, Kallen had written of his prospects for a culturally plural United States, pros-

---

*Grandfather of Evelyn Kallen, co-author of the first detailed analysis of ethnicity in Canada in 1974 and author of a revised work expanded into ethnic human rights in 1981.

pects that have since applied more to Canada (which he had visited often and knew fairly well) than to its southern neighbour. His hopes back then regarding the nature of ethno-racial-religious groups in a culturally plural Canada or United States ring with as much validity for today and tomorrow as they did over 60 years ago:

> The common language of the (culturally plural) commonwealth, the language of its great tradition, would be English, but each nationality would have for its own emotional and voluntary life its own...speech, its own individual esthetic and intellectual forms. The political and economic life of the commonwealth is a single unit and serves as the foundation and background for the realization of the distinctive individuality of each nation that composes it and of the pooling of these in a harmony above them all...a multiplicity in a unity, an orchestration...(Kallen, 1924:124).

Among the first Canadian academics to question publicly the assumptions and desirability of assimilation to Anglo culture (Anglo-conformity) was England (1929). He asked whether British culture in the developing urban-industrial Canada was really superior to immigrant culture. He saw value in the attempts to create a solidary Canadian people to offset the potential for "strife and anarchy" from the existence of immigrant communities in the cities and rural, "bloc" ethnic settlements of the Canadian West. But England also stressed the right of immigrants to maintain their ethnic individuality in some attenuated form. The question he posed was "can we achieve the transformation without injuring the best in the old-country heritage?" (England, 1929:169,173,176). This is still the essential quandary when considering, on the one hand, the nature and adaptation of Canadian ethno-racial-religious groups, and, on the other, the unity of Canada and Canadians.

Twenty years later, the issue was more clear-cut for Hughes (1948) regarding the relations of Anglo-Celts with French Canadians. Critical for the later study and legitimization of polyculturalism, for Hughes, was affirmation of "a group's right to exist on the basis of its cultural peculiarities" (1948:479). Because of his scrupulous implementation of his beliefs through detailed social studies of "les Canadiens," Hughes was accorded the honourific title of "father of ethnic studies" in Canada.

In 1963, Glazer and Moynihan's *Beyond the Melting Pot* brought ethnicity home to Americans by providing numerous instances of the persistence of "white" ethnicity there, despite the long-standing official ideology and practice of assimilationist policies. Four years later, as an integral part of Canada's own centennial celebration, the presence of and contributions by our many ethnicities were given nation-wide attention. So ready was the country's acceptance at that time of our own ethno-racial-religious diversity, that John Porter was moved to exclaim:

> If there is any basic, positive value expressed about the character of Canadian society...it is to be found in the notion of a pluralistic society. Canada is attempting an experiment in which the principle of ethnic differentiation is the most important. That is to say, it is creating a society in which various groups retain their identity (Porter, 1967:103).

Palmer (1977) has suggested that full public appreciation and the blossoming of academic study of ethnic-group dynamics and change in Canada have two sources: Canada's Centennial Commission, with its pluralistic bent and products (e.g., films, plays, music, artifacts)) and the Royal Commission on Bilingualism and Biculturalism (the "Bi and Bi Commission"). Special analysis of the so-called "other" (non-charter) ethnic groups in *The Cultural Contribution of the Other Ethnic Groups*, Book 4 of the commission's final Report directed everyone's attention to the great degree of cultural plurality, multilingualism, and ethnic dynamics that then existed in Canada. More, the Centennial and Bi and Bi Commissions revealed the necessity for social justice in ethnic relativity: that while Canada was to be proclaimed legally bilingual, this did not mean that there was or would be any official culture(s). All non-charter ethno-racial-religious cultures were recognized to be as valid and legitimate as the Anglo-Celtic and the French cultures.

From its beginnings, the political viability of Canadian Confederation had depended upon the co-existence of "deux nations" and the special status accorded to the French language and to Quebec as a province. The dual nature of Canadian society came to be transformed over time by the arrival of many other groups, and following the report of the Bi and Bi Commission, any thoughts of forcing the "newer" Canadians into the strictures of Anglo/Franco conformity became untenable. In part, this was due to the revitalized drive for independence within Quebec; enclosing "minority" group cultures within the boundaries of Anglo-Celtic culture would have been taken by Québécois as the first step toward their own annihilation. The predictable resistance by Quebec to uniculture prevented any attempts to do so. Interestingly, during the latter 1970s to mid-1980s, the efforts by the Parti Québécois government to restrict language use to French, and the cultural spinoffs from the policy that emerged, were combatted with equal vigour by the federal government, Anglo-Celt Quebeckers, and other non-French ethnic groups in the province.

Therefore, given the basic and necessary commitment to dualism since the post-Conquest years in Canada, it was not surprising that other ethnic, racial, and religious groups would also aspire to the preservation of *their* languages and cultures—ideally, as a constitutional right. This view was powerfully expressed by one Bi and Bi commissioner in a minority report, published as part of the first book of the Commission's report. The commissioner expressed his belief that regional minority languages required special protection, and he, therefore, proposed amendments to the British North America Act that would assure the same guarantees for minority languages as those recommended for French and English by the majority report of the Commission (Richmond, 1969).

Official government recognition of the cultures of the "other" ethnic groups—even if not their languages—came with the announcement in Parliament by Prime Minister Pierre Elliott Trudeau on October 8, 1971 of a policy of multiculturalism. The intent of this policy, according to Burnet (1975), is to affirm Canada's pride in all of the various ethno-racial-religious groups that comprise our population. The policy, since reaffirmed in the Canadian Charter of Rights and Freedoms (Constitution Act, 1982 Part I) further assures the non-charter (and charter) groups that if they wish to sustain their cultural identity, the federal government will encourage and support them in this.*

The enormity of change represented by this acceptance of all cultures was expressed by the Ukrainian-Canadian artist, William Kurelek, when he declared:

---

*New legislation, now (1988) before the House of Commons, Bill C-93 (The Canadian Multiculturalism Act) may further strengthen this assurance.

There is no longer any excuse for anyone in this country to be ashamed of his cultural background. Canada has a multicultural society. The days of Anglo-Saxon domination are gone, or nearly gone. The English have their own virtues and culture. We must not forget those virtues for in the days of their domination they gave our ethnic culture at least a breathing chance (Kurelek, 1977:55).

In somewhat the same way, Troper (1976) was typical of those who took a new look at the experience of ethnicity in Canada. By most, ethnic pluralism is now cast "not [as a passing stage but an ongoing Canadian phenomenon. Ethnicity is not just transplanted old world ways, but an outgrowth of life in the Canadian milieu." This "outgrowth" is also part of the ethnic-group transitions that comprise the focus of this book. The essence of the ethnic-group transitions in Canada was marvelously captured by the historian William Morton, when he observed that:

> There was at first, it would appear, no intention in creating a mosaic of settlement, still less to bring into being a social and cultural mosaic. That simply happened in the nature of things. The term mosaic in consequence passed into the common speech of Canadians and into the political rhetoric of the day....
> Migration to a new land and a new society affects [people] differently. Some wish entirely to cast off the old, and to begin afresh.... But to others the new land was an opportunity to remould the old society nearer to the heart's desires, preserving a continuity but using the opportunity to discard what had irked and to strengthen what appealed....
> All are strangers in a strange land.... It is therefore only realistic and in line with the nature of [people] to accept both the group and its continuation as long as it serves a social purpose.... The ethnic groups, it may be argued, if somewhat romatically, are a positive good in preserving elements of the organic society....
> What then, is the nature of Canadian society today, and what is its future, above all, what has its development to say about minorities?...
> Movement and evolution are continuous in the history and sociology of the minorities which make up Canada. To use Dr. Burnet's term, the kaleidoscope of the minorities is never still; the flashes of light are many, the moments of darkness tense, but the varying patterns in wheeling dissolve only to reform. (Morton, 1981:14,15,21,32,37)

I take a similar stance here: minority ethnicities have indeed been present throughout the entire period of human habitation of what is now called Canada, certainly long before the British conquest of Acadia and Quebec. There always has been change in Canada's ethnic composition, slowly over the decades of the nineteenth century, then more swiftly, until, by 1941, the Anglo-Celts of Canada had become a minority. The increasing diversity in ethno-racial-religious groups and the transition of immigrants into hyphenated Canadians led, eventually, to public recognition of the cultural contributions and characteristics of the non-charter ethnicities by the Royal Commission on Bilingualism and Biculturalism and, in turn, fostered an official multiculturalism policy.

My position here is, moreover, that as the ethnic condition in the social organization of Canada changed and as the character and patterns of social interaction altered, the norms describing ethnic-related behaviour changed as a result. It is these norms that came to be declared as official government policy. From this perspective, then, it was inevitable that, out of the historic Canadian dualism and given the large-scale immigration of non-charter peoples after both world wars, official pluralism would eventually emerge—that, given the base of biculturalism, multiculturalism was unavoidable.

To go even further, one can view the social ethic of Canadian society, with regard to non-charter groups, as shifting gradually from an initial assimilationist stance (an ascriptive means of defining people and of determining one's relation to them) to a stance of ethno-racial egalitarianism (a non-ascriptive means of definition).

MODELS OF INTERGROUP RELATIONS

Ethnically plural equality is, however, only one of several forms that minority-majority group relations can take. In 1978, Milton Gordon asserted that the principal variable in the relations of minority groups and their members to the majority group(s) and the host culture(s) on the one side, and to minority group members' sense and coherence of their ethnic culture on the other, is the ideology about interethnic relations in a nation, region, or city.

Gordon classified three ideological models of ethno-racial group relations that, together, seem to define the poles and the midpoint of an inequality-equality continuum for the potential of ethnic/group cultural existence. The first is the *assimilationist* model, wherein those of a minority ethnicity are encouraged or coerced to abandon their ethnic culture in favour of the dominant or "official" culture. Under this model, non-dominant or "unofficial" cultures can even be declared illegal, and those continuing to practise the non-official culture can be placed at legal risk. Despite almost 200 years of an official assimilationist policy in the United States, data demonstrate that assimilation was by no means entirely effective (Reitz, 1980:183).

At the opposite end of the continuum is *Liberal Pluralism*, emphasizing the absence and even prohibition of any legal, official, or unofficial government recognition of racial, religious, linguistic-cultural, or national-origin characteristics as having any special significance in the formation or implementation of government programs or practices. Buttressing this total equality under the law of all ethno-racial-religious groups, there is normally a prohibition against the use of ethno-racial criteria either for discriminatory purposes or for permitting group advantages.

Gordon's third ideological model, constituting the mid-point in the inequality-equality continuum, is *Corporate Pluralism*, wherein racial, religious, and/or cultural groups are formally recognized as legally constituted entities with official standing (or lack of standing) in the society. Social resources, such as education, occupations, residences, economic or political resources or awards—whether public or private—are allocated according to either the relative numerical strength of each ethnicity in the population, or some other formula emanating from the political process.

In some nations, of course, the "corporate" status of one or more groups in the national population is that of oppression—subordinate to the ethnically/racially/religiously different superordinate group—as is the condition of Blacks in South Africa. Several have suggested that Native Peoples in Canada are like an officially-oppressed corporate entity (Cardinal, 1969; Ponting and Gibbins, 1980; Frideres, 1983). Of a more beneficent character within Corporate Pluralism are those nations in which national elective office and/or political organization is structured according to formal representation of each ethnicity commensurate with their numbers; examples of these are Switzerland and Sweden. Linguistic and cultural rights often accompany the legal "corporate" ethnic rights in such nations.

Within both of the pluralist models, any egalitarian emphasis is on equality of condition and of opportunity, not equality of outcome. Within the Liberal Pluralism form, universalistic criteria of opportunity or access are applied with respect to all minority groups without distinction. Within the Corporate Pluralism model, there can be restrictions upon the operation of universalistic criteria for award or reward, possibly based upon inequality of access to resources stemming from the legally-defined superordinate-subordinate structure of the nation, and resulting in inequality of outcome. The infamous Asian Exclusion Act (1923) that was repealed only after the Second World War (1947) was accompanied, in many provinces, by the exclusion of Chinese from all professions, many other occupations, and from many educational programs.

Of the two forms of pluralism in Canada, Corporate Pluralism more nearly describes the linguistic relationship for Quebec, and Francophones, both within the jurisdiction of the Canadian federal government and within the provinces of Quebec and New Brunswick. Liberal Pluralism better characterizes the non-linguistic situation of the many non-French ethnicities in Canada. Indeed, what I earlier termed ethnic "relativity"—each ethno-racial-religious group having different values, structures, processes and cultural dynamics, yet official equality—is possible only under conditions of Liberal Pluralism, as is having an official policy of multiculturalism.

The dimensions of ethnic-group access to social resources and to cultural maintenance have been differently conceptualized by Evelyn Kallen (1982). Instead of Gordon's three models of equality-inequality in cultural privilege and maintenance, Kallen discussed four (1981:156–181), which in most respects overlap Gordon's three. The most egalitarian model, in terms of respect for ethnic difference in Kallen's scheme, is the polycultural *Mosaic*, of which the hallmark is cultural pluralism (cf. Gordon's Liberal Pluralism): making one nation with many peoples, each possessing its unique culture. The nation as a whole reflects these cultures in myriad manifestations. For Kallen, the *Melting Pot* (or Amalgamation) model partially reproduced Gordon's Assimilationist form. Under this model the policies and practices of social institutions are directed at amalgamating the originally different ethno-racial-religious groups into one nation and one people, different from any of the original ethnicities—even from the initially dominant group(s)—thereby creating one new culture—a "national" culture.

Representing one of the two models of cultural inequality is *Dominant Conformity* (Absorption), in which the ethnic minorities are assimilated to the dominant culture and in this process absorbed. The original subordinate cultures wither, as increasing proportions of the minority groups conform to the dominant group(s) culture(s). Dominant Conformity differs from the Melting Pot in that in Dominant Conformity there are assumptions of the subordinate cultures' being inferior either in content or viability. Their absorption into the dominant culture is viewed as either inevitable, or as a goal to be actively sought by the state through the application of negative sanctions in order to hasten the process. In the Melting Pot situation, by contrast, even the dominant culture(s), along with the minorities, alter over time, eventually amalgamating into a new, completely different unitary culture and people.

The most insidious of Kallen's four models is *Paternalism* (Colonialism), in which there is a dominant ethnicity and culture, with all others implicitly or formally defined as subordinate and inferior. In such nations, the subordinate groups comprise what George Manuel (a prominent Canadian Indian leader and author) has called the "Fourth World," that is, de facto colonies of the aboriginal peoples within a context of socio-political control by the superordinate ethno-racial group(s). Again, the applicability of this model to the situations of Blacks in South Africa and Native Peoples in Canada is obvious. This is not to say, however, that the conditions in Canada are as oppressively structured for our Native Peoples as for Black South Africans; the similarity lies instead in the groups' lack of power over their cultural and racial destinies. To carry the examination further, the most typical instances of Paternalism represent the aftermath of the conquest of aboriginal peoples and their lands; North, Central and South America, Africa, Australasia, and the Pacific Islands could all in lesser or greater ways demonstrate conditions of Paternalism. It should be emphasized, though, that Paternalism is not limited to subjugation of aboriginal peoples only; all non-dominant groups are subordinated and stigmatized, and experience sanctions preventing access to social resources equal to that of the dominant group.

In this way, Kallen's Paternalism is identical to the less-desirable possibility implicit in Gordon's Corporate Pluralism. Kallen's specificity in separating what is, in Gordon's category, one type into

two—Dominant Conformity and Paternalism—while not exactly
capturing the same aspects as Gordon, makes a valuable distinction
between the different dimensions of models of ethnic superiority.
None of Kallen's categories, however, accurately characterizes the
corporate nature of the French language in terms of federal jurisdiction and in the two officially bilingual provinces of Canada. The
advantage of Gordon's category of Corporate Pluralism is that it
points to the official exercise of power over at least some aspects of
culture that seems in Kallen's last two categories to be clouded. The
disadvantage of Gordon's Corporate Pluralism is that it fails to
capture the differences within a set of conditions ranging from
rather benign corporatism to extreme exploitation and official
oppression as instruments of legislated state authority and policy.
The formal power of the Anglo-Franco groups in Canada over the
culture and rights of non-charter groups, though, would seem to be
of an entirely different character from the power exercised by the
Afrikaner-British group over the Black majority and the other non-
white minorities of South Africa. It is not just the difference
between the oppressed being the numerical majority in that country, and the non-charter peoples being a numerical minority in
Canada, however. It should be apparent that official bilingualism in
Canada and the somewhat more oppressive linguistic policy of the
Parti Québécois and the subsequent Liberal government in that
province are both exceptionally mild by comparison with the mili-
taristic, unrepentant rule of suppressing Blacks' rights that is at the
basis of South African official policy. Further, few—even among the
Native Peoples in Canada—would declare their plight as being as
grievous as that of South-African Blacks.

It is just these differences in kind, not just in degree, that overlap
and cause ambiguity in Gordon's concept of Corporate Pluralism.
Even with the logical disadvantages of both of the pluralism typologies, though, it is clear that there are varying implications for the
nature of ethnicity, ethnic cohesion, and the direction and rate of
ethnic-group transitions under different models of ethno-political
policy which can be more clearly drawn from Kallen's categories.
And to the extent possible, it will be useful to inspect what trends in
ethnic cohesion there were in the shifts from the assimilationist
policies following Confederation, to the increasing de facto ethnic
pluralism later, through to the dynamics following the assertion of
official multiculturalism in 1971.

ETHIC IDENTITY IN CANADA

The key to understanding ethnicity in Canada, with its ethno-racial-religious pluralism on the one hand and its group and individual senses of ethnicity on the other, is the concept of *ethnic identity*. While ethnic identity has been a topic of scholarly study for many years (e.g., Driedger, 1975; Isajiw, 1975, 1981), the concept is not just an idea. As Driedger and his colleagues underscored in 1982, ethnicity "is still a very important preference for self identification and identification of others." This conclusion coming from their evaluation of many academic studies is backed up by the reality of the direct and central importance ethnic identity has in the daily lives of millions of Canadians.

To appreciate this fact, one has only to look at the 1981 Census data: more than 92% of the Canadian population identified themselves with one of the ethnicities in this nation. Almost all of the remaining 7.6% reported a multiple ethnic identity associated with two or three groups jointly. Of those reporting a single ethnic origin, nearly one-third were of non-charter groups. And, if one subdivided the "British" category into its (at least) four constituent ethnicities, the non-English, non-French ethnic-group segment of Canadians in 1981 amounted to about 43% of the entire population. Only a tiny fraction of Canadians failed to associate themselves with a single or joint "ethnic" identity of origin. Thus, it is clear that ethnicity is a major organizing principle in Canadian life.

Beyond this, a fundamental question exists: Why does ethnic identity and the phenomenon of "ethnicity" persist in Canada? In a real sense, it is tautological to answer this question by pointing to the ongoing inflow of large numbers of non-charter-group peoples beginning after Confederation or to refer to Canada's de facto and later de jure cultural pluralism. There seem to be no "facts" to help explain this most basic element of Canadian and ethnic social organization. There are, however, theoretical ways of coming to grips with the fact of ethnic cultural maintenance in this country.

First, Kallen (1982:79–80) has observed that if a nation's social organization is such that the major policies, laws, and practices are based on racist ideologies and supported by prejudice held by the public, then the boundaries of institutions "become ossified and virtually impenetrable by ethnic minorities." Such past conditions, then, would have led non-charter ethnicity members in Canada to remain, or to become, exceptionally dependent upon their cultural values, structures and processes because they had no readily accessible "Canadian" alternatives. Even if the Canadian social structure at an earlier time had not been virtually impenetrable, non-British/English and non-French people in Canada would still have continued to rely as much as possible on their ethnic peers, to keep up the majority of their social and economic interactions with them, and so remain loyal to the ethnic community values and practices. In this way, "ethnicity" came to comprise a parallel social organization for all those who were unable or unwilling to take on the physical and social characteristics of one of the dominant ethnicities: "ethnicity" and ethnic identity thereby persisted as a fundamental element of Canadian social organization.

Second, in earlier, more empirically-based work, Porter (1965:521,558) had put forth the argument that the persistence of ethnic identity and cohesion was a result of ethnic economic separation:"[I]t is the [ethnic] outsider who is conscious of the barriers and his own lack of the proper preparation to cross them. . . . This subjective component. . .will be perpetuated as long as ethnic differentiation is so highly valued" by the charter or by "minority" groups. Indeed, Reitz (1980:41), in reviewing theory and research on ethnic-group survival, carefully examined Porter's argument and concluded: "In other words, the Canadian mosaic...[was] actually a means of ethnic exploitation." Anglo-Saxon encouragement of the celebration of ethnicity, according to this perspective, was self-serving in that it was an attempt to maintain British supremacy and, as an unintended consequence according to Porter, assured the survival of non-British, non-French cultures in Canada.

Reitz (1980:38–39) pointed to a third conceptually different reason for continued ethnic cohesion in Canada: Clark's (1962) notion of the Canadian penchant for differentiating this country from the United States. Clark noted that "ethnic separation" seemed to be widespread not just among the French, other Europeans, and Asians in Canada, but also among the separate ethnicities that together are included under the "British" rubric. This pattern, so different from that seen by Clark as paramount in the United States, was part of Canadian government policy "to check American influences in Canadian cultural life." The implementation of this policy "involved the strengthening of the supports of ethnic group loyalties...through the preservation of Old World loyalties" (Clark, 1962:195–196).

A fourth possible reason for the maintenance of ethnic culture and identity in Canada was suggested by Isajiw (1978). Underlying Isajiw's theory is the ascriptive basis for social interaction and status that existed in Canada prior to the Second World War. Given the predominance of ascriptive criteria such as race, ethnicity, and religion, ethnic cultural survival was all but inevitable. However, after the Second World War, Canada became a state in which there was a shift from the use of ascriptive standards to the use of achievement-oriented criteria in many of the "public" institutions; formal education facilities, the economy, housing, and even politics have become subject to the non-discriminatory policies of human-rights legislation. Focusing on the technological culture of Canada today, Isajiw reviewed the literature on the persistence of Canadian ethnicity, alongside the emergence of technological culture, based on meritocratic criteria. The current reliance on technical qualifications, Isajiw's argument goes, reveals a special "time dimension" within the technological culture of work and school. Individuals subject to the technological culture are considered only in terms of some of their characteristics. Technological culture is attuned to the here and now; it cannot admit of the whole person, of personal or collective identity, of phenomena other than the instrumental and technical.

Ethnicity, in contrast, contains emphases which, Isajiw observed "link up with the remote...past...the seasons of the year, to the events in the life cycle." Isajiw's theory can be taken even further: the link of values and of identity with the eternal that are part of ethnic-group culture emphasize the human aspects of the whole social life, complementing the material and partializing aspects of the post-industrial urban culture of technological Canada. Indeed, were not ethnicity and ethnic identity still prominent in Canada, something very much like it would have to be invented; humans cannot live by technology alone!

Carrying this a bit further, we may speculate on the comparative situations in the United States and Canada. The United States has possessed fewer vital ethnic cultures than Canada—at least since the Great Depression, and especially today. This is, perhaps, the reason for the apparently stronger emergence there of the born-again-Christian phenomenon. What may have been born again was a sense of time-dimensioned identity, in the relative absence of ethnic identity. In Canada, where ethnic culture and identity remained healthy, the "rediscovery" of ethnic identity by individuals, ethno-racial-religious groups, and by governments legitimated the de facto maintenance of ethnicity in Canada. Nothing new had to be invented here, since the complement to universalistic, alienating technological culture had never lost its power to the point of being moribund. Ethnicity in Canada was live, vital, and needed, but it fulfilled a function different from that of earlier times.

ETHNIC DIFFERENTIATION

As indicated, an essential element in the analysis of the nature of ethnicity and ethnic groups in Canada is the degree to which an ethnicity becomes or is dissimilar—to other groups, and within each group. The process of becoming less similar is termed "differentiation," and besides the one axis of inter-group versus intra-group distinctions, we can also inspect the time dimension of differentiation: differentiation over time versus differentiation at the same point in time. What we end up with is four categories of differentiation which will be used in our analysis: the extent to which ethnicities have been dissimilar (1) over time from each other, (2) differ from each other at the same point in time; the extent to which subsets of the same ethnicity(ies) (3) became more or became less similar to each other over time, and (4) differed from each other at the same point in time. The first two dimensions of analysis can be thought of as macroscopic differentiation and the latter two as microscopic differentiation.

Differentiation can be traced along a continuum running from very little to extremely great—within both the macro- and micro-perspectives—not just over time, but also at the same date, depending on one's particular interest at any specific point. For example, we may at first be interested merely in characterizing the degree of between-group differentiation in the early part of this century and then go on to trace the extent of differentiation over time through to today. One could then progress to focusing on within-group differentiation some time ago—based, say, on generation in Canada, or gender, and then inspecting the degree of internal group differentiation today. This potential for analyzing how the nature of ethnicity in Canada has altered over time, or varied between ethnic groups at one date, is the most explicit, but only one of the manifestations of the "relativity" theory suggested earlier.

Since the late 1960s, there have been many excellent studies on the social organization of various ethnic groups.*

A work with analysis of more than two ethnicities is, however, exceedingly rare, especially one focusing on patterns of differentiation between multiple ethnic communities. The seminal research in this area was by Breton (1964) on the "institutional completeness" (organizational development) within each of several selected ethnic groups in Montreal. Breton has since gone on to theorize about two particular aspects of ethnic differentiation: the degrees of ethnic "enclosure" and "compartmentalization" that exist in various ethnic communities. For Breton (1978a) *enclosure* refers to the social boundaries a group develops that separate it from other groups and to the mechanisms used by the group to maintain these boundaries. Enclosure, therefore, should be viewed as involving the collective imposition of social boundaries on the group, whereby the networks of internal social relations are limited solely to members of that ethnicity-race-religion.

Compartmentalization is the related structure of formal organizations within the group that are parallel to those in the wider city or region. In essence, compartmentalization covers the extent of ethnic organizational development which operates to differentiate

---

*These works include among them Hill (1981), Christiansen et al. (1983), and Winks (1971) on Blacks; Chan (1983) on Chinese; Breton and Savard (1982) and Maxwell (1977) on French; Nagata on Greeks (1971) and on Greeks and Italians (1970); Greenglass (1972), Harney (1978), Jansen and La Cavera (1981), and Sturino and Zucchi (1985) on Italians; Lyman (1968) on Chinese and Japanese, and Maykovich (1971), Takata (1983) and Ward (1982) on Japanese; Rosenberg (1971) and Weinfeld et al. (1981) on Jewish; Frideres (1983) and Boldt and Long (1985) on Native People; Anderson and Higgs (1976), Higgs (1982) and Marques and Medeiros (1980) on Portuguese; Darkovich (1980), Lupul (1978), Petryshyn (1980), and Swyripa (1978) on Ukrainians; and Krauter and Davis (1978) on about a dozen groups. Also, Reitz's (1980) second chapter affords keen and concise insight into the social organization and history of ten ethnicities. In addition, the McClelland and Stewart-Canada Multiculturalism Directorate books eventually on about 25 groups—most of which are already in print—provide detailed analyses of each ethnicity's social organization, history, and culture in Canada.

and isolate the collective ethnic life of a group's members from that of other groups, and even from the city "life" as a whole. In this, there is an explicit inference of the group's separation from other groups both over time and at any one point in time. Subsequent to this work, Breton has conducted an empirical study (1981) of the perceptions of ethnic-group members about the degree to which certain ethnic community resources should be addressed toward a variety of issues and problems (e.g. discrimination, participation in selection of ethnic community leaders), and the more theoretically-bound concern about ethnocultural and linguistic resource production and allocation as symbolic media of exchange (e.g. use of the ethnic language in arts and cultural events) in Canada (1984), both being aspects of group-differentiation processes.

Another side of the group-differentiation question is the kinds of accomodations made by "minority" and "majority" ethnicities to each other within a city, region or nation. On this matter, Vallee Schwartz and Darknell (1957) distinguished between assimilation and differentiation. *Assimilation* was defined as the process by which two or more ethnicities become increasingly similar to each other. At the opposite end of this particular continuum was *differentiation*, the process or status of ethnic groups becoming or being less similar. Vallee and his colleagues observed that both may occur at the same time, not only among ethnic groups as a whole—as in majority-minority relations—but also within particular ethnic groups. Thus it is possible that at the same time one ethnicity is becoming more like the dominant-majority group(s) in some ways, it is differentiating from them in others. In any case, these researchers traced studies of ethnic differentiation in Canada back at least to 1938 and referenced each research interest in the cultural achievements of minority groups and the celebration of non-British/French cultural heritages.

A further aspect of ethnic differentiation touched on in the above study was microscopic differentiation—when subgroups of the ethnicity become separated or separate themselves from the larger ethnic community to form an autonomous body having a different ethnic identity and culture. This, what we call intra-group differentiation, has sometimes been a consequence of the newfound freedom in Canada as compared to the ethnic-group subordination and suppression experienced by such groups in the country of origin, for example: Byelorussians, Ukrainians,

Macedonians, Jewish, Hutterites-Mennonites, or Doukhobors. Even among the French or Blacks in Canada, and especially among the "British," there has been internal differentiation caused partially, it is conjectured, by ancestors settling in different locations. Such "structural differentiation" (i.e., separation of a subgroup from the larger community) relates to ethnic allocation of roles, rights, and facilities, while "cultural differentiation" concerns intra-ethnic variation in recreation, art forms, and other culturally expressive phenomena.

In 1975, Parsons proposed a new concept, wherein ethnic-group symbols are used to establish, re-establish or maintain a sense of individual identity—to counteract the universalistic thrust of urban technologically-based societies, in a fashion similar to the process later outlined by Isajiw (1978). Such "de-differentiation" is a compromise between restoration of a set of collectively held values, sentiments, and behaviours that immigrants brought with them and the recognition that many of the specifics of life in the current North-American societies were incompatible with the immigrant patterns. The de-differentiating tendency is, Parsons suggested, to select particular criteria and apply those as identifying symbols, as part of one's individual or group identity. Despite Parsons' label, this process is included here under the microscopic, intra-group differentiation rubric.

Glazer and Moynihan (1963:311–315) affirmed W. Herberg's (1955) interpretation of religion comprising one (or the predominant) element of ethnic identity in the United States. For these writers, religion, along with race, constituted the major arenas in which the post-war American search for post-industrial identity seemed to be pursued during the querulous, stormy 1960s.

Although there was always a greater freedom in Canada for the retention and practice of ethnic-group culture, cross-generation and temporal differentiation has also been discussed in this country. The process of ethnic-group adaptation can take place for those identified with the original immigrant tradition, that of either the pre-Depression or the post-war waves of massive movement to Canada. Contrasted with these groups are the rediscoverers, those who reclaim their ethnic identity later in life or in a later generation. Their commitment to the culture and whose utilization of ethnic institutions may be more symbolic than physically essential, represents a different kind of accomodation to Canadian life than that made by the immigrant and second generations, or even all generations in earlier times. In this regard, Isajiw (1975) asked two questions concerning the transplantation and reformulation of "ethnicity" within the Canadian matrix. First, what type and degree of symbolism is necessary for individuals and the collectivity to maintain ethnic identity; and second, what are the conditions that produce cultural "rediscoverers" in ethnic communities? Isajiw further suggested, as have I, that different ethnic groups in Canada may need different kinds and/or a different number or level of ethnic symbols as part of the resources needed to maintain ethnic culture and cohesion. Using data from Toronto's ethnic groups, Isajiw (1981) further examined these issues and found empirical support for his formulations, but of different forms for different ethnic groups.

To the extent that there was implicit or official opposition by government to ethnic-group identity maintenance, then there may well have been socially disastrous consequences—if one accepts the argument of Kovacs and Cropley (1971). They put forward the proposition that, with purely assimilationist objectives and practices as the mode of minority groups' relation to the majority culture (as in the past), alienation from the ethnic group inevitably attended those who assimilated. Moreover, the end result of an assimilation policy was not incorporation of "ethnics" into the majority culture, but, instead, marginality—being neither "ethnic" nor being accepted by the majority—a form of ethnic-group differentiation rarely investigated. Although Kovacs and Cropley do not suggest this, it seems possible that the much-studied crushing of the vaunted American spirit and military honour during the tumultuous 1960s through to the 1980s could have been an entirely unintended consequence of the sometimes fanatic actions by American governments to eliminate all vestiges of "un-American" character in its population—from the founding of the Republic through the post-Vietnam-War years into the era of Middle-East and Latin-American action: e.g., official denigration of non-Anglo or non-American culture, anti-Catholicism. Even today this drive to eliminate "un-American" elements in American society goes on: e.g., the increasing number of American states which have enacted "English only" language laws, even for the conduct of private business.

In contrast, the long-held recognition of cultural duality in

Canada and the more recent shift to official ethnic cultural plurality permitted not only integration by members of many ethnic groups in city-wide or nation-wide institutions, but also reduced the extent of cultural alienation (Kovacs and Cropley 1972). As well, the policy of cultural pluralism assures continued indentification with and pride in the minority ethnicity, given the will by group members to do so. The ideal for Canadians is not the denigration of minority culture and practice, but, instead, the celebration of ethnic-group culture as part of being Canadian.

What is still unresolved is whether the "two solitudes" of an earlier Canada have or can become "many solitudes." This book can only partially address that question. We need to ask yet another question: If the Canadian ethnic-relations dynamics have indeed led to a condition today of "many solitudes," is this the final result or merely a midpoint in ethnic-group transitions toward a future ethnically-plural state whose hallmark will be active, harmonious relations between the many ethnicities, rather than mere separate existences?

SUMMARY

The analysis in this chapter of the nature of ethnicity has emphasized that the bases of ethnicity in Canada are diverse—in part, dependent upon the unique characteristics of each particular group, but at the same time linked to geography and the official ideology concerning interethnic relations. In most respects, the nature of ethnicity and ethnic identity have been founded in the historic Canadian chartered duality, which gave rise to a particular form of ethnic-group differentiation. The permission for and the vitality of ethnic-group plurality in Canada in practice, if not always in law or formal policy, has, in any case, benefited the survival of minority cultures and peoples in Canada.

Seventeen years ago, moreover, the de facto ethnic pluralism engendered by the original Anglo-Franco duality matured into official multiculturalism—a combined Liberal/Corporate Pluralism in Gordon's terms, the Cultural Pluralism-Mosaic of Kallen's typologies. It is also quite clear that the nature of ethnic-group identity and cohesion must, therefore, be considered as variant, representing multiple transitions over the decades or between different generations. From being initially part and parcel only of the immigrant experience 50 to 100 years ago, "ethnicity" and ethnic-group identity have been transformed in the Canadian context.

Ethnicity and group cohesion in Canada today, therefore, can, perhaps, be best understood as evolving from the original duality, as reactions to the later overarching technological impersonality and universalism attending the post-industrial culture in the economy. It may indeed be that, instead of limiting individuals' statuses in Canadian society, ethnicity and ethnic-group cohesion has become the magnetism within and between the many peoples of Canada, the essence of being Canadian and of belonging to this country, and a vehicle for both individual and collective cultural and social freedom. What ethnic-group cohesion empirically was and now is, and what were the ethnic group transitions from yesteryear, comprise the remainder of this book.

Admittedly, the theory of or about Canadian ethnic groups set out here cannot by any means be considered as "grand theory" along the lines of Van den Bergh's (1981) conception of ethnicity as a biosocial phenomenon. Neither can the theory about ethnicities in Canada in this book be considered to be as rigorous a construct as the closely interrelated postulates of Schermerhorn (1970) or Francis (1976). Instead, what is developed here is a theoretical approach to outlining and explaining Canadian ethnic-group dynamics as they emerge from the observable working out of ethnic-group cohesion in Canada. The theory here, therefore, derives from the inseparable interaction between broad theoretical guidelines and empirical analysis. The result reflects, I hope, not just the reality of what ethnic-group cohesion has been and is in this nation, but also a theoretical lens by which that empirical reality can be explained and interpreted and which can be focused to provide a sharpened view for understanding.

CHAPTER 2

The Peoples of Canada

INTRODUCTION: APPROACHES TO ETHNICITY

Hughes (1948) established a critical principle for the study of ethnicity in Canada when he stressed that "[I]t takes more than one ethnic group to make ethnic relations..." and that "more can be learned...by studying the minority than by studying the dominant group." Fitting well into the strategy Hughes demanded was Lieberson's (1961) "societal theory of race and ethnic relations." Lieberson theorized that, in societies with more than one ethnicity, each group could be conceptualized—on the basis of history, if nothing else—as at least one indigenous group and at least one other group migrating into their territory. "Indigenous" in this instance did not necessarily mean aboriginal peoples, but rather a population sufficiently established in an area so as to possess institutions and the demographic capacity for maintaining some minimum form of social order through the generations. In addition to the earlier situation of the Canadian Indians, Quebec after the Conquest and British Upper Canada in the early 1800s come to mind here as examples. If different ethnic groups in contact with each other vary in the capacity to impose changes on the other group(s), then the imposing group can be defined as "superordinate" and the other(s) as "subordinate" in maintaining or developing a suitable socio-cultural environment.

Lieberson also distinguished between immigrant and indigenous subordinate groups, hypothesizing that the former would be more rapidly assimilated into the superordinate culture. Finally, he thought that immigrant subordinate groups would be subject to discriminatory and other control practices in non-conflictual ways, so as to enable the superordinate group to maintain its cultural and institutional hegemony.

Recasting Lieberson's superordinate-subordinate model of differentiation, the notion of "majority-minority" differentiation comes readily to mind. However, "majority" has meanings, in Canada at least, in addition to being a "superordinate" cultural or socio-economic power. For instance, "majority" in Canada suggests "charter group(s)" and the legalistic dominance conferred by the charter designation. As well, for the British/English and the French (especially Québécois), being dominant in cultural and socio-economic terms has been closely associated with numerical superiority: being the numerical majority conferred superordinacy in social power over the "minority(ies)." Given this, it could be predicted that the superordinate cultural and socio-economic power of the charter group(s) would lessen to the extent that the British/French lost their numerical dominance in Canada or its regions and cities. Here, we begin by examining the extent to which non-charter groups have increased their presence in Canada and what related structural alterations this has brought about. Other relevant questions underlying the analysis are the extent to which all ethnic groups in Canada today are, numerically, "minorities," and the complementary perspective, the degree of ethno-racial-religious diversity in Canada since the earliest times.

CANADA'S ORIGINAL PEOPLES

Humanity did not originate in what is now Canada. Apparently, neither *Homo sapiens* nor any of the earlier protohuman species were native to this land. When the first explorers and colonizers came to Canada, however, they did find the "New World" occupied by those we now call "Indians" and Inuit. (The name once given to the latter was "Eskimo," a Cree word for "eaters of raw flesh" (Jeness, 1977: 405)). The population of these original peoples in this era was between 220 000 and 300 000 Indians (Jeness, 1976: 1; Price, 1987) and about one-tenth that number, probably, of Inuit (Jeness, 1977: 422): roughly 250 to 330 thousand people occupying nearly ten million square kilometres.

Where did these people come from, and when? That they did not originate here seems conclusive from the total lack of archeological evidence of pre-human species that in several other continents established the emergence of modern humanity from pre-*Homo sapiens* species. It seems clear that, whenever they did arrive, they came across the Bering Strait and were, therefore, of Asiatic origin (Estabrook, 1982). But *when* these original peoples came is a matter of great controversy. Until recently, the general consensus was that Indians arrived here not more than 20 000 years ago (e.g., Jeness, 1977: 248). This figure was sometimes extended by some thousands of years, but that was considered the absolutely earliest time, due to the lack of a Bering land/ice bridge connecting our continent with the Sino-Russian continent for at least double the period prior to the most recent glacial era. Thus, as archeologists judged it, Indian migration to Canada was said to have been in the fairly recent past, and Inuit arrival much more recent, about 2000 years ago (Jeness, 1977: 248; MacLean, 1982: 2,131.)

New evidence, however, from archeological work in the Old Crow River area, 100 kilometres south of the Beaufort Sea in the Yukon, strongly indicates the presence of Canadian Indians going back, perhaps, 150 000 years, more than three times as long ago as had been believed. This would place the Indian migrants' arrival in Canada very shortly after *Homo sapiens* began to leave its ancestor, *Homo erectus*, during the Pleistocene era (Jopling, et al., 1981; Estabrook, 1982; Irving, 1987).

It seems likely, therefore, that at the beginning of the Anglo-European era in Canada, Indians had lived here for at least 100 000 years, and Inuit for about 2000 years. When Canada was "discovered" by Anglo-Europeans, almost every part of the country was occupied or claimed by some Indian or Inuit tribe. Those who came to exploit and later to colonize were usurpers in the eyes of the Indians and Inuit. At that time, the Indians were as culturally diverse among themselves as any of the non-Indians who later immigrated to Canada. There were more than 50 distinct tribes, each with its own language or dialect and possessed of its own particular manners and customs (Jeness, 1977: 2; Price, 1987).

When the French and later the British came to exploit the natural resources, colonize the land, and Christianize the indigenous inhabitants, the Indians numbered, as we have said, 250 to 300 thousand, and without their aid and support, the Europeans could not have established themselves. The Indians taught the whites how to survive physically and socially, indeed, how to thrive and enrich themselves on the land. In turn, the Anglo-Europeans converted the Native Peoples to Christian religions, obtained ownership of Indian lands, and drove most of Canada's original peoples onto reserves—too often on land unwanted and not useful to the British or French or other immigrants.

Another, even more devastating concomitant of the white occupation for the Indian (and later the Inuit) was contagious diseases. Jeness (1977: 249–264) summarized the transition: "The Indians taught the settlers woodcraft and the habits..." necessary for survival here. "They served them as guides and hunters.... Many tribes acquiesced quietly in the invasion of their territories.... Whether they resisted or submitted, all alike paid the same heavy price for their contact" with the colonists: "smallpox, which decimated them periodically from the early seventeenth century until the second half of the nineteenth.... Typhus carried off one third" of some groups, as did "pulmonary afflictions, especially tuberculosis...[which] at an early date and ever since have caused a high mortality.... Of shorter duration than diseases, but...almost equally destructive of aboriginal society, was alcohol. [It] destroyed the self-respect of the Indians, weakened every family and tribal tie and made them, willing or unwilling, the slaves of the trading-posts where liquor was dispensed to them by the keg" in exchange for furs valuable to the Anglo-Europeans (especially in their countries of origin) but of little importance to the Indians for maintaining their own life or culture. It was, however, this fur trade that some have emphasized as of critical importance to the economic development of Canada as a colony, that furthered the financial aims of the Europeans, but was also social and economic exploitation of the Indians (Woodcock, 1970; Creighton, 1961).

Disease and alcohol demoralized and destroyed the Indians just when they needed all of their energies to cope with the new conditions that suddenly confronted them. The old order that had developed over scores of millenia changed completely and abruptly with the coming of the French and the British. Economically and socially, the Indians were cut adrift from their geographic, life-maintaining, and social foundations at the very time when their numbers were being sharply decreased by previously unknown diseases. Canada's original peoples were, within a century, eclipsed. (Jeness, 1977: 249–264).

Through continued immigration, Anglo-Europeans and other groups came, more and more, to outnumber the declining Indian population, so much so, that, by 1851, in what is now Nova Scotia,

New Brunswick, Quebec, and Ontario, Indians comprised less than 0.5% of the colonial populations (Table 2.1). Indeed, 20 years later, they represented only somewhat more than that fraction, numbering about 23 000 (Table 2.1) within the organized boundaries of Canada.

By that time, the French, too, had become subordinate, at least in numerical representation, with the British making up nearly 63% of the four provinces' population in 1851, and almost that in 1871. The French accounted for almost the entirety of non-British Canadians (35%), complemented by a sprinkling of Blacks, Germans, other whites, and, of course, Native Peoples. For the Native Peoples, at that time including the Métis (mixed Indian and non-Indian ancestry), this was their lowest ebb since the intrusion of the white peoples. Thereafter, both the numbers and the proportional representation of Native Peoples, soon also to include the Inuit in the counting, increased in a somewhat cyclical pattern. Even so, through the era of what Native writers have called "The Great Swindle" of Natives' lands and civil rights (Cardinal, 1969: 39–50; Redbird, 1980: 17–25), the Native Peoples became numerically inferior and a socially conquered, culturally ravaged and suppressed group, until well into the 1970s.

THE NEW CANADIANS

After their conquest of Canada, concluded in 1763, the British actively pursued a policy of colonization and settlement, something the French had not done. According to French colonial censuses, (reported in the 1871 Canadian Census), the population of New France at the beginning of the seventeenth century was a mere 28 persons, and 50 years later it stood only at about 3200. Even after a century of residence there were just 17 204 inhabitants and after 150 years (in 1765), only about 70 000. There are no means, apparently, by which we can learn the comparative figures for the British population then, since a British colonial census seems not to have been taken until 1767, revealing that the residents of Prince Edward Island, Nova Scotia, and New Brunswick together numbered just under 13 500 (Kalbach and McVey, 1979: 21, 24). If we assume that most of Quebec's residents were French and most of the other colonies' British, the latter did not equal the French in size of population in Canada until about 1834, a half-century following the arrival of United Empire Loyalists (UELs) from the United States (Kalbach and McVey, 1979: 24).

Even so, it is known that ethno-racial diversity began during the French regime, first with the Indian-white differentiation, then with the transport of Black slaves to New France during the first half of the seventeenth century and later in British-Canadian colonies (Winks, 1971: 26).

The ethnic diversity of the population increased following the conclusion of the Anglo-French wars, initially in Acadia and Newfoundland after the Treaty of Utrecht in 1713 and then, finally, in the rest of New France after 1763 and the Treaty of Paris which ceded to Britain sovereignty over most of French North America. The effect of these two treaties was to very much increase the British presence in Canada and decrease that of the French. This was due in part to a difference in British policy concerning their colonies. French policy had de-emphasized French settlement of French North America in favour of exploitation of fur and other resources, Christianizing the Indians, and maintaining a military presence. With the advent of British control, however, populating the land with British settlers was given high priority by the new colonial governors—establishing farms, new townships, and centres of government—all looking forward to eventual permanent settlement throughout British North America.

The different colonial policies of France and Britain were to have far-reaching consequences. Since France had sought only to maintain an official political-military presence in her North-American lands, with only enough non-political, non-military colonists to support her primarily economic objectives, the population of French North America was always rather small. Indeed, even after more than a century of French occupation, the population of Quebec was well under 70 000. Since few French immigrants arrived in Canada thereafter, French Canadians necessarily had to rely upon natural increase to maintain their numerical standing in the country.

Of perhaps equal import for the French presence in Canada was the policy of deportation adopted by the British against the French in Acadia. The new political masters were unwilling to accept the Acadians' ready, self-proclaimed neutrality in the ongoing Anglo-French conflict because of the French government's attempts at creating a subversive population in Acadia. Thus, after 45 years of fairly faithful neutrality despite the urgings of French agents, almost all of the Acadians were uprooted by their British masters and, beginning in 1755, dispersed in small batches among the coastal British colonies or sent to French possessions and even France itself. Since the Acadians had constituted about one-fifth of the French in Canada, this, combined with the absence of French immigration after the conquest of Quebec, meant that the size of the French population in Canada was not merely constrained, but actually diminished by the time of the final establishment of British North America in 1763.

The next major shift in the ethno-demographic balance between the French and British groups in Canada came 20 years later, following the conclusion of the American war for independence. Beginning in 1783, about 35 000 "United Empire Loyalists" (UELs) immigrated to Canada. The largest portion of these, about 25 000 and almost all of British stock, went to Nova Scotia. About 3000 settled in New Brunswick, Prince Edward Island and Newfoundland. The other 7000 made up, in part, of Dutch, Scots and Germans came up the Hudson-Champlain route to the St. Lawrence Valley or via the Mohawk Valley to Lake Ontario and the Niagara region (Brebner, 1970: 107).

The myth continues that the UELs were entirely British. Yet, the national president of the UEL Association of Canada has emphasized that these refugees were not solely "Anglican...English" but included "Scotish, Irish and German Catholics...[and] Quakers... . Furthermore, that the loyalists were multicultural...cannot be denied. Many were Mohawks from upper New York State, many were Blacks, many were German, Swiss, Danish [or] Dutch; some were Palatines, French and Spanish" (Humber, 1983).

Even so, the ethnic diversity of Canada revolved about the British-French axis for over a century thereafter. From the middle of the 1760s, the population of the several colonies (primarily Newfoundland, Prince Edward Island, Nova Scotia, New Brunswick, and Quebec) increased dramatically. Since French immigration to British North America was extremely small, it is likely that almost all of the immigrants were British. Thus, during the 80 years after 1765, the increase in the population of Prince Edward Island from 500 to over 62 000 in 1848, the rise in Nova Scotia from under 12 000 to almost 277 000, the nearly 200-fold increase in New Brunswick to about 194 000, and the 13-fold increment in Quebec to almost 900 000 likely was almost entirely due to British immigration.

Looked at in summary fashion, the population of New France in 1754 amounted to about 55 000; in the four British colonies, the population was probably less than 10 000. From a base of about 65 000 at most, the population vaulted to 2.4 million, over 37 times as many, by 1851.* Given even the high birth rate and natural increase rate of the time (45 per 1000 for the French and perhaps 25 per 1000 for the British), the population rise was magnitudes above the potential from natural increase alone. So, immigration—mainly British—was the principal factor here. We can, therefore, conclude that in this crucial period, the ethnic nature of Canada changed from being primarily French and Indian to being primarily British.

In 1851, the populations of Nova Scotia, New Brunswick, Quebec, and Ontario, taken as a whole, were predominantly British (63%) or French (35%). The relatively few members of other ethno-racial-religious groups, in order of proportional presence were Native Peoples, Blacks, Germans, Italians, Jewish, and a sprinkling of others (Table 2.1).

Although there are no precise figures, it seems probable that the "British" was not a homogeneous group in 1851. In all likelihood, the Scottish comprised a larger portion of the British than did the English, and the Scots and Irish together numbered twice as many as the English. Certainly this was the case in 1871, and the numbers of Scots continued to be greater than those of the English until 1901.

At the same time, the proportion of the Canadian population made up of British groups began to decline after 1861. The French, too, continued to decrease as a proportion of the Canadian population. Both of these declines were due to the increased presence of Blacks, Native Peoples, Germans, Eastern and Southern Europeans, and Asians. By the turn of the century, the non-charter groups made up 12% of the Canadian population, compared to only 2% 50 years before. This increasing ethnic diversity was accentuated during the two decades before the Great Depression to the extent that non-charter groups were one-fifth of Canadians in 1931.

---

*The Census of Canada, 1870–1871, in addition to being the source for these estimates, provides a wide range of information concerning the French and British colonial populations for the more than 200 years before that date. (See Census of Canada, 1870–1971, Volumes 4 and 5.)

Table 2.1

Ethno-Racial-Religious Group Composition (in %) of the Canadian Population, 1851–1981

Year	Ethno-Racial-Religious Group										
	Arabic	Asian	Chinese	East Indian	Indochinese	Japanese	Korean	Black	British	English	Irish
1851	*	*	*	*	*	*	*	.4	62.6	*	*
1861	*	*	*	*	*	*	*	.8	66.7	*	*
1871	*	*	*	*	*	*	*	.6	60.5	20.3	24.3
1881	*	.1	.1	*	*	*	*	.5	59.0	20.4	22.1
1901**	*	.4	.3	0*	*	.1	*	.3	57.0	23.5	18.4
1911	*	.6	.4	.1	*	.1	*	.2	54.1	26.0	14.9
1921	0*	.7	.5	.1		.2	0*	.2	55.4	29.0	12.6
1931	*	.8	.4	.1	*	.2	*	.2	51.9	26.4	11.9
1941	*	.6	.3	.1	*	.2	*	.2	49.7	25.8	11.0
1951	*	.5	.2	.1	*	.2	*	.1	47.9	25.9	10.3
1961	.1	.7	.3	.2	*	.2	*	.2	43.8	23.0	9.6
1971	.1	1.3	.6	.6	*	.2	*	.2	44.6	29.0	7.3
1981	.3	2.6	1.2	.8	.2	.2	.1	.6	43.6	25.4	4.8

Year	Scottish	Other British	Central & So. Am.	Czechoslovak	Dutch	Filipino	French	German	Greek	Hungarian	Italian	Jewish
1851	*	*	*	*	*	*	35.4	.1	*	*	0*	0*
1861	*	*	*	*	*	*	30.8	.9	*	*	0*	0*
1871	15.8	.2	*	*	.9	*	31.1	5.8	*	*	0*	0*
1881	16.2	.2	*	*	.7	*	30.1	5.9	*	*	0*	0*
1901**	14.9	.2	*	*	.6	*	30.7	5.8	0*	0*	.2	.3
1911	14.3	.4	*	*	.8	*	28.5	5.5	.1	.2	.6	1.1
1921	13.4	.5	0*	.1	1.3	0*	27.9	3.4	.1	.1	.8	1.4
1931	13.0	.6	*	.3	1.4	*	28.2	4.6	.1	.4	.9	1.5
1941	12.2	.7	*	.4	1.8	*	30.3	4.0	.1	.5	1.0	1.5
1951	11.0	.7	*	.5	1.9	*	30.8	4.4	.1	.4	1.1	1.3
1961	10.4	.8	*	.4	2.4	*	30.4	5.8	.3	.7	2.5	1.0
1971	8.0	.4	*	.4	2.0	*	28.7	6.1	.6	.6	3.4	1.4
1981	5.9	7.6##	.2	.3	1.8	.3	27.2##	4.7	.6	.5	3.1	1.2

Year	Native Peoples	Polish	Portuguese	Russian	Scandinavian	Spanish	Ukrainian	Yugoslavian	Other European	Other	All Canadians
1851	.4	*	*	*	*	*	*	*	.2	.2	100.0
1861	.6	*	*	*	*	*	*	*	.1	.1	100.0
1871	.7	#	*	0*	0*	*	*	*	.3	0*	100.0
1881	2.5	#	*	0*	.1	*	*	*	.1	1.0	100.0
1901**	2.4	.1	*	.4	.6	*	.1	*	.5	.6	100.0
1911	1.5	.5	*	.6	1.6	*	1.0	*	2.6	.5	100.0
1921	1.3	.6	0*	1.1	1.9	0*	1.2	0*	2.4	.2	100.0
1931	1.2	1.4	0*	.8	2.2	*	2.5	.2	1.3	.1	100.0
1941	1.4	1.5	0*	.7	2.1	*	2.4	.2	1.4	.3	100.0
1951	1.2	1.6	0*	.7	2.0	*	2.5	.2	1.5	1.2	100.0
1961	1.4	1.8	.1	.7	2.1	*	3.9	.4	1.1	1.1	100.0
1971	1.4	1.5	.4	.3	1.8	.1	2.7	.5	.9	1.7	100.0
1981	2.0	1.1	.8	.2	1.2	.2	2.2	.5	1.0	3.9	100.0

Notes: *No data.

**No 1891 data.

0* = above 0, but under 0.051%

Included in Russian.

For British, includes some with multiple ethnic origins reported: two "British" ethnicities, or British and selected other ethnicities; for French, includes multiple ethnic origins reported: French and selected other origins.

Sources: Censuses of Canada

The groups that had the greatest growth in proportionate size (and thus in absolute numbers as well, see Table 2.1) were the various Asian groups, Dutch, Southern and Eastern Europeans, Jewish and Scandinavians. On the down turn side of the changing demographic presence were Blacks, Germans, Native Peoples and the charter groups, excepting the English and Other British (essentially, the Welsh).

The last few decades of the nineteenth century and the first two of the twentieth saw the populating of at least the southern tier of land to the Pacific and the growth of Canada's cities, largely through the immigration, for the first time, of non-charter-group members. During the following two decades, weathering the Great Depression and the Second World War, the ethnic mixture of the Canadian population changed little. Even so, it is noteworthy that between 1931 and 1941, the British group, for the first time in well over a century, contained less than one-half of the entire population (Table 2.1 and Figure 2.1). The post-war years brought even more dramatic changes in the ethno-racial mixture that has come to comprise the Canadian peoples.

Since the Second World War, Canada's ethnic composition has shifted markedly—away from the groups that formed the main components of the population as recently as the early 1940s. At that time, the non-British, non-French accounted for 20% of Canadians; today they are almost 30%. If one adds to the charter groups the "long-resident" ethnicities that in 1931 amounted to at least 1% of the non-charter groups—the Dutch, German, Jewish, Polish, Native, Scandinavian and Ukrainian groups—only 5% of Canadians would not have been included. In 1981, by contrast, the "recent immigrant" groups made up 12% of the population.

From another time dimension, we can see that, since 1951, the proportion of Canadians represented by Asians has risen fourfold (and that of the Chinese over sixfold); by Blacks tenfold; Greeks sevenfold; Italians threefold; Portuguese at least tenfold (Table 2.1). Between 1971 and 1981 alone, the number of Asians in Canada almost doubled (and the number of Chinese Canadians rose by more than one-and-a-half times); the number of Black Canadians increased nearly two-and-a-half times (and about 5.8 times over their number in 1961); the Greeks one-third more (and 1.7 times their number since 1961); the Portuguese nearly double (and at least 16 times their number in 1961).

The Canadian peoples in 1981 were of markedly different ethnic

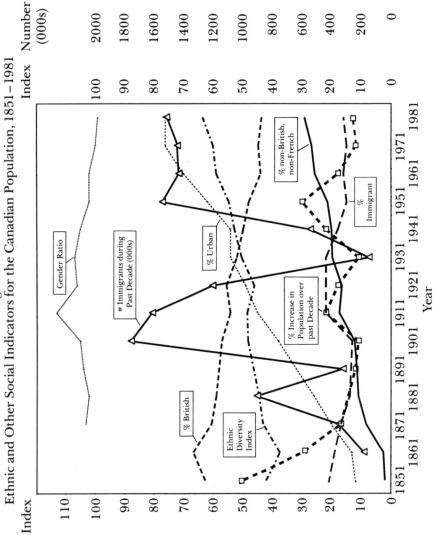

Figure 2.1

Ethnic and Other Social Indicators for the Canadian Population, 1851–1981 origins and races than at Confederation, and that change has been accelerating, particularly with regard to peoples who, at Confederation and even in 19o1 were all but absent, or present only in minute numbers. Canada today is becoming a newly-peopled nation compared to what it was originally, and that alteration continues. The rate of growth in the charter and other "long-resident" ethnicities is at best barely above the national norm. They form the backbone of Canada's peoples, but it is the newer ethno-racial-religious groups that are transforming the look of Canadians, a transformation that will have lasting effects.

ETHNIC-DIVERSITY INDEX

As Figure 2.1 demonstrated, the changing nature of the Canadian peoples is reflected and associated with many other alterations in the population. One of these reflections is the Ethnic-Diversity Index, a calculation of the average extent to which each ethno-racial-religious group (on which data could be found), as a percent of the entire population, varied from the largest ethnic group in Canada (the British).* An Index of 100 would indicate absolutely no variation in the degree each group was represented in the population, while an Index of 0 would be indicative of a population comprised totally of one ethnicity. The Ethnic Diversity Index was also calculated for five of the metropolitan areas in Canada, reflecting differences in regional location and ethnic mix of population. In Montreal, the majority group in 1851 was the British but thereafter it was the French. In Halifax, Toronto, Winnipeg, and Vancouver, the majority group was the British.

Because of the large number of French in Canada since at least 1851, relative to the number of British, the Ethnic Diversity Index for the nation was never very low. (Assembly of data for the seventeenth to early nineteenth centuries, if it was possible, would undoubtedly show a much greater diversity than existed in 1851.) Even so, the rise in the Diversity Index for Canada (Table 2.2) in the four decades following 1861 and in the 1921–1961 era, reflects the increasing presence of non-charter groups in Canada and the maintenance of the French as a Canadian people. The situation in

---

*The Index was calculated by 100 − (the sum of variations of each "minority" group from the "majority" group, divided by the number of "minority" groups).

Table 2.2
Ethno-Racial-Religious Diversity Index for Canada
and 5 Canadian Cities, 1851–1981

Year	Canada	Halifax	Montreal	Toronto	Winnipeg	Vancouver
1851	42.1	*	51.4	3.4	*	*
1861	37.5	*	57.4	4.1	*	*
1871	43.1	11.8	50.3	4.9	16.7	*
1881	44.4	14.5	47.7	7.0	17.6	*
1901	48.3	12.5	45.2	9.0	28.4	32.4
1911	48.5	14.0	48.1	15.0	39.8	21.9
1921	46.7	14.3	39.0	15.5	34.1	21.2
1931	50.4	16.0	38.2	25.2	41.9	24.2
1941	52.7	20.2	35.7	27.6	43.8	24.0
1951	54.6	22.0	34.5	32.8	52.5	30.5
1961	58.9	29.6	35.2	50.5	60.5	44.9
1971	60.1	28.3	37.7	57.1	62.3	49.3
1981	63.4	30.0	44.0	61.1	62.3	58.8

Notes: Higher index values reflect greater ethno-racial-religious diversity. The
index theoretically ranges from 0 (no ethnic diversity) to 100 (all ethno-
racial-religious groups are equally present in the population).
* no data.

Sources: Table 2.1 (above) and Censuses of Canada

Montreal, however, has been just the opposite: a long-term reduction until 1961 in the diversity of groups in that city, indicative of an
increasing domination of Montreal's population by the French,
then a small alteration in the pattern in the past 25 years.

The only other city to approximate the Montreal condition was
Vancouver, where the British majority became even more dominant in the population from 1901 through 1921. Even after the
Second World War, ethnic diversity there rose only slightly. Since
1951, though, a significant magnification in ethnic diversity has
taken place. The other three cities (Halifax, Toronto, Winnipeg)
each show a pattern of from mild to great transformation in the
ethnic mix of their populations. Halifax continued to remain the
most British of the cities and much less ethnically divergent even
when compared to Montreal. But still, in Halifax, the modest
increment in the Index since 1951 is evident.

Toronto is an extreme in Ethnic Diversity pattern, being almost
wholly British in 1851 and remaining so for about three-quarters of
a century. The massive immigration between 1921 and the Great

Depression, and again after the Second World War converted Toronto into a very multicultural place. Winnipeg, starting out with a less British-dominated population just after Confederation, became more diverse than Toronto, and it did so earlier. Today, it is likely the most ethnically diverse city in the nation, followed closely by Toronto. And since Canada's people are primarily urban dwellers, then, to the extent that the ethnic diversity patterns of Toronto, Winnipeg, and Vancouver become typical instead of those of Halifax or Montreal, to the same extent Canada will become increasingly more diverse. As these data intimate (and as later data point out more precisely), the periods of extensive immigration of non-British during the latter decades of the nineteenth century, plus the huge numbers of such immigrants following the two world wars have made Canadians a quite different people, progressively more ethnically, racially, and religiously diverse. Unless there is a marked change in the source of new immigrants in the years to come, compared to the 1951–1981 years, Canadians will continue to become even more diverse then they now are.

GENDER RATIOS OF CANADIANS

The Gender Ratio describes the degree of difference between men and women in some particular characteristic. Thus, it is a direct indicator of gender differentiation. The Ratio is calculated by multiplying by 100 the result of dividing the statistic for males (e.g., the number of males along some dimension, the number or percent of males with some particular attribute, etc.) by the statistic for females. Thus, to the extent the Gender Ratio exceeds 100, the statistic for males is greater than for females, and to the degree the Ratio is below 100, the statistic for females is greater than for males. We can, thereby, immediately judge the degree of difference between the genders along that particular dimension or with respect to that particular attribute (i.e., number in Canada, rate of language retention, religious affiliation rate).

Here, we are comparing the number of men in a particular ethno-racial-religious group to the number of women, both across groups and within groups over time (Table 2.3). Unfortunately, the earliest information dates from only 1911, which is well after the earlier periods of nation building through heavy immigration. Even so, as we shall see in the next chapter, 1911 was the year in which Canada experienced its highest-ever level of immigration. This wave of immigration had begun about a decade before and would ebb about five years later. So, 1911 does reflect the pre-First-World-War flow of immigrants that had begun shortly after Confederation and which peaked in that year.

In this period, the overall Gender Ratio of the Canadian population was at its highest point; thereafter, the number of men relative to that of women in Canada declined—considerably from 1911 to 1921 and more slowly from then on. That the national Gender Ratio for 1911 was so high was due, in large part, to the nearly as high Ratio among the British, who constituted so large a part of the population. It should also be understood that, in virtually every group from the earliest years of immigration, there were more males than females. Thus, the Gender Ratio was higher still in groups with much smaller populations than the Britishr all Asian groups, Greeks, Hungarians, Italians, Poles, Russians, Scandinavians and Ukrainians. Only among the Black, Dutch, German, Jewish, Native Canadian and especially the French groups was the ethnic-group Gender Ratio lower.

By 1921, however, the Ratio had declined in all groups and, except for a few ethnicities, would never again be as elevated. Indeed, even during the immigrant-heavy years of the 1950s and 1960s, the Gender Ratio remained close to parity in many groups. By 1981, the Gender Ratio reflects either an almost equal number of men and women, or a greater number of women than men in about one-half of the groups and especially in the charter and other groups who had been represented in the Canadian population for at least a century.

EXTENT OF URBAN RESIDENCE

Figure 2.2 and Table 2.4 describe the ethnic-group differentiation in the percent of the group that resided in urban areas, and the increase in this percent since 1871. The Figure 2.2 patterns make clear that, even at the time of Confederation, there were consistent variations in the tendency of some groups to be much more urban-oriented and for others to have a decided preference for rural residences. This remains true even today.

Among the most urban-inclined over the decades were: Jewish, Greeks, Italians, Asians, and Blacks. The more rural types included: first and foremost, the Native Peoples, then the Ukrainians, Dutch, Germans, and French. In the period 1871–1881, Russians were quite urban, but by 1901 they had become rural residents; for the Greeks and Asians, it was the other way around. Even so, the overall pattern is more one of regularity in transition than of great change or reversal. Slowly over the decades, the members of all groups became more urbanized and by 1981, with the sole exception of the Native Peoples and the Dutch, no ethnicity had less than two-thirds of its number living in urban centres.

Following the end of the Second World War, the pace of urbanization had increased to its highest rate, partly because the post-war immigrants had urban destinations, in contrast to the rural destinations of much earlier immigrants. In 1971 and 1981, the degree of difference between groups was one-quarter less than that of a century before. Notwithstanding, those groups who were either more urban or more rural in 1871 have approximately the same overall location in the urban-rural standings of the present era; on the whole, it is only the range between groups that has declined.

Since over one-half of all Canadians were urbanites by 1931, looking merely at the percent of the group that had "urban" residence becomes rather confusing. To clarify this, separate data are presented on the percent of a group's members that resided in large urban places of at least 500 000 population; this is more suited to analysis of trends in the recent decades (Table 2.5). Once more, the greater urban residence by particular groups is evident in the period before the Second World War: Jewish, Greeks, and Italians. In contrast, Asians, Czechoslovaks, Dutch, Germans, Hungarians, Native Peoples, Poles, Russians, Scandinavians, and Ukrainians were predominantly rural.

Fifty years later, the patterns of difference are substantially the same. For the Asians and Blacks, however, major change occurred after the Second World War; they became primarily residents of large cities. The groups that in 1921–1931 were least resident in such large centres continue to live elsewhere today; whereas, Jewish, Italians, Greeks, Chinese, and Blacks are pre-eminently city-dwellers.

The extent to which members of an ethnicity are urbanized, including residence in Canada's largest centres, can have a strong impact on many dimensions of a group's culture and social structure. For instance, to the extent that the group's members are urbanites, there is greater likelihood of cultural forms adapting away from the traditional or immigrant cultures to forms more

Table 2.3
Gender Ratios in Canadian Ethno-Racial-Religious Groups, 1911–1981

Ethno-Racial-Religious Group

Year	Arabic	Asian	Chinese	East Indian	Indochinese	Japanese	Korean	Black	British
1911	*	1501	2790	8574	*	502	*	109	112
1921	*	614	1533	*	*	197	*	108	105
1931	*	437	1241	*	*	145	*	110	105
1941	*	312	785	*	*	130	*	108	104
1951	*	186	374	118	*	115	*	*	100
1961	*	134	163	*	*	107	*	102	100
1971	110	111	112	109	*	103	*	94	98
1981	120	105	102	107	127	101	91	92	97

Year	Ctrl. & So. Am.	Czechoslovak	Dutch	Filipino	French	German	Greek	Hungarian	Italian
1911	*	*	110	*	103	110	578	152	322
1921	*	120	108	*	101	109	261	111	147
1931	*	195	110	*	101	110	179	162	128
1941	*	130	107	*	101	107	161	127	121
1951	*	126	105	*	100	104	*	120	126
1961	*	118	106	*	100	104	*	122	115
1971	*	115	107	*	99	103	111	115	111
1981	93	110	107	79	97	102	109	109	109

Year	Jewish	Native Peoples	Polish	Portuguese	Russian	Scandinavian	Spanish	Ukrainian	Yugoslavian	All Canadians
1911	110	103	*	165	149	164	*	135	*	113
1921	103	103	120	*	123	131	*	118	238	106
1931	102	105	129	*	120	138	*	120	337	107
1941	102	105	116	116	118	128	*	113	165	105
1951	103	104	117	*	111	119	*	111	151	102
1961	103	103	112	*	106	112	*	109	130	102
1971	101	*	106	106	99	107	105	104	117	100
1981	102	98	103	103	97	107	102	100	109	99

Notes: * no data.
  Gender Ratio = (# Males / # Females) × 100.
Sources: Censuses of Canada

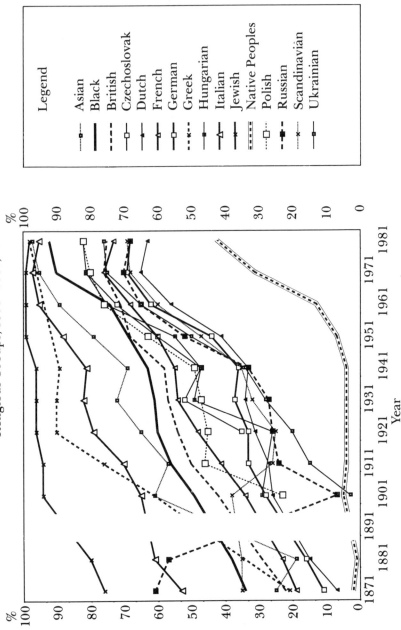

Figure 2.2
Extent of Urban Residence (in %) Among Canadian Ethno-Racial
–Religious Groups, 1871–1881, 1901–1981

compatible with the technological post-industrial values and structures that exist in the cities. Further, the cities are sites in which intra-group social interactions are more likely to occur. This is due to the greater concentration of a particular group within a geographically limited area and to the higher potential for proximity of residence among ethnic group members. Each of these leads to the early and sustained development of ethnic social, religious, economic, artistic, and other institutions to serve the ethnic-group population much more so than would be possible in places without these advantages of ethnic concentration.

In the cities also, there is often a greater mix of ethnicities and so, more opportunity for interaction by people of one group with those of a variety of other ethnicities, races, and religions. Thus, the nature of the socio-cultural forms of the urban members in any particular ethnicity is likely to be somewhat different from those of ethnic members residing in rural areas. Residence in the cities, therefore, affords both advantages and disadvantages for the preservation and adaptation of ethnic community values, structures, processes, and contents (e.g. arts, literature, occupations, economic emphases). We might expect, perhaps, that groups whose members have been urban residents in large numbers and proportions for several decades or even generations have been able to develop and maintain their transported culture and its structural supports, albeit in forms rather different from those that existed in the home country, or in Canada's rural areas, and which exist today in the home country. The other side of this connection between ethnic cohesion and urban residence is the possibility of ethnic assimilation to the dominant culture that existed in the past—in most of Canada, the Anglo-Celtic culture.

SUMMARY

In almost every respect, the ethnic, racial, and/or religious situation in Canada today differs from that of a century or more ago. The peoples of Canada have become immensely more diverse, not only in the much greater variety of groups, but also in the increased membership of each group currently. Canadian ethnic groups have also moved from male dominance toward gender parity; while some ethno-racial or religious groups had more than twice as many males as females, today's figures reflect the pattern of more mature, gender-balanced communities.

Table 2.4

Extent of Urban Residence (in %) Among Canadian Ethno-Racial-Religious Groups, 1871–1981

Year	Ethno-Racial-Religious Group									
	Arabic	Asian	Chinese	East Indian	Indochinese	Japanese	Black	British	English	Irish
1871	*	25	*	*	*	*	34	22	24	25
1881	*	19	19	*	*	*	38	29	31	30
1901	*	61	61	*	*	35	49	42	45	41
1911	*	57	63	*	*	37	56	50	54	47
1921	*	65	73	*	*	40	60	54	56	51
1931	*	72	83	*	*	47	61	57	59	55
1941	*	69	78	*	*	46	63	58	60	56
1951	*	79	87	*	*	62	*	68	67	63
1961	*	89	93	*	*	80	74	71	72	69
1971	*	95	97	*	*	89	90	76	*	*
1981	96	97	98	96	96	92	92	75	*	*

Year	Scottish	Other British	Central & So. Am.	Czecho-slovak	Dutch	Filipino	French	German	Greek	Hung-arian
1871	17	19	*	*	7	*	19	11	21	*
1881	23	30	*	*	15	*	23	16	*	*
1901	38	44	*	*	26	*	34	28	61	29
1911	48	52	*	*	27	*	41	33	76	*
1921	52	55	*	35	31	*	48	33	90	26

Year										
1931	57	58	*	52	34	*	54	37	90	49
1941	57	60	*	47	33	*	55	36	89	47
1951	66	70	*	60	41	*	60	44	*	55
1961	71	75	*	72	56	*	68	62	*	75
1971	*	*	*	81	65	*	76	69	*	81
1981	*	*	97	82	63	98	73	68	98	82

Year	Italian	Jewish	Native Peoples	Polish	Portu-guese	Russian	Scandi-navian	Spanish	Ukranian	Yugo-slavian	All Canadians
1871	76	2	*	*	*	61	35	*	*	*	20
1881	80	1	*	*	*	57	35	*	*	*	26
1901	94	5	*	23	*	7	38	*	3	*	38
1911	94	4	*	46	*	24	26	*	15	*	45
1921	96	4	*	45	*	26	25	*	20	49	49
1931	96	4	*	47	*	27	32	*	28	55	54
1941	96	4	*	49	*	33	35	*	34	54	54
1951	99	7	*	63	*	52	47	*	50	*	62
1961	99	13	*	76	*	65	60	*	65	*	70
1971	99	31	*	80	*	70	68	*	75	*	76
1981	98	42	98	82	97	68	69	96	76	*	76

Notes: "urban" residence, as applied here, is according to the criteria in each census, rather than the present one.
There is no data for 1891.
* no data.

Sources: Censuses of Canada

Table 2.5

Extent (%) of Residence in Places with 500 000 or More Population among Canadian Ethno-Racial-Religious Groups, 1921–1981

Year				Ethno-Racial-Religious Group					
	Arabic	Asian	Chinese	East Indian	Indochinese	Japanese	Black	British	Central & So. Am.
1921	*	7	10	*	*	0*	11	12	*
1931	*	9	10	*	*	1	13	13	*
1941	*	11	13	*	*	1	16	18	*
1951	*	38	*	*	*	*	*	22	*
1961	*	48	*	*	*	*	*	25	*
1971	*	64	65	*	*	61	67	28	*
1981	74	78	82	75	65	74	73	35	87

Year	Czecho-slovak	Dutch	Filipino	French	German	Greek	Hungarian	Italian	Jewish
1921	2	4	*	16	2	39	1	33	61
1931	17	3	*	18	3	40	12	35	60
1941	15	5	*	21	4	47	11	38	69
1951	*	9	*	22	7	*	*	43	74

1961	*	15	*	26	15	*	*	*	58	76
1971	35	20	*	32	22	*	*	35	65	87
1981	48	29	86	41	30	84		49	74	92

Year	Native Peoples	Polish	Portuguese	Russian	Scandi-navian	Spanish	Ukrainian	Yugoslavian	All Canadians
1921	0*	9	*	3	1	*	2	6	13
1931	0*	11	*	5	2	*	3	10	14
1941	1	13	*	5	3	*	6	11	18
1951	*	22	*	21	13	*	13	*	22
1961	*	30	*	30	18	*	17	*	26
1971	10	35	*	27	21	*	29	*	32
1981	31	50	76	35	33	83	44	*	41

Notes: * No data.

0* = under 0.51%.

Sources: Censuses of Canada, 1921–1931 data from statistics on cities; 1941–1961 data from statistics on Census Metropolitan Areas; 1971–1981 data from statistics by size of place.

Urbanization has been another major influence on the nature of the Canadian peoples. While certain groups continue to maintain above-average residence on farms or nearby rural areas, most ethno-racial-religious groups have become urbanites. This trend has focused the social power of ethnicities, because the members have become more proximate as the urbanization process went on; and low diversity of ethnic groups has been transformed into a great diversity of cohesive, geographically sizeable, and potentially powerful memberships.

Yet, a fundamental question that remains to be answered is whether the shift to urban ethnicity has, in the modern era, been more of a benefit or a disadvantage to the multiple groups in Canada. Rural isolation carried with it the potential for high ethno-religious cultural maintenance. Urban proximity of a group's members also portends association with other ethno-racial-religious groups and the potential for cultural assimilation.

Given the striking changes in the makeup of Canada's peoples, we need next to inquire into the immigration process—people coming from outside Canada and settling here—before going on to questions of ethnic cohesion. What we have established thus far are the bare outlines of changes in the peoples that have made up Canada.

## CHAPTER 3

Immigration to Canada

INTRODUCTION: IMMIGRATION AS A POPULATION DYNAMIC

Immigration has been an important population dynamic in Canada for a considerably longer time than the thirteen decades for which immigration statistics exist. From the first European contact, there was much immigration, but it was a long time before systematic records were kept. Even today, there is little precise information on the number or characteristics of those who leave this country. When one discusses the "number of immigrants to Canada," one is speaking of the number of persons who were officially counted as entering Canada from another country with the intent of making this country their permanent place of residence. Our sources of information are inexact concerning figures and/or the definition of immigrant but, this is all that is available for the study of who, and how many moved to Canada from elsewhere during any specified years.

Thus, granting the problems of counting involved, it is still probable that immigrants have accounted for something like one-third to one-half or more of Canadian population growth over any decade's time. During the periods of relatively high immigration—the late 1800s through the 1920s—it is likely that immigrants represented close to or more than the entirety of population growth (Table 3.1). Obviously, such calculations must have left out something: emigration figures—immigrants to Canada who later left or Canadian-born residents who moved. Despite this unavoidable omission the results still underline the importance that immi-

Table 3.1
Immigration to Canada as a Ratio to Natural Increase and as a Percent of
Population Increase in Canada, 1861–71 to 1971–81

Decade	Births minus Deaths (000s)	Interdecade Population Increase (000s)	Immigration (000s)	Immigration /Natural Increase Ratio	Immigration as % of Cdn. Population Increase
1861–1871	651	395	183	.28	46
1871–1881	723	636	353	.49	56
1881–1891	714	508	903	1.26	178
1891–1901	718	538	326	.45	61
1901–1911	1120	1836	1759	1.57	96
1911–1921	1230	1581	1612	1.31	102
1921–1931	1360	1589	1205	.89	76
1931–1941	1222	1130	150	.12	13
1941–1951	1972	2502	548	.28	22
1951–1961	3148	4229	1543	.49	36
1961–1971	2703	3330	1429	.53	43
1971–1981	2119	2775	1440	.68	52

Sources: 1861–71 to 1951–61, F. Hawkins. *Canada and Immigration*. (Montreal: McGill-Queen's University Press, 1972), p. 371; 1961–71 to 1971–81 figures from CEIC: Canada Immigration Statistics (annual issues); Statistics Canada: *Vital Statistics* (annual issues); and Censuses of Canada.

gration and immigrants have had in the growth of the Canadian population over the past century and more. Even the most conservative interpretation of Table 3.1 would have to admit of the undoubted significance of immigration for the growth of our population.

Beyond this, Figure 3.1 shows that, in every aspect of immigration, there have been cycles of increase and decrease, rise and decline of rates in one or another indicator. Most dramatic are the extreme variations in the volume of immigration over entire decades. The rise in immigration volume can also be seen to have inversely influenced the proportion that British made up of all immigrants and increased the portion of immigrants who said they were coming to settle in Ontario. The proportion of immigrants coming from the visible minorities, in a different trend has increased steadily since 1951. Of older origin has been the decline in the extent to which men have comprised the immigrant flow and the small change during the twentieth century of the extent to which immigrants have been a segment of the entire population.

In brief, before the Second World War, immigrants were—much more so than today—British and male. In the most recent decade portrayed, the proportion of visible-minority immigrants was magnitudes higher than the proportion of British immigrants. Gender parity has also characterized recent immigration. These phenomena, it should be noted, have obtained during an era of extremely elevated levels of immigration; whether any significant changes will take place during the 1980s—other than the admission of considerably fewer immigrants—only time will tell.

IMMIGRANTS THROUGH TIME

Table 3.2 summarizes the history of immigration into Canada, according to: (1) ethno-racial-religious groups, (2) the periods of major immigration, and (3) the predominant occupations of the immigrant groups.*

The long-term trends of immigration are depicted in Figure 3.2. The history of immigration into Canada since 1852 can be differentiated into seven periods (Figure 3.2). The first period, 1850 to 1880, was one of steady but low immigration; in only one year did as many as 50 thousand immigrants arrive. Second, between 1880 and the mid-1890s there was an abrupt rise (1880–1890) followed by a gradual decline (1890–1896) to even lower levels than had existed before. This marked the first, large, decade-long period of sustained immigration in Canada's experience, greater by far than any of the previous waves, including that of the Loyalists a century before. It was this mass of immigrants in the ten years following 1880 that began in earnest the population of the Canadian Prairies and the West by means other than internal migration.

In the third period, economic recession combined with internal political problems in the first half of the 1890s had the effect of cutting immigration to almost nothing (Brebner, 1970:330). The

*More detailed histories of ethnic groups in Canada are available in such journals as *Polyphony* (published by the Multicultural History Society of Ontario) and *Canadian Ethnic Studies*, as well as in the *Generations* series of books about dozens of ethno-racial-religious groups (published by McClelland and Stewart in co-operation with the Ministry for Multiculturalism for Canada).

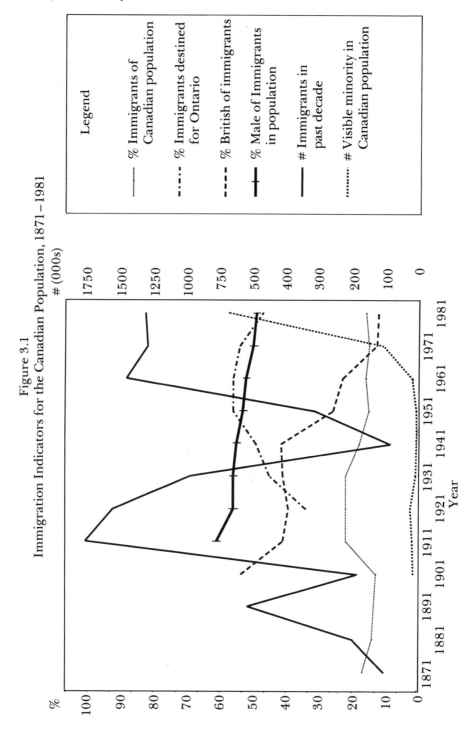

Figure 3.1
Immigration Indicators for the Canadian Population, 1871–1981

Table 3.2
Immigration of Selected Ethno-Racial-Religious Groups into Canada

Group(s)	Date(s)	Major Occupation(s)
Native Peoples	Pre–1600	All occupational roles of self-contained societies
French	1609–1755	Fishing, farming, fur trading + supporting occupations: military, blacksmithing, etc.
Loyalists from U.S.A.: Mennonites, Blacks, Germans, English, Scots, Quakers	1776 to mid-1780s	Farming
English & Scottish	mid-1600s on & 1815 on	Farming, skilled crafts
Germans & Scandinavians	1830s to 1850s & c. 1900, 1950s	Farming Mining, city jobs
Irish	1840s	Farming, logging, Construction
Blacks from U.S.A.	1850s to 1870s	Farming
Mennonites & Hutterites	1870s through 1880s	Farming
Chinese	1855 & 1880s	Panning gold Railway building, mining
Jews	1890s to 1st WW	Factory work, skilled trades, small business
Japanese	1890s to 1st WW	Logging, service employment in city, mining, fishing
East Indians	1890s to 1st WW & 1970s	Logging, service employment, mining Skilled trades, professions, farm work in B.C.

Table 3.2   Continued

Group(s)	Date(s)	Major Occupation(s)
Ukrainians	1890s to 1914 1940s to 1950s	Farming Variety of occupations
Italians	1890s to 1st WW 1950s to 1960s	Railway building, other construction, small business Construction, skilled trades
Polish	1945–1950	Skilled trades, factory work, mining
Portuguese	1950s to 1970s	Factory work, construction, service occupations, farming
Greeks	1955 to mid-1970s	Factory work, small business, skilled trades
Hungarians	1956–1957	Professions, variety of other occupations
West Indians	1950s 1967 on	Domestic work, nursing Factory work, skilled trades, professional, service occupations, contract farm labour
Central/South Americans	1970s and 1980s	Professions, factory and service occupations
Vietnamese	late 1970s to early 1980s	Variety of occupations, including self-employment

Source: Cross-Cultural Communication Centre (no date)

election of 1896 saw both an end to the recession and the assumption of power by the Liberal Party led by Wilfrid Laurier. Under Laurier, and with improved economic conditions throughout the world, Canada experienced its greatest period of growth—both economically and in population: well over three million immigrants arrived over the next two decades (the fourth period). Indeed, between 1910 and 1913 alone, more than 1.3 millions arrived in Canada, a not inconsiderable proportion of the entire population in that era (Hawkins, 1972: 371–372).

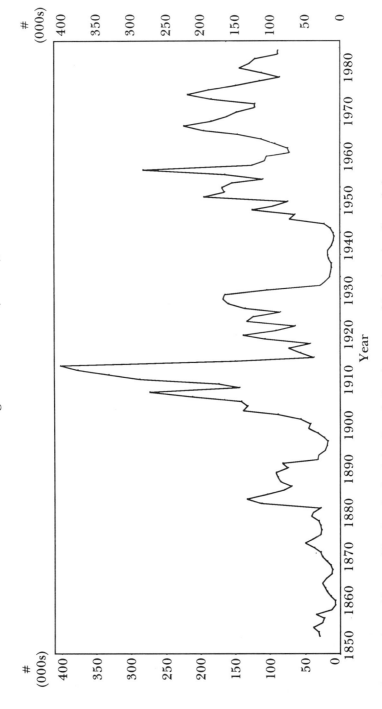

Figure 3.2

Number of Immigrants to Canada (in 000s), 1852–1980

Sources: Annual issues of *Immigration Statistics*. Canada Employment and Immigration Commission. (Ottawa: Minister of Supply and Services Canada.)

The fifth period in the long-term trends of immigration is the 17 years following 1913, which saw an abrupt decline in immigration because of the First World War and then see-saw alterations until the late 1920s. The sixth period began in 1930 when the number of immigrants declined to almost nothing and remained that way through the Great Depression and the ensuing war years. With the ending of the Second World War (the seventh period), immigration began again and has continued apace, never falling below 70 000 immigrants per year since 1945 and frequently exceeding 150 000 in a year. Since the war, the number of immigrants admitted has taken on a saw-tooth pattern—declining somewhat over a half-decade, then rising back to about the original level over the next half-decade and so forth.

Overall, while the levels of immigration since the Second World War never reached the enormous peak of the 1910–1913 period, neither has it declined to ever being very low. And, while the pattern of numbers is a jagged one (Figure 3.2), the immense post-1945 immigration has added nearly 5 000 000 people to Canada's population through 1980, an average of about 140 000 per year. This exceeds the levels of all previous eras in Canada, with the exception of the dizzing height of the first two decades of the twentieth century. Moreover, it appears from all indications that the level of immigration will continue at a moderately high level throughout the 1980s and 1990s, even if not at the very elevated level of the 1950s and 1960s.

In terms of regional distribution of immigrants in Canada, the prevailing trend ever since 1921 has been a tripartite one: Ontario has been the most popular site of destination, accounting for about one-half of all immigrants; Quebec the Prairies, and the Territories together with British Columbia have, collectively, attracted from somewhat fewer to somewhat more immigrants than Ontario; the Atlantic region has been the least-sought destination, but always a small proportion have settled there. For the last 40 years, this has been a quite stable pattern, and there is little in the immigration policies and forecasts that might alter this picture. In fact, given the nature of recent immigration, there is every reason to predict that the dominance of Ontario (and of the cities of southern Ontario) will at least continue and, perhaps, even strengthen.

IMMIGRANTS' DISTRIBUTION AMONG ETHNICITIES

Unfortunately, the analysis of trends in immigration with respect to the proportion or number of immigrants in each ethno-racial-religious group has been possible only since the turn of this century. The category of pre-1901 immigrants combines those who came here at various times: all who were immigrants in Canada at the time of the 1901 census. Data between 1901 and 1980 on distribution by ethnic group are differentiated by the period of immigration, and are drawn, not from the census, but from immigration statistics (Figure 3.3). Figure 3.3 illustrates in a rather gross fashion the numerical predominance of the British ethnicities in Canadian immigration throughout the entirety of post-Confederation times until the 1970s. Even when immigration fell to exceptionally low levels, the British still constituted the bulk of those coming to this country.

If the reader can follow the intricate path of each ethnicity, it will become evident that, excepting the preponderance of British and excepting the period 1931–1940, each group has a rather different history of passage here. For instance, immigration of a fairly large number of Polish is reported for 1901–1910, but that number declined rapidly thereafter and increased to moderate numbers only after the beginning of the Second World War. In contrast, Dutch immigrants were relatively few until the Great Depression and Second-World-War era when their numbers rose sharply then dropped once more by 1951, and have remained low since. The immigration of Greeks is rather like that of the Dutch until the war period, when it rose considerably and remained quite high through 1980.

German immigration shows a rather saw-toothed pattern, with marked declines during the two war periods, but higher than most other groups during the 1921–1930 and 1951–1961 decades. Italians (allies of Canada in the First World War but not in the Second) had a still different immigration trend: high in numbers between 1910 and 1920 and rising to become the second-largest immigrant group in the 1951–1971 period, well over 150 000 immigrants per decade. In contrast, French immigration has always been quite low, even during the period 1951–1970, when the average number of French immigrants per decade was not even 50 000.

As indicated earlier, the British no longer comprise the largest

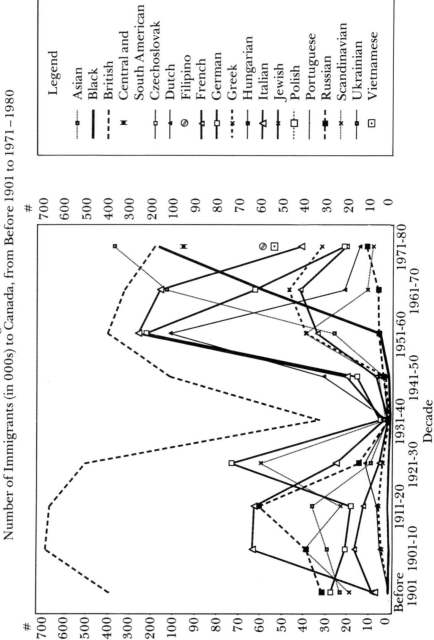

Figure 3.3
Number of Immigrants (in 000s) to Canada, from Before 1901 to 1971–1980

immigrant ethnicity. A downward trend in the number of immigrant British has been evident since 1960, and, by the end of the 1970s, Asian immigration (excluding the Filipinos) was double the number of British. Moreover, the number of Black immigrants (West Indians, Africans, *not* including any Black-American immigrants) was almost as great as that of the British.

Another group that became sizeable in the 1970s were those from Central and South America. Although this area is very large, immigrants to Canada were too few to be categorized separately until the period 1971–1980, when they constituted almost one-half the number of the British. Finally, we consider the Portuguese, who constituted a tiny number of immigrants into Canada for perhaps three centuries, but whose numbers have been counted only since 1901. Before the Second World War, the number of Portuguese immigrants (both mainland and Azorean-Madeiran) was, at its highest, about 1000 per decade. Following the war, however, the number accelerated sharply and continuously, so that from 1971 to 1980 Portuguese represented the fifth-largest immigrant group.

Thus, the numbers of immigrants have changed along at least three dimensions: (1) the numbers from one ethnicity in the past relative to others then and today; (2) the numbers within the same group over time; and (3) the rank of various groups in the past relative to today's situation. Through the 1960s, the British constituted the largest category of immigrants. During the post-war years, the number of immigrants in several other groups was close to that of the British, a pattern quite different from that prior to the war. By the 1950s, the number of immigrant Italians, Germans and Dutch was close to the British level; jointly, those groups greatly exceeded the British.

At the same time, and even more so over the next 20 years, other ethno-racial groups were becoming much more dominant as immigrants to Canada. The 1960s saw the emergence of Chinese, Japanese, East Indian and other Asian immigrants; West Indians and other Black immigrants; and the Portuguese and Greeks bolstering the Italians in the immigration of Mediterranean peoples to Canada. Then in the 1970s, the pace of Asian and Black immigration accelerated; the number of British immigrants continued to decline, and, for the first time, large numbers of Central-South Americans, Filipinos, and Vietnamese became significant immigrant groups. By 1980, the ethno-racial nature of immigrants into Canada was very much different from what it had been early in the century and even so recently as 1950. In terms of both ethnicity and race, recent immigrants to Canada are much more varied than has ever been the case before; a sign, perhaps, of the future rather than a reflection of the past.

Inspecting the proportional representation of each ethno-racial-religious group among Canada's immigrants since the end of the nineteenth century accentuates these shifts and alterations in immigration patterns much more sharply than looking at numbers of immigrants (Table 3.3). Of all pre-1901 immigrants identified in the Canada census of that year, over one-half were British; any other ethnic group comprised well under one-tenth. Of these, Asians, Germans, Russians, and Scandinavians were the most prominent of the groups identified. (It is likely also that had Ukrainians, as such, been identified by immigration or census officials, then they also would have been prominent. At that time however, Ukrainians were not categorized and even later were included under diverse labels; the term "Ukrainian" did not come into use until 1921 for some analytic dimensions and 1931 in others.)

The information concerning the years from 1901 and later are from actual immigration statistics, rather than the census. It is evident that the immigrant stream was less made up of British than those reported in the 1901 census as British immigrants; in all probability, the proportion of immigrants that were British had been declining for several years prior to 1901. Even so, in the first decade of the twentieth century, the British were still the predominant immigrant group by an order of eight magnitudes, compared to the next largest group, the Polish (41% vs. 5% respectively). The British continued to dominate the immigration rolls, even during the Great Depression and through the 1940s.

In the decades before the Second World War, a variety of European groups slowly increased their proportional representation among immigrants. In the first decade of the century, there was an increased proportion of immigrants from Italian and Polish groups. The second decade saw a higher proportion of Italians again and of Russians and Ukrainians; the 1920s had higher than previous levels from Czechoslovak, German, Hungarian, Jewish, Polish, Scandinavian and, again, Ukrainian categories. The Depression and earliest war years saw more Czechoslovaks, Hungarians, Jewish and Ukrainians immigrate, while the 1940s were marked by a higher percent of Dutch, Italians, Polish, and the

continued flow of Ukrainians. In that decade, groups having conspicuously lower rates of immigration—but for entirely different
reasons—were the Asians Hungarians and especially the Jewish,
whose proportion dropped thirty-fold when compared to the previous decade.

However, the war years and the reorganization of Canada and
other nations in the closing years of the 1940s resulted in a radical
change in the sources of immigrants for Canada during the 1950s.
The earlier exclusionary laws and discriminatory policies, which
had limited immigration from the Asian countries, and of Jewish,
were largely eliminated or, at least, greatly moderated. Too, Bri-
tons were apparently more concerned with rebuilding their cities
and their war-ravaged economy: neither the number or the proportion of immigrants from Britain in these years came close to those
of the pre-Depression years. The level of post-war immigration,
though, was higher than in the decade immediately preceding the
Great Depression, primarily because of much greater immigration
from the many parts of the world previously excluded by Canadian
law or policy. With the 1950s came new and more egalitarian
policies for increased immigration; these combined with the building desire to emigrate on the part of some people in almost every
country of the world to effect great changes in the nature of
immigrants to Canada.

With the decrease of British immigration, greater emphasis was
now on Asians, Dutch, Germans, Hungarians, and, especially,
Greeks, Italians, and Portuguese. At best, these three latter groups
together made up only 3% of all immigrants in the pre-
war/Depression decades, but in the 1951–1960 period they constituted almost 20%. The 1960s saw the continuation of this trend,
with Southern Europeans constituting 18% of immigrants. Also,
the 1960s included a major increase in the importance of Asians
(especially Chinese and East Indians) and Black West Indians. With
the end of the 1970s, it became apparent that Greek and Italian
immigration was lessening, while the Portuguese comprised a
larger share than before. British in this most recent period comprised less then one-seventh of immigrants; this represented more
than a threefold decline from the proportion British had made up
of all immigrants to Canada 30 years before.

The 1970s brought other major alterations in the immigration
flow. Asians came to comprise almost one-third of all immigrants—
including a new group, the Vietnamese. They were also some new

Table 3.3
Percent Distribution of Immigrants to Canada, by Ethno-Racial-Religious Group and Decade,
Before 1901 to 1971–1980

Ethno-Racial-Religious Group

Decade	Asian	Chinese	East Indian	Japanese	Vietnamese	Black	British	Central & So. Am.	Czechoslovak	Dutch	Filipino	Finnish	French	German
Before 1901 #	5.6	4.2	.3	1.2	*	.2	53.5	*	*	.3	*	*	2.0	6.7
1901–10	1.8	.6	.3	.8	*	0*	40.9	*	0*	.3	*	.7	1.0	1.2
1911–20	2.1	1.7	0*	.4	*	.1	39.1	*	.1	.4	*	.6	.7	1.1
1921–30	.7	.4	0*	.3	*	.1	40.9	*	2.3	.9	*	1.4	.4	5.9
1931–40	.8	0*	.2	.6	*	.1	40.6	*	3.7	.6	*	.3	.7	3.0
1941–50	.6	.5	.1	0*	*	.1	41.2	*	1.1	6.3	*	.2	1.3	3.2
1951–60	1.7	1.4	.2	.1	*	.3	25.8	*	.4	7.1	*	1.0	2.1	14.3
1961–70	9.1	3.2	2.4	.3	*	4.2	22.9	*	.3	1.5	*	.4	3.0	4.4
1971–80	29.2	7.6	7.4	.5	3.6	11.5	12.8	6.7	.3	1.0	1.4	.2	1.4	1.5

Decade	Greek	Hungarian	Italian	Lebanese	Jewish	Polish	Portuguese	Russian	Scandinavian	Ukrainian	Yugoslavian	All Groups
Before 1901 #	.1	*	1.7	*	*	*	*	7.7	4.5	*	*	100.0
1901–10	.2	.6	3.8	*	2.9	4.6	0*	2.3	2.3	.3	.7	100.0
1911–20	.3	.3	3.7	*	1.7	2.1	0*	3.5	1.3	3.3	.4	100.0
1921–30	.3	2.4	2.0	*	4.0	3.9	.1	1.2	4.9	4.8	1.7	100.0
1931–40	.4	2.5	1.9	*	3.2	2.6	0*	.5	1.5	5.0	1.8	100.0
1941–50	.4	.7	4.1	*	.1	7.3	.1	.7	1.1	4.6	1.1	100.0
1951–60	2.5	3.0	15.9	*	.9	2.4	1.4	.3	2.5	.9	1.9	100.0
1961–70	3.3	.6	11.2	*	2.0	1.3	3.9	.4	.8	.4	2.4	100.0
1971–80	2.2	.4	2.9	1.9	.4	1.0	5.6	.8##	.6	##	1.7	100.0

Notes: * No data.

0* = under 0.051%.

1971–80 figure for Russians includes Ukrainians.

"Before 1901" figures are based on the number of immigrants in Canada at time of the 1901 census, by Place of Birth.

Total includes many from the United States, undifferentiated by ethnicity.

Sources: Royal Commission on Bilingualism and Biculturalism. *Report: Book 4*. (Ottawa: Information Canada, 1970), pp. 238–245; CEIC, annual statistics on immigration.

groups: Central and South Americans, Lebanese and Filipinos. From widely separated parts of the globe, these three new categories together represented almost one-eighth of the immigrants to arrive here between 1971 and 1980. Another group, not new by any means, but much greater in their relative share in the process were Blacks (mostly West Indians), who made up almost as great a proportion of immigrants as the British.

If one uses a rather restrictive definition of "visible minorities" as including only Asians and Blacks (the number and proportion of immigrant Indians and Inuit to Canada have been infinitesimal), then visible minorities represented less than 1% of immigrants before 1960 and only about 13% in the 1960s. In the decade, 1971–1980, however, they made up about 41% of all immigrants here. If, moreover, the definition of visible minority is expanded to include Filipinos, Lebanese, and Central and South Americans—as many of these peoples perceive themselves to be in Canada and as many "white" Canadians declare them to be—then the visible minorities made up 54% of immigrants to Canada in the period 1971–1980. Immigration to Canada, then, has become increasingly variegated in the post-war era. It has become a rainbow of peoples with a broad spectrum of cultures and a concert of languages—a river of immigrants quite different from that before 1940.

PERCENT IMMIGRANT WITHIN EACH ETHNICITY

At one point in Canada's history nearly three centuries ago, all non-Indians and non-Inuits were immigrants to Canada. Likewise, for all ethnic groups subsequent to the "founding" ones, all members were at some time immigrants to the country. As a matter of fact, the percentage of immigrants within each ethno-racial-religious group at different points over the years provides a ready picture, from a different perspective, of the immigration history of the various groups. For instance, one can speculate that, to the extent that the proportion of a group's immigrant members has decreased over the years, then, to the same extent, immigrants have had a lesser influence on the maintenance and alteration of the group's ethnic structure and culture. Conversely, the extent to which the proportion of immigrants within a group has risen and how quickly it has risen, could provide cues to any shifts in the group's structure and its cultural content. Thus, the percentage of immigrants within a particular group is a useful index to both the immigration process of that group and to a likely source of change in cultural maintenance processes and outcomes.

Estimates of the degree to which each group had immigrant membership were calculated from place-of-birth data in the censuses prior to 1921. Therefore, there are figures on the percentage of immigrants in ethnic groups from 1871 to 1921 (Table 3.4). From 1921, the statistics have been directly cross-tabulated in the censuses. For many ethnicities, there were no specific data until at least a decade after a large number of immigrants had arrived in Canada (e.g., Czechoslovaks, Hungarians, and Ukrainians). For other groups, the numbers of immigrants were relatively low and spread over time, and the census officials became aware of a "new" and sizeable ethnicity only a considerable time after immigration had begun. Thus, for groups like the Dutch, the Germans, the Greeks, the Italians, and the Scandinavians, immigration to this country began so far back and/or had progressed so gradually that by the time the group was listed as a distinct category the proportion of immigrant members within the group was relatively low, although in many of these instances, later waves of immigration changed this condition.

Overall, Canadians have always been, in a substantial measure, immigrants; the proportion of immigrants in the entire population has never been below one-eighth, and it has been almost as high as one-quarter. In fact, for over three decades, 1911 into the 1930s, more than one-fifth of Canadians were immigrants. As Table 3.4 implies and as we haved already noted, there were several ethnic groups other than the British, French, and Native Peoples that were long-present in Canada at the time of Confederation; most of the Germans, Italians, and Scandinavians were Canadian-born.

The waves of immigration beginning near the end of nineteenth century and continuing until about 1930 are reflected largely in the presence of immigrant ethnic groups coming for the first time to Canada—Asians, Czechoslovaks, Hungarians, Poles, and Ukrainians. In addition, Greek, Italian, Jewish, Russian and Scandinavian immigration also increased in numbers during this era which saw the Prairies and the West populated and the transition of Canada from an almost totally agricultural country to one whose residents were more urban than rural.

By the time the Great Depression was testing the fortitude of Canadians, the decline in immigration was transforming most of

Table 3.4

Percent Immigrant of Canadian Ethno-Racial-Religious Groups, 1871–1981

Ethno-Racial-Religious Group

Year	Arabic	Asian	Chinese	Filipino	East Indian	Indochinese	Japanese	Black	British	Central & So. Am.
1871#	*	*	*	*	*	*	*	*	23	*
1881#	*	100*	100*	*	*	*	100*	*	18	*
1901#	*	98	98	*	*	*	98	4	13	*
1911#	*	97	97	*	*	*	93	*	20	*
1921	*	87	93	*	*	*	73	25	26	*
1931	*	71	88	*	*	*	52	20	25	*
1941	*	59	80	*	*	*	39	*	20	*
1951	*	48	69	*	*	*	27	*	16	*
1961	*	46	61	*	*	*	22	*	14	*
1971	*	61	62	*	84	*	24	45	12	*
1981	91	74	75	*	77	94	27	72	12	91

Year	Czechoslovak	Dutch	Filipino	French	German	Greek	Hungarian	Italian	Jewish	Native Peoples
1871#	*	*	*	0*	12	*	*	21	*	*
1881#	*	*	*	0*	10	*	*	42	*	*
1901#	*	1	*	1	9	20	*	63	*	*
1911#	*	7	*	1	10	74	91	76	*	*
1921	56	17	*	3	28	69	51	57	60	1
1931	72	20	*	3	30	57	72	47	56	1
1941	61	16	*	2	24	50	58	39	49	0*

Year										
1951	55	25	*	2	21	61	52	41	43	1
1961	46	36	*	2	27	67	57	59	38	*
1971	49	35	*	2	25	63	48	54	37	2
1981	51	37	92	2	25	61	52	53	36	4

Year	Polish	Portuguese	Russian	Scandinavian	Spanish	Ukrainian	Yugoslavian	All Canadians
1871#	69##	*	69##	36	*	*	*	17
1881#	63	18	63	49	*	*	*	14
1901#	*	*	*	59	*	*	*	13
1911#	*	*	75##	57	*	75##	*	22
1921	48	*	50	62	*	46	85	22
1931	53	*	46	56	*	43	91	22
1941	42	*	38	44	*	35	82	18
1951	44	*	34	34	*	30	98	15
1961	40	*	27	27	*	23	74	16
1971	33	74	23	22	*	18	75	15
1981	38	76	23	22	79	15	*	16

Notes: * No data. No 1981 data.

estimated from data on place of birth.

1871, Polish and Russian combined; 1911, Russian and Ukrainian combined.

0* = under 0.51%.

100* = over 99.50%.

Sources: Censuses of Canada; except for 1971 underlined figures, which are from W.C. Kalbach and W.W. McVey. *The Demographic Bases of Canadian Society.* 2d ed. (Toronto: McGraw-Hill Ryerson, 1979) pp. 202.

these groups into being majority Canadian-born. The even more limited immigration of the war years continued the trend, so that, by 1951, all groups but the Chinese, Czechoslovaks, Greeks and Hungarians, had more Canadian-born members than immigrants. The post-war immigration altered that situation for many of the ethnicities. What the changed nature of post-war immigration sources brought about, was the division of Canada's ethnic groups into (1) a category of long-resident groups whose level of immigration continued to decline steadily or to remain at a level whereby the majority of the group remained Canadian-born versus (2) the category of other groups who experienced an often very rapid increase in the number and proportion of their memberships who were new immigrants.

Stable or declining immigration levels were the course for Japanese, British, French, Germans, Jewish, Native Peoples, Polish, Russians, Scandinavians, and Ukrainians. In contrast, post-war increases in the group's percent of immigrants characterizes Chinese, Blacks, Dutch, Greeks, Italians, and Portuguese. Of the 24 distinct ethnicities listed in Table 3.4, 13 have over one-half their membership comprised of immigrants. By contrast, only seven of the groups have immigrants making up one-quarter or less of the group. The Japanese and Native Peoples are the only visible-minority groups with a low proportion of immigrants, while there are six "white" ethnicities with at least one-half the group's composition being immigrants.

Finally, immigrants of the last 20 years have included many more entire families and/or women than was ever the case at the beginning of this century. The most recent development in immigration to this country has been the much-increased flow of adults coming here for their formal education in Canadian colleges and universities.

SUMMARY

Immigration to Canada has been subject to many changes: in ethno-racial composition, in religious composition, in the balance between genders, and in family units or reunification of families. Increasingly since the Second World War, immigration to Canada has been from regions of the world less prominent in the earlier waves. This rainbow of immigrants has, over the past 30 or so years, made Canada much more richly diverse in ethnic origin, race, and religion.

The 1950s and 1960s saw heavy immigration from Italy, Greece, and Portugal/Azores. The later 1960s also marked the beginning of a great number of visible-minority immigrants: Blacks from the West Indies and Chinese and East Indians from Asia. These last three groups increased their representation in the 1970s, and this decade also witnessed the first sizeable immigration of Filipinos, many groups from Southeast Asia, and people from Central and South America ("Hispanics"). The 1980s and beyond will, undoubtedly, witness the development of new immigration trends to Canada. Likely, this will include even more Latin Americans, more Southeast Asians, and perhaps the first sizeable movement of Africans to Canada (including Blacks) along with both Christian and Moslem Middle Easterners.

There can be no doubt that immigration will continue to be a major population dynamic in Canada and that the flow of immigration from the traditional and more recent sources will combine with even newer sources to make the last two decades of this century an era of still different mixes of incoming peoples. Because of this, the Canada of 2001 will be a different ethno-racial-religious mix from what it was even in 1981. Immigration has always had a strong effect in Canada, and there seems every reason to expect a continuation of population change from the immigration of the present decade. In turn, this will effect ethnic cohesion in both present and new Canadian ethnicities.

It seems likely that Canada's current major immigration policies with respect to flow and country of origin will remain for the near future; family immigration will continue to be prominent, along with even more liberal emphasis on family reunification through immigration to Canada. Undoubtedly, however, new trends among immigrants and in immigration policy will emerge in the 1980s and 1990s. At the time of writing, much controversy had recently erupted over government constraints on the admission of persons claiming to be refugees. While the emphasis in the late 1980s on preventing illegal refugees and deporting them consumed much media space and political rhetoric, this will have relatively little influence on the overall immigration flow into Canada during and beyond the 1990s. Moreover, this hardening of policy will probably be short-lived, given that a substantial increase in the number of immigrants has just been suggested, to compensate for a Canadian birthrate that has been, in recent years, below even the replacement level.

PART 2

ETHNO-CULTURAL MAINTENANCE IN CANADA

INTRODUCTION

After a certain number of people from a particular part of the world had immigrated to Canada, there began a process of settlement which involved two separate, simultaneous, and often contradictory phenomena: (1) establishing the ethnic, racial or religious group *as a group* in this country and/versus (2) adaptation by individual members, families, and the group as a collectivity to their new Canadian home in each and all of its physical, social, and political dimensions. The first of these phenomena was dependent on a great variety of factors, including: the size of the group; the gender balance; whether the group settled in the city or the country; the group's geographic distribution across Canada; the extent to which the imported ethnic culture varied from the ("ethnic" or "secular") culture in the locale(s) of settlement; the extent to which the ethnic culture varied from the semi-official British/French culture of the region; the size of the continuing immigration flow of the group; and, later, the proportion (and influence) of the group's membership who were immigrants to Canada.

In addition to these factors internal to the ethnic group, there were many extra-group influences, often hard for formal social analysis to pin down: the policy of the federal, provincial, and municipal governments toward a particular group, in terms of immigration of its members and the transplantation of its culture, race or religion in Canada; the course of the acceptance-rejection of the group in the locale(s) of settlement, which was, in part, based on the degree to which a pluralistic-egalitarian philosophy was held by the governments and people of Canada at a particular time; and, finally, the economic needs of the regions and the nation. Together, these and other factors conspired to frame the social structure for a group's physical and cultural establishment in Canada and its subsequent maintenance over the following decades and generations. These structural properties can be compared to a human skeleton, the framework which shapes the external physical structure; Part 1 of this book has already described many parts of this skeletal structure.

Extending the analogy to the human body, the second, often counteracting, phenomenon—that is, the immigrants and their descendants learning about, utilizing and becoming comfortable with the socio-cultural currency of Canada, while simultaneously evolving the means for continuing their culture here—can be compared to the circulatory system that enables life to progress and modify. This second process usually meant acquiring an understanding, if not always a fluency, in the English or French languages; use of the public schools for their children even when those schools employed curriculum and methods that served to disengage the youth from their immigrant parents' culture and its practice. If local circumstances combined to permit members of an immigrant or other minority group to resist the assimilating aspects of the national or regional culture and its institutional agents, then the outcome was the continuation of the immigrant cultural heritage as the dominating influence in the ethnic community and as the life-blood of its survival. It often required extreme efforts by the immigrant families and their community leaders to sustain their culture in the face of powerful external forces for assimilation. For some, adapting to the host society meant the rapid uprooting of the immigrant culture, even when a large number of people in the ethnicity resided within the same jurisdiction. For other groups, it meant the development of a siege mentality, to survive the blows from outside the ethnic collectivity, and the evolution of their Old-World culture into one able to withstand and, if possible, fit in with the influences intruding into the ethnic community.

It is the processes, transitions and outcomes of cultural establishment among the various ethno-racial-religious groups of Canada that is the focus of Part 2. Heretofore, ethnicity and ethnic groups have been treated as though they were all the same. But, of course, they were not and are not now. Indeed, on almost every dimension of cultural maintenance that will be examined from here on, each ethnicity can be placed on a different point on each particular ethnic-maintenance continuum. It is on the axis of differentiation that the analysis of ethnic-group cultural changes and outcomes is conducted here. This will first involve a synthesis of cultural maintenance theory, followed by a conceptual-empirical inspection of the five central mechanisms by which ethnoculture has been continued in Canada.

CHAPTER 4

Theory on Ethnic-Group Cultural Maintenance

INTRODUCTION: CONTRIBUTIONS OF BRETON, ISAJIW, DRIEDGER

The initial multi-group comparative study of the structure of ethnic identity in Canada was probably that by Breton (1964) on the "institutional completeness" of various groups in Montreal. More recently, Breton (1978a) went on to elucidate another critical dimension of ethnic differentiation—the extent to which ethnic communities have parallel social networks and institutions. This dimension is distinguished into the degrees of "social enclosure" and "compartmentalization" that exist in each ethnic community.

For Breton, *enclosure* refers, first, to the existence of social boundaries between an ethno-racial-religious group and other groups and, second, to the mechanisms used by a group to maintain these intergroup boundaries. Enclosure, therefore, can be seen as involving some degree of collective assertion within a group, so that the networks of social relationships are restricted as much as possible to members of the ethnicity, race, and/or religion. It takes only a moment to recognize that among the central mechanisms of ethnic enclosure are ethnic language retention, residential proximity, maintenance of the traditional or at least the same religion, and marriage within the ethnic group. These are some of the most powerful forces in existence for the erection and maintenance of ethnic boundaries within which members of the group can be enclosed. Each of these is dealt with in coming chapters.

Breton's concept of *compartmentalization* refers to the related structure of formal institutional organizations; that is, the degree to which each ethnic group in a particular locale has developed a set of institutions of its own paralleling those in the wider city outside the ethnic community. In essence, then, compartmentalization covers the extent of the group's institutional completeness, the concept introduced by Breton in 1964. This concept includes such factors as ethnic sub-economics, churches, educational and cultural facilities, media, and other organizations to serve the members of the ethnic community. Together with the elements of enclosure, these factors refer to the nature of intra-ethnic relations and the separate networks of ethnic interactions that exist. Theoretically, at least, we should be able to differentiate among groups as to the particular ethnic mechanisms employed in attempting to establish ethnic enclosure, the contours of the ethnic community boundaries and how they have changed over the years, and, finally, the comparative degrees of success in achieving ethnic enclosure and/or compartmentalization.

Breton (1978b) believes that what has been happening in recent years in Canada is the emergence of a view that it is possible to consciously mould the mechanisms and institutions of an ethnic community to take into account the specific differences of one group from another. In this view, rather than sociologically considering the ideal city or national organization as culture-free and having some invariant or stable form, ethnic-group social institutions are coming to be accepted as mechanisms combining creativity and experimentation in the best ways so as to incorporate ethnic diversity into a multicultural country like Canada. In Canada, it is difficult, if not impossible, to define any cultural forms possessed by the smaller minorities in our population as "non-conforming" cultural aspects. Thus, what were in the past labelled as "deviant" cultural forms, Breton has inferred, should today be accepted as representing different points in the range of the possible forms which ethnocultural structural dimensions can take and still be "Canadian."

Isajiw (1978), addressing a related topic, the nature of ethnicity in post-industrial Canada, characterized it as a link with the past that is central to understanding the persistence of ethno-racial-religious variations in cultural forms within a quite technological society. Whatever symbolic meanings these many extracted cultural patterns may have to those who are involved with them today, they share one thing: feelings of identity. Ethnic cultural patterns, even if completely torn away from their original temporal and social contexts, have, in Canada, become representative of people's roots. Such symbols, Isajiw asserted, are necessary for the support of personal identity.

Hence, in any research for personal identity, ethnicity, race, and/or religion become relevant because through their ancestral dimension, people can, at least symbolically, experience belonging. The ethno-racial-religious bonds contribute to personal and collective identity through transmittal of a sense of the eternal. This temporal, culture-bearing (and culturally diverse) character is in direct contrast to the post-industrial, technological tendencies of fostering individual autonomy, universality of "culture-free" requirements, and impersonality in interactions and methodologies. Thus, the technological nature of Canada today actually heightens the need for personal and collective identity and, ironically, creates the search for identity so noticeable in today's mass society. Cultural maintenance or renewal constitutes one significant direction that the need to search out one's identity has taken in Canada since the Second World War—particularly for the Canadian-born. For immigrants, ethnic cultural maintenance has cushioned the shock of immersion in today's Canadian, urban, technological society (Isajiw, 1978).

Another very important contribution to the comparative analysis of ethnic-group cultural structure is that made by Driedger in a long series of publications (1975; 1976; 1977a; 1977b; 1978; Driedger and Church 1974; Driedger, et al., 1982). In part, this work has been directed at the same concerns as those of Breton and Isajiw, but has gone beyond mere conceptual elucidation to inspect the actual structures and strengths of ethno-religious cultural identities and forces. Driedger's formulations look to the mechanisms through which Canadian-born members of different cultural groups have worked to maintain or even increase the vitality of their ethnic identities.

Synthesizing the theoretical and empirical conclusions of these investigators, we can postulate that ethnic-group identity probably performs a function in today's society different from that of the past. While enclosure and compartmentalization were objectives of ethnic cultural maintenance in past decades, the emphasis today is more likely on complementing the technological, so-called "culture-free" mass society. Indeed, as Isajiw has pointed out, if Canadians did not value ethno-racial-religious-group identity so highly, something else very much like it would have to have been found to counteract the powerful individualist, alienating influences of the achievement-oriented Canadian economy. The primary source of ascriptive, temporally based personal identity in Canada is the sense of belonging one derives from membership in an ethnic group, a racial group, and/or a religion (Isajiw, 1978). Today, when even (or especially) the founding groups are "minorities" in the numerical sense, ethnic-group culture can be likened to the house from which one emerges to interact on a regular and personal basis with those from other houses, or even other neighbourhoods.

In a very real sense, then, the sociological structure of Canada is partially founded on ethnocultural cohesion within the various groups and the varying forms of ethnic social organization that exist among the groups. *Cohesion* is employed here as a criterion of ethnocultural maintenance in Canada, a referent to the degree of vitality in group identity and in social structure. Specifically, ethnic cohesion indicates the extent to which an ethno-racial-religious group is able to retain its membership, and, in that sense, it is an outcome measure regarding group cultural maintenance. Since it is suggested that the particular ways in which a group adapts and changes over time influence its degree of ethnocultural cohesion, then what we are inspecting when we study cultural cohesion and the nature of ethnic social organization in a group is the result of all forces to date which influence people to remain members of a particular ethnicity. The patterns of ethnic-group behaviour and interaction are the aspects of ethnic cohesion most often studied for the simple reason that they are moderately susceptible to observation, and often even quantification, while the philosophical and other purely cognitive bases for ethnoculture and ethnic cohesion are relatively unobservable, even while being of considerable import (Retiz, 1980: 90–100).

SOURCES OF ETHNIC-GROUP IDENTITY

There are three sources, or typologies of ethnic-group identity or cohesion in all: the Collective, the Individual, and the External.

The most fundamental source of ethnic-group cohesion or identity is the *Collective* type. Each ethnic, racial, and/or religious group defines—either explicitly or implicitly—its own criteria for including persons within their ethnic collectivity. Collective criteria of ethnic culture and cohesion include: ethnic, racial, and/or religious ancestry; country of origin; cultural practices (including language); and the nature of people with whom interaction occurs. In some groups, ethnic criteria—that is, secular cultural practices—comprise the core of the collective definition of identity. In other communities, racial and/or religious characteristics, and definitional criteria involving these, will be of primary concern. What the different forms of Collective ethnic cohesion share are, first, the sense of collective socio-emotional "pull" toward sharing and contributing to the ethnic identity and, second, the exclusion of all who do not meet the criteria of ethnic belongingness. Indeed, the Collective level of ethnocultural identity and cohesion represents the antithesis of cultural (and structural) assimilation to the dominant group(s) in Canada. Therefore, the Collective measure of cohesion is roughly equivalent to the extent of ethnocultural group "survival."

Some individuals, however, consider and announce themselves as members of a group, even though they may not meet one or more of the Collective definitional criteria, or may have repudiated membership in the group previously. This *Individual* kind of identification with an ethnic group can sometimes occur even when the person meets very few of the criteria—when the principal mechanism for being identified as a member of the ethnicity is the decision and statement of the person. For instance, someone may look "white" and be accepted by others as such, be a second- or later-generation Canadian, and have few of the several characteristics that would suggest the person was a Black, yet the person identifies him/herself as a member of the Black group. Such individual identification with an ethno-racial-religious group is by no means a frivolous declaration, but it is a different ethnocultural identity outcome than would have occurred 20 or more years ago. Such Individual ethnic identifications have their origins in a family background of membership in the group one or more generations back, followed by a combination of circumstances that would, otherwise, have permitted the person to "pass" as "white" or an Anglo-Celtic.

Indeed, until the mid-1970s, many such people would actively have sought to so "pass." Not appearing to be a visible minority in skin colour, hair or facial features; speaking English (French) without an offshore accent; and believing that social and socio-economic goals would be more easily and quickly attainable without the taint of being identified as a member of a non-British group, many persons in the past avoided any "ethnic" connections and projected themselves as "non-ethnics." Undoubtedly, this has been the case for literally thousands, perhaps hundreds of thousands of people in Canada over the past 200 years.

For some, of course, this was impossible because of skin colour or some other readily classifiable "minority" characteristic. Such persons sought protection from discrimination within the confines of their ethnic community to the extent it could provide this and, when the occasion presented itself, vilified the notion of "passing" or of leaving the ethno-racial-religious collectivity.

In contrast, most of those who had succeeded in passing, who had "escaped" what they saw as the confines or disadvantages of an ethnic, racial or religious collectivity and who had made their way in an Anglo-imitative existence in Canada, made no effort—and avoided any opportunity—to reidentify with their original ethnic heritage. Intermarriage perhaps, lack of interaction with "ethnic" people, the absence of accent in combination with a "Canadian" skin-facial appearance permitted these people to search out the possibilities of being immersed in the "majority," of being like the British, and so reap the benefits from this kind of persona common to the era of the late 1800s through to the 1960s.

With multiculturalism as government policy, following upon the celebration of ethnic peoples and their contribution to Canada during the Centennial activities of 1966–1967 and the publicizing since 1971 of the diverse ethnic, racial, and religious character of Canada, a different kind of perception and a different kind of search began for those who had before avoided "ethnicity." People who looked and spoke like one of the British-Canadian groups began identifying themselves with their ethnic heritage. People who, in many cases, met few of the Collective ethnic criteria began to characterize themselves in terms of their parents' or grandparents' ethnicity. Even people who neither looked nor sounded like "minority" persons began to enter the fringes of ethnic-group activities, with the objective of recapturing in their lives an approximation, at least, of an ethnic-group identity. Other people who looked "white" began to object to racial affronts and discrimination, identifying themselves as Black, or of the Native Peoples, or simply as antagonistic to ethnoracial insult. Others, who spoke unaccented English (French) and had only a scant acquaintance with Italian, Ukrainian, Polish or some other language, either sought out places where their young children could learn the language of their parents or grandparents or encouraged their children to enroll in voluntary, after-school courses in the ethno-racial-religious heritage of their ancestors.

Indeed, it is by no means uncommon in my ethnicity courses, for my university students (about half of whom are mature students with families of their own) to recall how they or another individual or family worked to recapture their ethno-racial-religious heritage, having lost it in their parental or grandparental generation in Canada. What is of most direct relevance from this is that the resumption of the ethnic identity is an individual decision to become something they were not but which their ancestors were. This Individual identification with a non-English ethnicity or non-white race is quite independent of the collective ethnic community not just in its origins, but often in its implementation. This makes the alteration in ethnic identity clearly an individual act, even if there was a social stimulus (i.e., official multiculturalism and its sequelae) to the ethnic revival.

The existence of an Individual ethnic identity level is also pointed to by the ready and voluntary identification of people with a non-English ethnicity, even when they have no deep involvement in the local ethnic community. An example of this is again provided by some of the students in my ethnicity courses over the years. While preparing their term research paper, many observed that, while they (and usually their parents) readily identified with their ethnic origins, this identity was rather superficial in that they knew little of the parameters of the local ethnic community and seldom participated in ethnic community activities. Indeed, some, who had no doubts as to their ethnic identity, never, or only rarely, interacted with other members of their ethnicity.

While such people unhesitatingly identified with an ethnicity, they often had no plan (and sometimes a fear) to explore their ethnicity further. These people, combined with those who actively refrain from identifying themselves with an ethnicity (e.g., "I'm just a Canadian."), but who later clothe themselves in a new ethnic-group identity, have, quite obviously, come to this new identity very much separated from any collective influences. So, while there are several different paths by which people come to profess an ethnic identity separated from collective activities and intra-ethnic interaction, the quality of their cultural identity being a quite Individual one is common.

It should be noted, though, that currently, there seems to be a moderately widespread trend for people possessing an Individual ethnic identity to seek ways by which the potential in that Individual identification can be realized through greater participation in ethnic community activities. Sometime during the months that the course lasts, a sizeable minority of my ethnicity students state that the pleasure and knowledge obtained in studying and doing field research into their ethnic community was the most valuable product of the term's work and that, as a result, they are now mildly active in their ethnic community's organizations and services.

Probably, in a less directed and intense fashion, such public ethnic festivals as Toronto's Caravan perform the same function. Ethnic newspapers and other media also have a large and ready audience, it would seem, in those with an Individual ethnic identity and who seek more information and involvement in their ethnic communities, if they still exist. Thus, in these times, there exists a strong possibility that, for many with an Individual ethnic identity, the cultural messages of today will result in their becoming participant in the Collective ethnic identity to a much greater extent than was true earlier in their own lives or in earlier generations.

In a different way, the Collective and Individual levels of ethno-racial-religious identity are related in a behavioural way to the third type of cultural identity—*External*. Certain persons, because of purely external characteristics, such as skin colour, facial features, kind of clothing, and or accent (or even presumed attributes of a group's members) are labelled, often pejoratively, as "Blacks," "Asians," "aliens," and so on. Usually, such acts are characterized, to some degree, by inaccuracy, as in the labelling of anyone with a dark skin as "Black" or "Pakistani" (not to mention the more derogatory terms). The inference of this labelling of anyone visibly or audibly deviant from the popular conception of the "Nordic type" is that, in some external way, they are somehow "not-Canadian" and/or that such persons can "never become Canadian"— whatever those phrases mean. Such characterizations and bases for labelling people as "different" were, of course, the manifestations of prejudicial attitudes and discriminatory behaviour in the past.

Such *External* definitions of ethnic identity are so inapt and socially destructive because they are made by non-group members and are founded in the conceptions, experiences, and subconscious fears of the labellers. At best, then, External definitions of ethnicity have at their heart muddled misconceptions about the other group and, at worst, a total lack of knowledge, understanding, and even respect. The External definition really has little or nothing to do with the true characteristics of a group, its social patterns of organization and celebration, or the differences between the group and other Canadian ethnic, racial or religious groups.

In these ways, then, the External definition of ethnicity and ethnic identity are entirely different from the Collective or the Individual definitions of ethnic identity. Because the External definition is so divorced from reality and can have such segregative, discriminatory consequences, it is the most dangerous of the sources of ethnic-group identity. The Collective form of ethnic identity, even in its most ethnocentric form, has much less potential for social damage because its usual extreme outcome in the past or today has been to bolster voluntary group isolation from the other Canadian peoples. Even when this has occurred, there has usually been an eventual integration in extra-community institutions, like the economy, education, and politics.

The External mode of assigning ethnic identity, however, tends to retard this intergroup integrative process, even if this was not its original intention. And, today, this usually generates an atmosphere that is corrosive of mutual understanding, acceptance as equals, and co-operation for the attainment of common goals between the definers and the defined. In these ways, then, the External definition, because of its being such a common phenomenon is the most deleterious of the three sources of ethnocultural group identity.

Ironically, however, because of their negative nature, External definitions of ethnic identity probably have the effect of strengthening group ethnocultural cohesion. This is because the more an ethno-racial-religious group perceives that non-group members are incorrectly and denigratingly assigning persons to the group on the basis of false criteria, the more a group perceives that non-group members have erroneous beliefs about the group and/or are contemptuous of the group's beliefs or practices. And the more such external labels proffer an inferior, despised group status, then the more the group members may feel under siege. High group cohesion and extreme efforts to survive the siege by maintaining the highest level of ethnocultural identity would be the natural modes whereby ethnic-group dignity was assured. But even when External definitions of ethnic identity are seldom imposed, groups which have sustained a high Collective definition of identity will also tend to have higher ethnic cohesion than groups in which Collective definitions are weak, or challenged by Individual identity definitions that do not contain group interaction or collective cultural survival as dominant themes.

The garrison mentality—feeling it necessary to maintain very strong ethnic cohesion in the face of derogatory External definitions—was probably quite common in past decades. But the change in tenor of Canada's ethnic peoples' attitude toward each other has likely diminished not only the frequency and power of negative External definitions, but also the ethnic-group reactions to them. This is not to suggest that Collective identities are less prevalent today than in the past, but that External ethnic labelling has decreased in recent years. Eventually, though, only extensive research will define the situation. What has also changed is the strength of association between the two and the nature of each.

Breton (1981), for instance, has published data that are very much suggestive of a still very powerful Collective identity among many but not all of the Toronto groups that were studied. Isajiw (1981), Kalbach (1981), and Driedger et al. (1982) have also emphasized the salience that ethnic-group identity has for people, but it is unclear as to whether the Collective or the Individual definition is the more prominent. What all of these studies do tend to confirm is that the power of ethnocultural group identity is a principal complement to the strength of group cohesion and that, probably, the two together are the major vehicles for group ethnocultural survival in Canada.

INFLUENCES ON ETHNIC-GROUP COHESION

There are a variety of factors involved in ascertaining the depth of group ethnocultural cohesion of various groups. The first of these is the *size of ethno-racial-religious-group membership*. As defined by responses to the Census, this was discussed in Chapter 2. Likely of equal import is what we call *Territorial Concentration*, the proportion a group represents of the total population in a city, a region or the entirety of Canada. The higher the proportion is, the greater is the "concentration" of the group in the particular "territory" relative to other groups. Thus, for instance, a group with a certain number of people in Ontario would have that great an Ethnic-Group Size and a certain level of Territorial Concentration. However, this group, with the same Ethnic-Group Size would have a much higher Territorial Concentration in Alberta or some other province. Thus, the importance of both of these indicators. Territorial Concentration in Canada was analyzed in detail in Chapter 2.

Language Retention, as an index of the extent to which the ethnic or heritage language is still understood and used in speech has been put forward as perhaps the single most important indicator of both the Collective identity definition and of ethnocultural cohesion. See, for instance, de Vries and Valee (1980), Joy (1972), Rayfield (1976) Reitz (1974; 1980) or Wardhaugh (1983: esp. 176–197). Language Retention is examined in Chapter 5, both in terms of "mother-tongue" maintenance in Canada since 1921 and, more recently, home use of the heritage language.

Chapter 6 covers ethnic group *Residential Concentration*, another important factor in ethnic group cohesion. Here again, there are two facets covered, providing both the macroscopic and microscopic perspectives on ethnic cohesion. The large-scale image of Residential Concentration of each group among the regions of Canada is covered first. We then go on to the proximity of residence within each group inside five Canadian cities. This micro-view assesses the changes in the degrees of intra-city Residential Concentration over a relatively long period.

In Chapter 7, the extent to which the traditional ethnic religions have been able to maintain affiliation by group members—*Religious Monopoly*—is assessed. While concentrating on the extent to which the members of an ethnoracial group belong to the same religion, we shall also note the principal minority religions important in each ethnicity.

One further contributor to the strength both of ethnic-group cohesion and of intergenerational ethnic-group identity maintenance is *Endogamy*: the extent to which adults in a group are married to persons from the same group. Endogamy is analyzed (in Chapter 8) from the perspective of marriage within the same ethnic group, though marriage within the same religion is also mentioned. Included here also is fertility as another dimension of ethnic family maintenance.

The concluding chapter in this Part addresses *Institutional Completeness* in an ethnic community, albeit in a preliminary way (Chapter 9). Very little work has been done on this central influence since Breton's 1965 seminal advancement of the concept in Canada. At the present time this subject cannot be easily (if at all) researched as a Canada-wide phenomenon, like Language Retention or Religious Monopoly. Thus, what is undertaken here is an exploration of the theoretical parameters of Institutional Completeness and an expansion of their dimensions beyond the initial ones used by Breton (1965) and Driedger and Church (1974). In this, I cover the variables relevant to the investigation of Institutional Completeness in particular ethnic groups in a particular geographic location. Also proposed are a delineation of institutional sectors and a methodology by which this most important factor can be investigated.

ETHNIC-GROUP COHESION IN CANADA

It is to be expected that the various elements involved in Canadian ethnic-group cohesion have differed not just between different groups or within the same group over time, but also between the different group-cohesion measures themselves. Most or all of the factors introduced above must once have been very high, perhaps close to 100% in many of the ethnicities, especially in those early times when a large proportion of the group was comprised of immigrants. Unfortunately, however, data from those earliest post-Confederation years are not yet available in a form permitting computerized analysis of group cohesion or the underlying structural variables. For most of the group-cohesion influences, the available census data begin with either the 1921 or 1931 census. Figure 4.1 presents the macroscopic Canada-wide trends for five of the ethnic-group-cohesion aspects, along with two of the structural indicators.

For cohesion statuses since 1951, the cohesion factors can be divided into those corresponding with high(er), moderate or low levels of cohesion. The variable that has the highest level (inspection of Fig. 4.1 reveals) has been Ethnic Endogamy, which represents the condition for a great majority of Canadians. Next are three other cohesion factors, which in 1981 averaged about 50%–54%: Ethnic-Language Retention, Religious Monopoly and Religious Endogamy (at time of marriage). The lowest of the five group-cohesion influences traced for 1981 in Figure 4.1 was Residential Concentration (proximity of residences) at about 35%.

Interestingly, while the proportion of the non-charter groups in

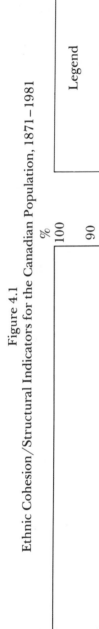

Figure 4.1

Ethnic Cohesion/Structural Indicators for the Canadian Population, 1871–1981

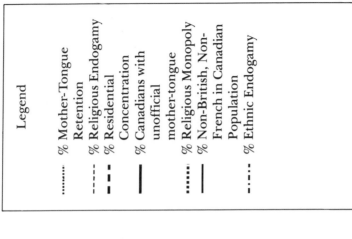

Legend

.... % Mother-Tongue Retention

– – – % Religious Endogamy

▪ ▪ ▪ % Residential Concentration

——— % Canadians with unofficial mother-tongue

▪▪▪▪▪ % Religious Monopoly

——— % Non-British, Non-French in Canadian Population

–▪–▪ % Ethnic Endogamy

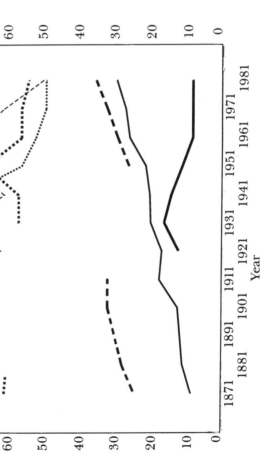

the Canadian population has steadily increased since Confederation, all but one of the five group-cohesion variables being analyzed
in Figure 4.1 declined over the three or four decades prior to 1981.
The exception, residential proximity within cities, is doubly out-
standing, having risen between 1951 and 1981, but, nevertheless,
still very much the weakest of the ethnic-cohesion measures.

It should be recognized that the patterns for the two large
charter ethnicities strongly influence the overall patterns depicted
in Figure 4.1. Of course there are great, sometimes even extreme,
variations in group cohesion between the various ethnicities. Further, we will see that there sometimes have been very great shifts in
one or more factors of group cohesion within the same group(s)
over time. Each of these and other threads will be traced in the
following chapters.

Of course, the contribution of each of these elements to cultural
maintenance within ethnic communities is obvious. It is, however,
their collective contribution that is theoretically of greater consequence to the ethnic community, particularly through the interaction of the various cohesion mechanisms, in producing a cumula-
tive dynamic in ethnic-group culture that goes beyond their
individual effectiveness.

It takes no great insight to appreciate the fact that the size of the
membership in a city's ethnic community enhanced the likelihood
of social interactions among people in the ethnicity, thus leading
not only to higher language retention, the possibility of carving out
an ethnic residential territory in the city, and sufficient variety
within the ethnic community membership to help assure the selection (supply) of potential marriage partners within the ethnicity,
but also to providing support for the development and sustenance
of ethnic institutions, especially the establishment of the ethnic
place of worship. In turn, a high degree of language maintenance
benefited the retention of the ethnic culture and its practice,
especially the fine arts and folk celebrations. Too, language retention undoubtedly helped to preserve the practice of the ethnic
religion in Canada.

Creating ethnic institutions provided arenas of interaction for
use of the language and practice of the ethnic culture, as well as
opportunities for youth and adolescents to associate with fellow
group members, looking forward to within-ethnicity marriage.
These ethnic community organizations also contributed to the
continuance of the groups' religion(s) and cultural practices not

only for the immigrant developers of the community long after the initial settlement period, but also for the Canadian-born generations. Similarly, the existence of high residential concentration, especially within the cities, enabled the concentration of ethnic-group members necessary for continuing the daily use of the ethnic language; it also stimulated demand for ethnic goods, including cultural ones and thereby the formation and use of ethnic retail outlets and cultural and recreational organizations; and, finally, was especially essential in the founding of ethnic churches within easy transportation distance.

Factors that would generally be considered "causative" factors of ethnic-cohesion mechanisms can readily be seen to also be interdependent on others, and outcome benefits from a high level of other ethnic-group cultural possessions. Given the retention of language, residential concentration and the maintenance of the ethnicity's religion, along with the institutions that enabled cultural survival in Canada, the knowledge of the ethnic community's cultural power soon spread to other locales, including the country of origin. This knowledge has been and will continue to be the means of attracting new members of the ethnic group to that city or region. Indeed, this is, at least in part, the reason that Toronto, for instance, contains the largest Black, Chinese, Filipino, Italian, Japanese, Jewish, Latin American, Portuguese, and Southeast-Asian communities in Canada today.

As we have already said, it is the synergism of these factors that underlies ethnic-group cohesion in urban Canada. We must keep in mind, therefore, that none of these ethnic phenomena exist or can be analyzed in isolation. Yet few empirical studies of ethnic-group cultural retention have considered more than one ethnic-cohesion mechanism. Exemplary in their broad coverage of different ethnic-cohesion attributes and the documentation of the interaction between them in multiple ethnicities have been Reitz's (1980) examination of ethnic-group survival, and several of the reports from the Ethnic Pluralism Study of multiple groups in Toronto: Breton (1981), Isajiw (1981), and especially Kalbach (1981). It is just this recognition of the mutual interdependence of the many ethnic-group supports that became the central point in Darroch and Marston's (1987) carefully reasoned model of urban ethnicity patterns.

So, what must be studied is as many as possible of the forces at work in that aspect of the daily life of communities that we here reference under ethnic-group cohesion. In this book, the history and contemporary patterns of some of the major mechanisms of ethnic community maintenance are examined but always with the understanding that even when only one is being inspected, the outcomes delineated comprise only a part of the total mosaic.

CHAPTER 5

Ethnic Language Retention and Use

INTRODUCTION: THE FUNCTIONS OF LANGUAGE

If culture is regarded as a system of symbols, and language is one of the most important elements in that system, we would expect to find a close parallel between changes in ethnic language retention in Canada and changes in ethnic cultural content and practice. Stated another way, the more that members of Canadian ethnicities learn a new language (i.e., English and/or French) the more they will learn of and participate in a new culture and vice versa (Rayfield, 1976). Wardhaugh (1983: 176–197) has said the same, that language is a or the principal mainstay of minority culture in Canada.

Furthermore, it has been argued by Brazeau (1958) and by the author(s) of Book 4 of the Report of Royal Commission on Bilingualism and Biculturalism (1970) that cultures of the "minority" or "subordinate" ethnicities can be maintained only when the cultures are employable in all areas of life. According to this theory, if language is not functionally applicable in all areas of social life, then the remainder of the cultural factors is endangered: culture and the language that serves as its vehicle cannot be dissociated. Language allows for self-expression and communication according to the unique cultural logic. Therefore, those who care about their cultural heritage usually care also about their ancestral language (Royal Commission, 1970: 13).

One of the functions of language postulated long ago by Sapir (1933) was that it constitutes a powerful social force that binds a group together. For Sapir, language was not merely a vehicle for the expression of thoughts, perceptions, sentiments, and values that were characteristic of an ethnicity. Language also represents a fundamental mode of collective social identity. Casting Sapir's formulations into testable hypotheses, Reitz (1974) used original survey data, finding support for the theory. Language retention, Reitz discovered, was in itself an important prerequisite to ethnic community participation, independent of generation in Canada or family ethnic characteristics. However, language seems also to represent only one aspect of cultural survival. This fact relativizes language, making of it a desirable cultural attribute, but not, theoretically a *sine qua non* for maintaining ethnic-group culture. Moreover, Breton (1978a) has suggested that the ethnic language retention can change in ways different from other aspects of an ethnic culture. Of perhaps more import to Breton is the fact that the retention of any cultural content in Canada, including language, does not seem to be possible without the development of ethnic institutions.

Others have different views on the essentiality of the ethnic language's remaining unchanged or being the superstructure for other cultural aspects. On the one hand, there is the reality that ethnoculture is by no means bound solely to the ethnic language in all groups. Indeed, many languages can serve to express the culture of an ethnic group: the ethnic heritage language, English, French, or some other language. Furthermore, speaking one or both of the official languages of Canada does not prevent ethnic-group members from expressing their cultural thoughts and an ethnic way of life. It seems possible, then, that people can speak English or French—and even be linguistically assimilated to one of these languages—without adopting an "Anglo" or "Franco" culture. Indeed, this hypothesis implies that an ethnoculture can be maintained even though English or French is the language of communication (Lamerand, 1977). For example, Binns (1971) early noted differences between different Ontario ethnic groups in the forms and extent of practice and celebration of their ethnic culture, as well as the expectation of cultural maintenance by their children. Significantly, cultural maintenance was not eschewed by Anglophone members of the ethnic groups in this study. This conclusion is supported by many of the findings in Isajiw's (1981) report on Toronto groups.

The other side of the cultural coin is the adoption of Canadian (or Ontarian or Torontonian) characteristics into an "ethnic culture." Ziegler (1977) reported that the children of Italian immigrants, grown and, for the most part, feeling completely at home in Toronto, planned to remain permanently in Canada. They spoke English more often than Italian (some were almost totally assimilated to English). But, they were marrying Italians and using a variety of techniques to insure that their children would be fluent in Italian as well as English. What is clear, Ziegler concluded, is that, for them, family and cultural-linguistic ties have not only survived migration to a totally different social milieu, but have, in fact, been fortified by it.

Relatedly, Danesi (1983) has pointed to how the adaptation or learning of the ethnic language in Canada has integrative aspects for people *as Canadians*, quite aside from the functions language fulfills for ethnic communities. That is not to say that the adaptation of the ethnic language or learning the ethnic language as a "heritage language" in school does not also have a very beneficial result in terms of assuring ethnocultural survival. But for Danesi, the more important results of what becomes bilingualism is the greater sense of comfort both within and outside the ethnic group collectivity and the apparent academic performance benefits accruing to bilingual students.

Thus, when examining the information on the degree of and differences in ethnic-language maintenance, we must keep in mind that: (1) language is part and parcel of group ethnoculture, at least in most Canadian ethnicities; (2) the question about the extent to which the cultural survival of groups depends on ethnic-language retention is still very much unsettled. Cultural survival in at least some ethnic communities may be less or not at all dependent upon language use than is the case in other ethnic communities; and (3) the possession of an unofficial language can have desirable outcomes for members of ethnic communities *as Canadians* (or as residents of a province, or a specific city).

MOTHER-TONGUE RETENTION WITHIN GROUPS

The "Mother-Tongue Retention Rate" refers to the extent to which those persons who might be considered "ethnically" eligible continue to understand the ethnic mother tongue. Generally, this is calculated by dividing those members in a particular ethnic group who continue to understand the traditional ethnic language(s) by the total number of persons in that ethnicity. This calculation is a somewhat conservative one and yields a Mother-Tongue Retention Rate, expressed as a percent figure, which can, theoretically, vary from 100% to 0%, the latter figure being indicative of complete linguistic assimilation within that ethnic group. A more liberal interpretation of this indicator, and the one employed here, is the percent obtained when one divides the number in a non-British, non-French ethnicity who reported a mother tongue *other* than one of the two official languages, by the total number in that ethnic group (x 100). Of course, for calculating the French Mother-Tongue Retention Rate, the number of those from within the French ethnic group who reported their language as French comprise the numerator.

Although the method of accounting mother-tongue according to ethnic origin has varied somewhat between that used from 1921 to 1941 and the reporting method employed since 1951; the data from 1921 on are essentially equivalent. Throughout the analyses, I have selected the kind of data and the mode of calculation that seemed best-suited to the nature of the question being studied. Thus, though form and method of census data and statistical array may have differed slightly, I work on the premise that close equivalence between data from different eras is more preferable than excluding all data or methods that are not precisely identical. The intent here always is to inform on the most probable pattern of ethnic transition, and when it appeared that the data could not meet the criterion, the figures were excluded. When there are estimates, usually by myself, but occasionally by or with staff of Statistics Canada, these are sincere efforts to inform as accurately and soundly as possible, always with the debatable justification that estimated information is vastly superior to total absence of any indication.

One further caveat remains, concerning the mother-tongue

within the British group. Patently, those of an English ethnic origin would have English as their mother tongue. But what is the mother tongue of the British who are of non-English ethnic origin? The number of persons who spoke Celtic was reported in 1931 to amount to 32 000 persons; Celtic was then the thirteenth most-frequently held language. Its history in Canada is about as ancient as that of English, and in some regions of Canada its use as the common tongue was great, e.g., our "New Scotland" province in the Atlantic region. So, is the heritage language (the mother tongue) of Canada's Irish, Scots, and Welsh the Celtic tongue or the English dialects? Strictly speaking, the obvious answer might seem that the heritage tongue of the Celtic peoples of Canada (about 16% or so of the entire population in 1981) is Celtic. However, it is apparent that, even in 1931, the use of the Celtic language had already declined considerably in Canada, as it had in Scotland, the Republic of Ireland, Ulster, and Wales. Today in Canada, it is virtually extinct as a mother tongue and as a home language. Thus, I have considered the English language as the mother tongue of Canada's Celts. Quite inconsistent with this, but for informational purposes, the rate of Celtic Mother-Tongue Retention has been included as a subcategory of the British languages (Table 5.1) but English has been used as the criterion for the entire British category there and on Figure 5.1. In Tables 5.2 and 5.3 later on, dealing with very specialized comparisons between rural and urban rates, and of Mother-Tongue versus Home-Language Retention, I have reported the English-based British-language retention rate.

Thus cautioned, we can consider three possible patterns of ethnic cultural differentiation that might have occurred. One possibility could have been that emphasis upon the use of one (or both) of the official languages in the economy, schools, politics, and other institutions in Canada would have led to an "Assimilating" pattern of mother-tongue retention—continuous decline in retention and perhaps even at an increasing rate to, or almost to, language extinction. The "Maintaining" pattern could be expected for some groups who may have experienced lowered cultural cohesion—here in the form of diminished Mother-Tongue Retention—but for whom, at some point in recent decades, the decline stopped and retention remained at the same maintenance level. Particular ethnicities too, especially ones composed primarily of recent immigrants might have a high and maintaining level of language continuance. Of course, the English and French languages likely have been Maintaining at quite high levels within their respective heritage ethnicities.

The final pattern that could be projected is that in which an ethnicity had experienced either an Assimilating or a Maintaining language level which, in recent (post-war) years, had shifted to increasing language retention: a "Returner" cultural-cohesion pattern. This pattern could be based in either post-war immigration or a return to a language in the second or third generation, triggered by the de facto and eventually de jure multicultural situation in Canada.

Figure 5.1 and Table 5.1 permit us to test the extent to which each of the cultural differentiation models outlined above meshes with the real experiences of the ethno-racial-religious groups. As can be readily seen, the Assimilating model seems to explain the lowering language retention rates in a majority of the groups between 1921 and 1951 or later. However, only the East Indians, Native Peoples, the Jewish, and probably the Scandinavians have experienced persistently lower Mother-Tongue Retention Rates each decade through 1981. To a limited degree, the French have been experiencing lowering linguistic levels, but, the pronouncement of Québécois personages notwithstanding, with so high a language retention, the French are more properly characterized as exhibiting a Maintaining pattern. The same is certainly true for the British and probably for the Asians: both patterns of Mother-Tongue Retention have remained relatively high, though the Asians (particularly East Indians and Japanese) have shown moderate language-loss rates over the past four decades.

Of the 20 groups for whom time series are portrayed, nine of them appear to have a sustained resurgence in language retention rates since 1931 (Dutch), 1951 (Greek, Italian), 1961 (Czechoslovakian, Yugoslavian) or 1971 (Hungarian, Polish, Russian). Of these, the return to the language among the Dutch, Czechoslovaks, Hungarians, Russians, Italians, and Yugoslavs are the most spectacular, rising from close to or well below the 50% level to markedly higher Mother-Tongue Retention Rates thereafter, and in 1981.

Thus, only three or four groups of those inspected here have an Assimilating pattern linguistically; a few more are Maintaining, while most of the ethno-racial-religious groups have become Returners in terms of language rates. To be true, the overall trend during the past 65 years has been toward declining Mother-Tongue Retention Rates (Figure 5.1). It is also very evident that linguistic

Figure 5.1
Mother-Tongue Retention (in %) Among Canadian
Ethno-Racial-Religious Groups, 1921–1981

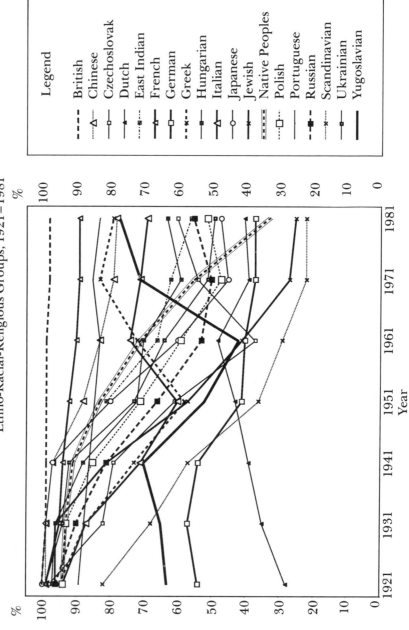

cohesion is, on the whole, holding to a stable or rising level. While language levels may not rise to the very high ones of 1921–1931, neither does it seem likely that many groups will have their language's die out among their members in the near future. However, for the Jewish and perhaps for the Native Peoples and the Scandinavians, ethnic-language extinction may, unfortunately, be very near. Not only have these three groups few immigrants among their current membership, relative to their total numbers, but it is also unlikely that they will receive sufficient immigrants in the future to revive their flagging language maintenance.

Data not shown here reveal that the major difference according to generation in Canada* regarding ethnic-language retention within the group is between immigrants and those born in this country. As readily predictable in all groups but the British, French and Native Peoples, the Mother-Tongue Retention level among immigrants is from one-quarter to over six-times higher than that of the second and later generations. The lack of significant intergenerational differences within the two charter groups is very likely due to the linguistic protection and encouragements afforded the respective languages by the official status the languages have enjoyed since the Act of Union of 1841. This has been even more secure since the Official Languages Act of 1969.

Even so, there is no lack of reports that demonstrate the linguistic vulnerability of the French outside their territorial stronghold of Quebec. It may come as a surprise to some that the British are susceptible to exactly the same linguistic injury as the French. In Montreal in 1971, for instance, only 77% of third- and later-generation British still had English as their mother tongue (Herberg, 1980: 62).

The increasing urbanization of Native Peoples since 1941 so closely parallels the decline in their ethnic-language level of retention that a casual influence from urbanization can be reasonably inferred (though this will be tested more explicitly later in this chapter).

With this cross analysis of ethnicity and Mother-Tongue Retention, the between-ethnicity patterns remind us that the real situa-

---

*"First" generation = Immigrant to Canada.
"Second" generation = Born in Canada with at least one immigrant parent.
"Third or later" generation = Born in Canada to Canadian-born parents

Table 5.1

Mother-Tongue Retention Rates (in %) among Canadian Ethno-Racial-Religious Groups, 1921–1981

Year	Arabic	Asian	Chinese	East Indian	Indochinese	Japanese	Korean	Black	British
				Ethno-Racial-Religious Group					
1921	*	99	99	*	*	100*	*	*	100*
1931	*	99	99	*	*	99	*	*	99
1941	*	91	97	*	*	97	*	*	99
1951	*	74	88	81	*	80	*	*	99
1961	67	68	83	66	*	60	*	*	99
1971	*	65	79	62	*	45	*	*	98
1981	56	68	78	56	83	47	77	2	98

Year	English	Celtic	Czechoslovak	Dutch	Filipino	French	German	Greek	Hungarian	Italian
1921	*	*	89	28	*	99	54	95	97	94
1931	99	1	82	35	*	95	57	87	96	87
1941	99	1	79	39	*	94	54	73	88	71
1951	99	0*	61	43	*	92	41	58	72	60

1961	99	0*	37	48	*	90	40	72	70	74
1971	97	1	54	39	*	89	37	83	59	71
1981	98	0*	60	40	64	89	37	79	63	69

Year	Jewish	Native Peoples	Polish	Portuguese	Russian	Scandinavian	Ukrainian	Yugoslavian
1921	96	94	94	89	96	82	99	63
1931	96	93	93	*	90	68	94	65
1941	81	91	85	*	81	57	92	70
1951	57	83	71	*	66	36	73	52
1961	41	71	59	83	53	29	64	42
1971	27	55	47	85	50	22	51	71
1981	25	33	51	83	55	22	49	77

Notes: *No data. 100* = over 99.50%. 0* = under 0.51%.
Sources: Censuses of Canada.

tion within ethno-racial-religious groups in Canada is not readily amenable to unvarying rules of social order, but seems, instead, to follow a path of its own, often unexplainable by observers and participants alike.

URBAN-RURAL RESIDENCE

While rural/farm-resident members of ethnicities overall enjoyed higher language retention until 1961, thereafter the difference between the Mother-Tongue Retention of farm residents and their urban cousins declined, until urban residents were higher in retention. Table 5.2 displays this phenomenon within each ethno-racial-religious group.

First, there are considerable urban versus rural differences in language-retention rates within almost all groups during at least one period since the Second World War. Only among the British and perhaps the French was there no or only a small variation over all dates. In most groups also (ignoring for the moment, whether urban or rural residents had higher language retention) the absolute extent of difference between urban and rural people declined over time.

In 1951, the rural residents in 12 of the 15 groups covered had from slightly to markedly higher language-maintenance rates than those of their ethnicity who lived in the urban parts of this country. Of the remaining, only one group, the Chinese, had higher Mother-Tongue Retention by their urban dwellers. In the Polish and British groups, essentially identical language levels existed for both rural and urban residents in 1951. Ten years later, of the original 12, in only three groups did farm dwellers possess higher Mother-Tongue Retention: Japanese, French and Native Peoples. At that date, four ethnicities were characterized by a higher language maintenance among urban members of the groups: Chinese, Hungarians, Italians, and Jewish. The other eight groups had equal language rates, or nearly so, for both farm and urban dwellers.

In these two decades, the greatest variations in language retention were among Native Peoples, whose urban members had language-retention rates under half that for their farm cousins. Among Hungarians, Italians and Jewish, 1951 rates favoured farm residents, but by 1961 this had shifted to favour the city members of these ethnicities. Within the Czechoslovak, Dutch, German, Russian, Scandinavian and Ukrainian groups, 1951–1961 saw a shift from farm dominance in language retention to almost identical levels for both farm and urban people.

In 1971, only four of the seventeen ethno-racial-religious categories were marked by much higher language retention among farm residents: Germans, Native Peoples, Russians, and Ukrainians. Eight of the thirteen other groups had from moderately to greatly higher language rates among urban residents. Only the British rates showed no difference at all by residence between 1951 and 1981. Among the French, the rural residents had much to a bit higher ethnic-language maintenance at all dates.

In 1981, there seem to be even more groups in which the trend was for language maintenance to be weakened by the isolation of rural residence. In contrast, there were at least nine ethnicities then of the total of seventeen in which urban residence clearly facilitated the continuance of the ethnic tongue, likely because of the concentration and proximity of group members in these centres. It is not mere coincidence, moreover, that, in 1981, the groups with either a more consistent and/or higher urban superiority in language maintenance were, by a wide majority, ethnicities with a history of urban residence. Thus, there may well be a cause-effect relationship over the decades between urban residence and higher ethnic-language retention. Also, the increasing urbanization of most groups from 1971 to 1981 appears to have led to almost uniformly higher retention of the ethnic language by these urbanities. Only among Native Peoples were rural residents clearly superior in Mother-Tongue Retention (E. Herberg, 1986).

GENDER VARIATIONS IN LANGUAGE RETENTION

Probably the first definitive investigation into gender variations in Mother-Tongue Retention was by Coats and MacPhail (1924: xviii) using 1921 Canadian census data. They concluded that there were strong gender differences, of women experiencing language loss more slowly then men. Coats and Macphail speculated that this was because women were not as much "employed in pursuits which bring them intimately in touch with persons speaking English or French."

Since the very large immigration of the 1950s and 1960s, which was much more comprised of entire family units, there have been constant first- or second-hand accounts that immigrant (and even

Table 5.2

Mother-Tongue Retention Rate (in %) within Canadian Ethno-Racial-Religious Groups, by Farm/Rural-Urban Residence, 1951–1981

Year and Residence	Ethno-Racial-Religious Group									
	Asian	Chinese	East Indian	Japanese	British	Czechoslovak	Dutch	French	German	Greek
1951: Farm	*	79	*	89	99	65	45	95	53	*
Urban	*	86	*	75	99	61	20	91	32	*
1961: Farm	*	77	*	65	99	39	39	94	42	*
Urban	*	83	*	59	99	38	39	89	42	*
1971: Farm	88	69	*	46	98	44	39	92	45	52
Urban	79	81	*	46	98	59	37	89	36	75
1981: Rural#	62	68	59	40	98	52	37	93	45	60
Urban#	70	78	59	49	97	67	41	90	45	80

	Hungarian	Italian	Jewish	Native Peoples	Polish	Portuguese	Russian	Scandinavian	Ukrainian	Unofficial Language Total
1951: Farm	70	58	55	80	56	*	47	42	75	67
Urban	61	52	53	37	55	*	31	31	71	50
1961: Farm	54	43	29	72	44	*	25	28	59	56
Urban	64	75	34	35	44	*	26	28	59	52
1971: Farm	52	33	15	52	42	83	41	24	67	47
Urban	70	73	27	30	48	89	23	21	33	49
1981: Rural#	54	56	**	41	33	77	52	22	56	41
Urban#	75	72	25	11	54	88	69	24	53	51

Notes: * No data.
** Too few cases.
# Estimated.
Sources: Censuses of Canada.

Canadian-born) women are considerably more isolated than men from extra-family, extra-ethnicity influences because of their lesser fluency in an official language. Such claims typically are presented as a given, without substantiation, and the claim—as made—becomes the basis for wide-ranging suggestions for social remedies (e.g., Ng, 1982).

However, independent analysis of the relevant 1921 census data and figures from subsequent years does not verify Coats' and MacPhail's conclusions. Looking at the statistics, controlling for gender and generation in Canada and for both generations combined in a group, no immigrant group could justly be characterized as having a female language-retention rate significantly higher than the male rate in 1921. Indeed, in that year, only the Czechoslovak and Ukrainian immigrant females had even a marginally higher retention rate than immigrant males. More frequent were the four immigrant groups that had higher male ethnic-language rates than groups with higher female rates. Among the Canadian-born as well, the case for higher language retention by females was just as weak. Neither the 1971 nor 1981 data (the only years since 1921 for which comparisons are possible) revealed any considerable variations by gender, even when immigrant-Canadian birth status is controlled.

So, contrary to both the Coats and MacPhail and the Ng claims, women in neither generation were generally higher in Mother-Tongue Retention Rates, although they are higher in 1971 and 1981 than 50 to 60 years before. Moreover, whatever basis there is for the female isolation-language-retention thesis is grounded more in the Canadian-born and in a particular few ethnicities, such as the Dutch and Italians.

A case can be made for ignoring the generation in Canada and for inspecting the entire group for gender differentiation in language-retention rates. When this is done, it becomes apparent that, as the rate of language retention fell between 1921 and 1951, the Gender Ratio of retention generally increased (i.e., less gender difference, or higher male rates), peaking in 1951. In most groups, the post-1951 Gender Ratios of language-retention rates have declined to levels at or close to gender parity. It is not coincidental, I think, that, after 1951, there came the great waves of family-unit immigration that augmented the numbers of both genders in every ethnicity and could well have lessened isolation for both genders at that time.

HOME LANGUAGE COMPARED TO MOTHER TONGUE

"Home language" in the 1971 and 1981 censuses is defined as the language "usually" employed as the medium of communication in the home. Data on this aspect of ethnic language was first collected in the 1971 census. We can, thus, compare the 1981 rate of using the ethnic language as the usual home language with only the 1971 rate. However, we can compare the Home-Language Use Rate to the Mother-Tongue Retention Rate for both these dates.

Ordinarily, if the ethnic language has not been maintained, it would be impossible to have the ethnic language as the home-use language. The only exception to this, as we shall see, is in the case of the British. However, the possibility exists that, even in cases where the ethnic language is retained in other groups as the "Mother Tongue," this language can be abandoned in favour of one of the official languages as the tongue utilized in the home. Thus, the general rule that can be developed from this logic is that (except for the British) the Home-Language Use of the heritage tongue cannot be greater than the Mother-Tongue-Retention Rate for most ethno-racial-religious groups in Canada.

The ratio of Home-Language Use (of the heritage tongue) to Mother-Tongue Retention, therefore, should be *below* 100 (100 indicating parity between Mother Tongue and Home Language). And, as the statistics in Table 5.3 demonstrate, this is indeed the situation. However, the deficit between Mother Tongue and Home Language varied considerably, both between groups in 1971 and 1981, as well as within the same group over the decade. Further, not all the changes over that decade have been for the worse, in terms of language maintenance.

Table 5.3 is the only one in which, for special comparison purposes, the "British" language rates were calculated on the conceptual basis of their being comprised of two separate categories of ethnicities: the English group, and the Celtic people (Irish, Scots and Welsh). Thus, the rates of British language retention, so much lower than on Table 6.1, are the result of the nearly total loss of Celtic language retention in Canada. Home-language use was also calculated using the English-Celt dichotomy.

Only the English ethnic group was in the situation wherein Home-Language Use of the ethnic language (English) was higher—

Table 5.3

Mother-Tongue Retention Rate (in %), Home Use Rate of the Ethnic Language (in %), and Ratio of Home Use to Mother-Tongue Retention Among Canadian Ethno-Racial-Religious Groups, 1971 & 1981

Language Index		Ethno-Racial-Religious Group								
		Arabic	Asian	Chinese	East Indian	Indochinese	Japanese	Korean	Black	British
M-Tongue Retention	1971	*	65	79	62	*	45	*	*	64
	1981	56	68	78	56	83	47	77	2	57
Home Use	1971	*	54	62	44	*	24	*	*	65
	1981	36	52	61	45	83	26	57	1	60
Ratio: Home/M-T	1971	*	83	78	71	*	53	*	*	102
	1981	64	76	84	80	100	56	75	33	105

		English	Celtic	Czechoslovak	Dutch	Filipino	French	German	Greek	Hungarian	Italian
M-Tongue Retention	1971	97	1	54	39	*	89	37	83	59	71
	1981	98	0*	60	40	64	89	37	79	63	69
Home	1971	99	0*	29	10	*	85	14	70	33	58

Use	1981	99	0*	27	8	36	85	12	62	26	48
Ratio:	1971	102	3	54	25	*	96	38	84	56	78
Home/M-T	1981	100	6	45	19	56	96	31	78	41	69

		Jewish	Native Peoples	Polish	Portuguese	Russian	Scandinavian	Ukrainian	Yogoslavian	Unofficial Languages
M-Tongue Retention	1971	27	55	47	85	50	22	51	71	49
	1981	25	33	51	83	55	22	49	77	49
Home Use	1971	13	43	23	74	23	3	23	44	27
	1981	10	24	23	67	23	3	17	44	27
Ratio: Home/M-T	1971	48	78	49	83	46	14	45	62	55
	1981	39	74	45	81	41	12	34	57	55

Notes: *No data.
Sources: Censuses of Canada.

albeit only barely—than Mother-Tongue Retention. This finding suggests that some of these people, living in Quebec or elsewhere in the condition of an ethnic minority, have succumbed to a certain degree of linguistic assimilation, but still use English in the home.

It must re-emphasized that a group's being characterized by a high or low ratio of Home-Language Use to Mother-Tongue Retention makes no necessary inference regarding the actual level of either language dynamic. Theoretically, a group with either a high or low Mother-Tongue Retention Rate could have either a high or low ratio of Home-Use-to-Mother-Tongue Retention, depending entirely on the level of the Home-Use rate, relative to the Mother-Tongue Retention. What the ratio here does is to describe, in a purely numerical way, the degree to which the Home-Language Use level diverged from the Mother-Tongue Retention Rate.

That understood, the first dimension that we can inspect here is the magnitude of the Home-Language Use/Mother-Tongue Retention Ratio—that is, in ethnicities other than the English, the extent to which Home-Language Use was below Mother-Tongue Retention. This deficit was especially great among Celts, Scandinavians, Dutch, Germans, Jewish, Ukrainians, Russians, and Polish. In each of these ethnicities, the level of Home-Language Use was under one-half and down to one-ninth that of Mother-Tongue Retention. At the other end of this continuum, the highest correspondence between Mother Tongue and Home Language was among the Indochinese, French, Chinese, Portuguese, East Indians, Greek, Koreans, and Native Peoples, in that order. Each of these eight ethnicities had a ratio of from 100% to 74%; high indeed, considering that only ten of the 25 groups arrayed here met a 70% Rate criterion.

It was indicated above that there was no necessary *theoretical* link between the level of Mother-Tongue Retention relative to the degree of Home-Language Use, in terms of the ratio of one to the other. There is, nevertheless, a readily obvious *empirical* correlation of Mother-Tongue Retention and Home-Language Use. It seems quite significant that only two of the eight groups with a large deficit between Mother Tongue and Home Language in 1981 had a Mother-Tongue Retention Rate above 50%. And, of the eight ethnicities with the highest ratio here, only one had a Mother-Tongue Retention Rate under 50%. Thus, groups with a high Mother-Tongue Retention Rate tended also to have high use of the ethnic language as the medium of communication in the home. Correlatively, for ethnicities in which Home-Language Use was low, the Mother-Tongue Retention was also depressed.

The other dimension of investigating the relation of Home-Language Use to Mother-Tongue Retention is the degree and direction of change in the ratios of the two language measures between 1971 and 1981. Excluding the five ethnicities for whom time-shift data were not available at time of writing, the other 20 groups can be put into two polar categories plus a middle one. To begin with, there is one category of ethnicities that were characterized by either an increase in the Home-Language to Mother-Tongue Ratio, no change in the ratio, or only a slight decrease in the ratio over the decade. This category of essentially high-level Home-Language maintenance included eight groups. In order of decade shifts from increment to slight decline, they were: the East Indians, Chinese, Japanese, French, English, Greeks, Portuguese and Native Peoples.

At the other extreme, in order of greatest decade decline in the Home-Language/Mother-Tongue Retention Ratio, were: the Jewish, Italians, Dutch, Hungarians, Ukrainians, and Czechoslovaks; most registering from almost a one-half to a one-fifth decline in the ratio over the ten years. The other ethnicities, six in number (Celts, Germans, Poles, Russians, Scandinavians, and Yugoslavs), comprise the middle collection, having had more decline in the Home-Language/Mother-Tongue Retention Ratio that those in the "high" category, but considerably less than those in the "low" category.

Finally, the summary ratio of Home-Language Use to Mother-Tongue Retention for all the non-charter ethnic groups considered together (bottom row on Table 5.3) was stable at 55% from 1971 to 1981. This suggests, perhaps, that the use of the ethnic language has reached some sort of plateau—at least with respect to the level of Mother-Tongue Retention over all the non-British, non-French ethnicities in Canada.

The truly significant question to ask in all this is whether the Home-Language Use/Mother-Tongue Retention Ratio will continue to remain as high in the future, given the likely transition of Canada from a nation with high immigration from the 1950s through the 1970s, to one of lesser immigration in the 1980s. This could lead to the increasing significance of the second, third and later generations in language retention/use. The only data available on this essential issue is from my five-city analysis of ethnic phenomena and change (E. Herberg, 1980). The data on the adult (age 20 or older) populations of Halifax, Montreal, Toronto, Winnipeg, and Vancouver were combined and analyzed by generation in Canada for the 1971 ratio of Home-Language Use to Mother-Tongue Retention. As earlier data demonstrated (Table 5.2), urban residents in many groups have higher language retention rates than rural residents. Thus, the language figures for the five-city statistics should also be somewhat more elevated than they were for those covering the whole of Canada.

As expected, the Home-Language Use/Mother-Tongue Retention Ratio was highest for immigrants in all groups but the French (with whom the 3rd,+ generation had the largest ratio). And again, excepting the French and this time also the British, all groups were characterized by a huge decline in ratios between the immigrant and second generations. The ratios in the second generation are from nearly one-half to nearly three-quarters lower compared to the immigrant generation. Over all non-charter groups combined, the second generation's ratio was two-thirds lower than in the immigrant group.

Further, excepting the two charter groups and the Scandinavians, the Home-Language/Mother-Tongue Retention Ratio for the 3rd,+ generation is even lower than in the second generation, by a considerable margin. This is due primarily to the fact that Home-Language Use declined through the generations in these five cities much more than did Mother-Tongue Retention. Indeed, in these cities, we are faced with the ironic situation of Home-Language Use declining in the 3rd,+ generation among some groups while Mother-Tongue Retention either diminished only slightly or became even higher in the 3rd or later generation, compared with the second.

These varied patterns suggest one or more of three outcomes: (1) The likelihood of continued declines in the extent of Home-Language Use, especially with regard to the level of ethnic Mother-Tongue Retention, as the influence of the Canadian-born generations increases in the future; or (2) some groups (e.g., Chinese, East Indians, Germans, Greeks, Italians) are either retaining the ethnic Mother Tongue in the third or later generation at a rate higher than in the second generation or (more likely); (3) the ethnic language is experiencing a rebirth or renewal in the 3rd,+ generation, and this is a harbinger of renewed strength in the use of the ethnic language in the home in the years to come.

Actually, it is probable that, in some ethnicities, both Mother-Tongue Retention and Home-Language Use will continue to decay in all generations including the immigrant aggregate as it has already in some ethnicities. In other ethnicities, it is quite possible that language growth will occur, particularly in the Canadian-born generations and very likely more among the 3rd,+ generations than with the second. If this "returner" pattern is occurring (and we will not be able to ascertain this until the 1991 census, if even then, because the 1981 and 1986 censuses did not include a question on parental birthplace), then we might also expect to see a favourable impact in these groups on Home-Language Use. For a sizeable fraction of ethnic-group members, it seems, therefore, not untoward to expect at least an interruption, and, perhaps, even a remission in the loss of ethnic-language retention and/or use.

Now that school children can maintain their ethnic language or even learn it for the first time in schools where there are Heritage Language Programs, the likelihood of legitimation of a "minority" ethnicity and retention of an unofficial language is greater. During the 1970s and 1980s, such programs existed in most of the Canadian provinces. In Ontario alone, over 76 000 students were enrolled in Heritage Language Programs during 1980 (Danesi, 1983), and this number may have increased since. This successful school-related program has had three major effects in addition to the youths simply learning the ethnic languages. First, participation by youth in a Heritage-Language learning experience apparently encourages greater use of the ethnic language in the home (Keyser and Brown, 1981). Second, a favourable attitude to non-English, non-French ethnicities and languages is generated which, in turn, creates greater tolerance and respect for linguistic-cultural retention and practice. Finally, Heritage Language training in elementary school not only tends to facilitate majority (official) language learning, but also to bring many and wide benefits to these youths' cognitive development (Danesi, 1983).

Given that a significant fraction of students are already enrolled in Heritage Language Programs, and given that the benefits to these students in other aspects of their education are being documented and recognized, there is every likelihood that the enrolment in these programs will continue to rise. Since these programs also promote a favourable attitude not only toward one's own ethnic heritage, but also toward that of others, the stage has been set for a greater degree of retention/rediscovery, maintenance, and domestic use of the ethnic language by these youth and their parents.

SUMMARY

From 1941 to 1961, Mother-Tongue Retention, or continued knowledge of the heritage language, was on the decline for the unofficial ethnic languages. During those two decades the degree of unofficial language maintenance had dropped by one-quarter, compared to only eight to ten percent between 1921 and 1941. Since 1961, however, the rate of language deficit has not exceeded one-sixteenth, and in the decade 1971–1981, the rate of language retention among the non-British, non-French considered in a summary fashion remained stable at 49%.

This new, changed state of language maintenance seems due to a much more varied pattern of language retention that has emerged in recent decades. There were almost universally high rates of Mother-Tongue Retention in the 1921–1941 era and then sharp declines by most groups through 1961 or 1971. Both charter groups have retained high levels of language retention since 1921. In contrast, the period from 1961 to 1981 has shown remarkable language-retention recoveries among all ethnicities dealt with here except Jewish, Native Peoples, Scandinavians, and, perhaps also Germans and Dutch. Since the language retention in the two Canadian-born generations in all these groups but the Native Canadians is much lower than among the immigrant members, the fact that these groups have recently had relatively few immigrants to bolster language maintenance bodes ill for future Mother-Tongue Retention among those ethnicities.

Some ethnic groups have either maintained high levels of language retention or improved the group's overall rate of maintaining the ethnic language probably because of the great numbers of immigrants over the last few decades: Chinese, East Indians, Indochinese/Vietnamese, Portuguese, Greeks, Czechoslovaks, and Hungarians among them. Only some of the latter groups, however, have been able to arrest the decline in home use of the ethnic language. Even so, the overall Home-Language rate has remained the same since 1971 (27%, vs. 49% for unofficial Mother-Tongue

Retention). Very likely it will stay this way or, perhaps, increase modestly in response to a possibly improved rate of Mother-Tongue Retention. This can be postulated as one scenario on the basis of (1) the increasing respect for ethno-racial-religious diversity and differences in Canada and the maintenance of cultural practice; and (2), more directly, the development, spread, and success of Heritage Language Programs in the schools of most Canadian provinces.

Notwithstanding all of this, the level of Mother-Tongue Retention in certain groups must be close to what would ordinarily be considered the brink of language extinction. Home-Language Use of the heritage tongue is lower than Mother-Tongue Retention in all non-British groups; in many groups it is markedly lower. Even with the apparent stability in recent language-retention levels, there may be too low a floor in certain groups for the existing language maintenance to enable the conduct of ethnic practices and the continued life of their ethnocultures. If it is true, as theorized at the beginning of this chapter, that the ethnic language is the lifeblood of most groups' cultures in Canada, then the next question, obviously, is: How has the decline in language retention since 1921 affected other mechanisms of cultural cohesion in Canada? The question we must answer in subsequent chapters is whether, low and decreasing language retention in many groups, has brought in its wake a corresponding pattern of decline in other mechanisms of ethnic-group cohesion.

CHAPTER 6

Residential Concentration

INTRODUCTION: CONCEPTIONS OF RESIDENTIAL CONCENTRATION

"Residential Concentration," as used here, means the degree to which members of each of the ethno-racial-religious groups reside in proximity to others in the group. It can be considered as a kind of socio-geographic phenomenon, representing an "objective" face of ethnic social organization and requiring no social or social-psychological explanations. It can also be viewed as the social outcome of intergroup dynamics, as in the residential "segregation" concept (Richmond, 1972; Kalbach, 1980; 1981), or the residential "isolation" notion (Driedger and Church, 1974). In either case, the theoretical kernal is, simply, the extent to which members of a group reside near each other. In its purely empirical measure, "concentration" of residence implies nothing about the reasons for this concentration within a particular ethnicity.

Use of the segregation or the isolation concepts and the calculation methodologies developed for them, involves the almost inevitable assumption that ethno-racial-religious-group identities and differences cause residential separation between groups. Because of this, the residential segregation or isolation concepts generally carry pejorative connotations of superiority-inferiority, majority-minority, superordinacy-subordinacy—a heavy load of cultural conclusions to be carried in a concept. For this reason, I prefer to focus on the differentiation that can be demonstrated in the residence patterns of the ethnicities and to become concerned about segregation or isolation only as interpretations of empirical results and not as unavoidable *a priori* attributions.

There are two major ways by which one can assess the residential concentration tendencies of ethnic groups: (1) concentration within the several *regions of Canada* and (2) concentration within its *cities*.

REGIONAL CONCENTRATION OF RESIDENCE

The regional distribution of the ethno-racial-religious groups in Canada is the simpler of the two kinds of residential concentration perspectives. It has long been thought, for instance, that the cultural features of Franco-Canadians are, in very large part, due to the centuries-long concentration of the great majority of this group in the province of Quebec. At the risk of being geocentric, a quick index of the concentration tendencies in each Canadian ethnicity is the percent of the group residing in Ontario. That province is chosen for the fact that, since Confederation, it has been the place of residence for more Canadians than any other.

Figure 6.1 depicts the proportions of the various ethnic groups that have been resident in Ontario; the time period covered is that since Confederation. The statistics are drawn from figures on the proportion of each group that resided in each of the regions of Canada during this same time frame, but not included here. Looking at the within-Ontario patterns, it quickly becomes clear that this province has, increasingly, become the residence for many groups, in contrast to a smaller number of groups whose Ontario representation has been stable or declining. The first category includes: Asians, Czechoslovaks, Greeks, Hungarians, Italians, Jewish, Polish, Portuguese, and Ukrainians. Among most of these ethnicities and especially among Asians, Italians, and Portuguese, there has been a marked increase in Ontario residence since the Second World War. In the second category are the Dutch and Black groups which show a variation on the post-war Ontario increment. In both groups, the period from 1871 to 1941 was one in which the proportion of the group residing in Ontario had declined from about 70% to approximately one-half of that. Then, in the post-war decades more of their respective groups either migrated or immigrated to Ontario, particularly among Black Canadians.

A third category is represented by the Russians and French, who have tended to have a fairly steady, small percentage of their people

Figure 6.1

Percent of Canadian Ethno-Racial-Religious Groups Residing in Ontario, 1871–1881, 1901–1981

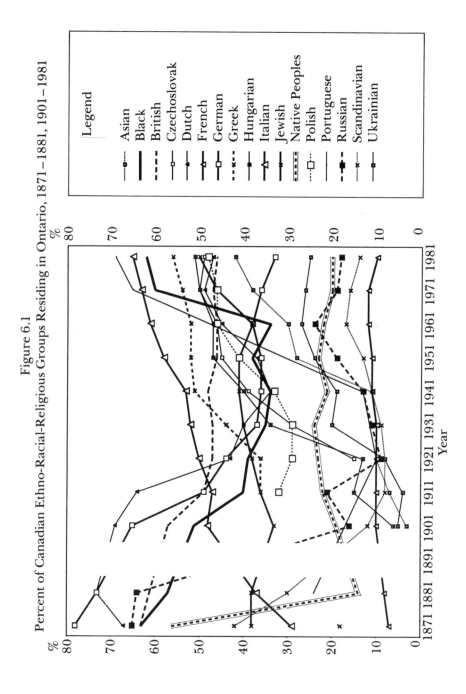

in Ontario. The final pattern to be found in Ontario is the long-range decline, between 1871 and 1981, for British, Germans, Native Peoples, and Scandinavians. The pattern for Natives is somewhat artificial, since at the time when they are represented in Figure 6.1 as having almost 60% residing in Ontario (1871), the base for calculating this included only the four original provinces in Confederation and excluded everything north and west of southern Ontario.

Of the seventeen groups on Figure 6.1, the Portuguese, Italian, Black, Greek, Hungarian and Jewish groups were, in 1981, most highly concentrated in Ontario, with at least half their people in that province. Those having only one-fifth or less of their members in the province were the French, Scandinavians, Russians, and Native Peoples.

Data not presented here reveal that these Ontario patterns convey only part of the concentration dynamic of ethnic groups in Canada. In 1901, nearly all Asians lived in British Columbia and most Hungarians in the Prairies or Territories. In 1871, two-thirds of the Greeks were concentrated in the Atlantic provinces, and more than one-half of the Italians and Jewish were resident in Quebec. The earliest data on Portuguese—1921—show the largest proportion to be in the Atlantic region, and in that year more than two-thirds of Czechoslovaks resided in the Prairies and Territories. Today, from one-half to more than two-thirds of all these groups are concentrated in Ontario.

Since Confederation, as suggested above, the concentration of Asians in British Columbia has shifted from 88% in 1901—and 99% of Chinese in 1881—to only 29% and 34% respectively in 1981. In 1871, more than one-third of Canadian Blacks resided in the Atlantic region; a tiny fraction lived in Quebec, and most of the rest in Ontario. Today, almost the same percent as that of 1871 are in Ontario; about one-quarter live in Quebec, but only 2% are in the Atlantic region.

Quebec as the region of concentration for the French has declined only a little since 1871, from 86% to 79% in 1981. The region of concentration for Russians has shifted from Ontario in 1871 and 1881 (64–65% in both years, and 4% in British Columbia) to British Columbia in 1981 (40% versus 18% in Ontario). Scandinavians have experienced the same kind of regional transfer: 20% in the Prairies during 1881, compared to 52% in 1981. Among Ukrainians, the Prairies as the locale of greatest concentration declined from pre-Depression highs near or above 90%, to 59% in 1981, the major change coming after the Depression with a greatly expanded portion residing in Ontario.

To determine whether that and similar shifts in Ontario concentration were the result of internal migration—to escape the worst of the rural Prairie economic collapse—or of the change in destination by immigrants during the 1921–1931 and post-1951 decades that figured so much in those periods of heavy immigration to Canada would require more specialized analysis than is possible here. Considering the immigration trends covered in Chapter 3 and the fact that, in most ethnicities, immigrants comprised a minority of group members, it seems quite likely that both internal migration and immigration to Canada were involved in the site shifts of group residential concentreation. Further, the major shifts, whether due to internal migration or immigrant shift in destination, were greater during the three decades following the Second World War than in the one or two decades before.

What none of the figures here consider, and what the statistics in Chapter 2 cover only in a summary fashion, is the massive shift from rural to urban residence. This transformation, beginning well before the Depression, was accentuated after the war and, thus, probably involved a majority of immigrants. What we do not know, however, is the extent to which the rural-to-urban relocation in Canada also overlapped and was part of the shift in region of residential concentration as well. Again, it is probable that some "double" residential relocation—rural to urban plus relocation between regions—took place, but in which groups this was particularly notable only further detailed research will reveal.

There are, however, four lines of transition that present themselves concerning this. First, members of groups that were largely rural could have migrated to urban places within the same region, and later—even decades later—members of the group moved to the urban centres in other regions. A second possibility is that the rural-to-urban migration took place as part of a shift between regions—a simultaneous double transition. Each of these two changes implicitly cover the Canadian-born generations. Immigrants, however, could have shown different patterns that would have yielded the summary outcomes reflected in Figure 6.1, and those just described. Thus, immigrants of certain groups, early on, may have settled on the farms occupied by their Canadian-born relatives and then, later, migrated to the region's towns and cities.

Or—the second possibility—immigration just before or following the Second World War might have been to other regions, in fact, to the cities of regions other than those in which their Canadian predecessors dwelt. Undoubtedly, there are additional variations on the migration-immigration theme that are involved in the combined rural-to-urban and regional redistribution experienced by many Canadian ethnicities.

Finally, whatever the history of past versus present regional residential locations, most of the ethno-racial-religious groups are concentrated in one or more regions of Canada to a degree exceeding the proportion of the entire Canadian population possessed by the region in 1981. Such regional concentrations are: Chinese, Japanese, and Russians in British Columbia; Germans, Native Peoples, Scandinavians, and Ukrainians in the Prairies and the Territories; and East Indians, Blacks, Central and South Americans, Greeks, Hungarians, Italians, Jewish, and the Portuguese in Ontario. These are, of course, over and beyond the traditional home ground of the French in Quebec. Within the Atlantic region, though, about all the ethnic residential concentration that exists is among the British, while every other group seems to be under-represented.

Notwithstanding the 1981 residential concentrations in regions, there has been, over the years, a drift by certain groups away from the locales originally settled after the initial large waves of immigration—a drift directly contrary to the westerly migration trend of the late nineteenth and early twentieth centuries. The Asian shift from British Columbia to Ontario began in the opening decades of this century. The most abrupt of these transitional movements was the forced reconcentration of the Japanese during the hysteria following Pearl Harbor; in 1941 only 1% of Japanese lived in Ontario; almost all the rest were concentrated in British Columbia. Ten years later and continuously thereafter, at least 40% of Japanese had (or had been) relocated in Ontario, with only a little more than one-third maintaining residence in British Columbia. Today, the relative concentration of residence in these two provinces by the Japanese is just about equal, a far-different pattern from that of early 1941.

In the same period, late nineteenth to early twentieth century, Czechoslovaks, Hungarians, and Polish have shifted their residential concentration from the Prairies to Ontario. The Scandinavians and Ukrainians have maintained their concentration in the

Prairies. Even so, some of the former moved west to British Columbia after 1945, and a larger fraction of the Ukrainians than before are now in Ontario, this latter transition beginning in the 1921–1931 decade. Moving west from the Atlantic region sometime after the Second World War, the current centralization of residence in Ontario by the Portuguese is likely due, in large measure, to the great influx of this group since the late 1950s. The only other major westward movement by an ethnicity in Canada has been that of the Russians from the Prairies to British Columbia, commencing in the late 1920s; by 1981 more Russians (many of them Doukhobors) held residence in British Columbia than in the adjacent region.

The Germans and Dutch appear to have been the only ethnicities to have experienced the relocation of their residential concentration from Ontario to the Prairies (+ Territories)—between 1901 and 1931 among the Germans (including Mennonites and Hutterites) and beginning ten years later in 1911 among the Dutch, but being established in the Prairies by the time of the Depression. As unique as this pattern is, the post-war residence dynamic of the Dutch is even more unusual, reversing the 1911–1931 shift back to residential concentration in Ontario since 1961.

These multiple and quite varied alterations in regional Residential Concentration within Canadian ethnicities only partially reflect the opening of the Prairies, Territories, and British Columbia to settlement following 1881 and the attendant increase in the proportion of the entire population there expanding from a miniscule figure at Confederation to 30% in 1981. Indeed, the eastward or westward migration of residence to Ontario by the several groups discussed above goes counter to the trend of the major directions of population change in the respective regions. This lack of congruence to national population shifts and especially running counter to them, seems to render still further evidence, if more were needed, of the impossibility of applying generic linear explanations to the transitions manifested within and by ethnic groups in Canada. More to the point, the most apt interpretation of the regional ethnic Residential Concentration patterns is that each must, at least to a large extent, be considered as a phenomenological outcome of the very different values, structures, and processes extant in each group.

ETHNIC RESIDENTIAL CONCENTRATION
WITHIN URBAN CENTRES

As indicated at the beginning of this chapter, regional concentration of ethnic-group residence is but one of the two ways by which Residential Concentration can be assessed. The other is the degree of concentration within one or more urban centres. In a fashion somewhat similar to looking at regional concentration, the within-city(ies) method also aims to ascertain the extent to which members of each ethno-racial-religious group reside in proximity to other members of their group. This dimension of ethnic residential patterns originally derives from a model of urban growth and succession put forward in 1925 by the University of Chicago demographer and developer of human ecology, Burgess.

In this model, it was hypothesized that immigrants of the same ethno-racial-religious group coming to a city would settle close to each other in one of the areas of the city, initially close to the city's central business district, and there establish an ethnic community. Over the following years, and particularly with the second and later generations, members of the ethnicity would leave the residentially concentrated ethnic enclave for other parts of the city. Over the intervening years, the theory goes, the second and later generations, having been socialized to the dominant culture (through formal education and such) and perhaps even the immigrant generation (through assimilation brought on by integration with people outside the ethnic enclave) would disperse to different areas of the city and to ethnically mixed neighbourhoods. Thus, according to this "assimilation" theory, the degree of ethnic residential concentration would decline over time in direct proportion to the assimilation of group members into the dominant ethnicity's culture.

The essential dynamic for the immigrant members of a minority ethnicity was the separation of ethnic-group residence from that of the majority ethnicity or, for that matter, from any other group. One way of ascertaining the degree of this separation—arriving at indices of residential *segregation* or *isolation*—is through calculations made from census-tract data. Segregation was different from isolation, both in meaning and method of calculation.

The first analysis of ethnic-group residential "segregation" in Canada was conducted by Hurd (1942) as part of the precedent-setting 1931 Census of Canada monographs. For Hurd, who built on American concepts and methods, residential segregation meant

Table 6.1
Urban Ethnic-Group Residential
Segregation in Canada, 1931

Ethnicity	Index	Rank	Ethnicity	Index	Rank
French	105	2	Polish	308	8
Scandinavian	174	3	Hungarian	404	9
German	176	4	Ukrainian	540	10
Dutch	189	5	Italian	809	11
Russian	289	6	Native Peoples	845	12
Czechoslovak	292	7	Jewish	896	13

Source: W.B. Hurd. *Racial Origins and Nativity of the Canadian People.* Census of
Canada monograph (Ottawa, 1942), pp. 563, 639.

the extent to which the average concentration of ethnic-group residence in Canadian municipalities exceeded that of the British majority group(s). Thus, the British became the comparison group, with a hypothetical index of 100 and a rank of 1. All other groups were found to have much higher indices of concentration of residence, some, over eight times higher (Table 6.1).

No index for the Chinese or any other Asiatic ethnicity was calculated, nor for the Asiatic group as a whole. Hurd (1942: 563) observed that "Asiatics are omitted for the reason that an index of segregation is apt to be misleading." Hurd, however, failed to suggest in what way, exactly, the datum on Asian residential segregation would be "misleading," and the puzzle remains today, so far as I know.

In any case, Hurd's statistics clearly demonstrate a wide degree of ethnic residential differentiation, documenting that, in 1931, the residential patterns of the French, Scandinavians, Germans, and Dutch in Canada's "municipalities" (i.e., the cities) was quite similar to that of the British groups. Those of the Italians, Native Peoples, and Jewish (plus Asians?) were least like that of the British. Another group Hurd unfortunately did not include was Canadian Blacks, who very likely would also have been categorized near the end of the residential segregation continuum opposite the British. Despite these gaps, this first Canadian examination of Residential Concentration proved to be most informative.

Regrettably, none of the census reports since 1931 have included data or analysis bearing on ethnic residential patterns, although there have been studies based on census data. With three exceptions, all of the investigations I was able to find that focused or even touched on ethnic-group residential phenomena were limited to only one urban site, and measured residential "segregation" from the British and/or the degree to which the residences of members of the various ethnic groups varied from a hypothetical average over all ethnicities. Even the three exceptions of Balakrishnan (1976), Balakrishnan and Kralt (1987), and Richmond and Kalbach (1980: 189) utilized one of these two lines of analysis, but each provides a multi-city perspective on residential situations of multiple ethnicities.

Most of the work in these residential "segregation" studies has either been based on or included Toronto. Altogether, the earliest works after Hurd's came in the late 1960s (Marston, 1969) or early 1970s (Darroch and Marston, 1971; Driedger and Church, 1974; Richmond, 1972; and, more recently, Kalbach, 1981). Three of these involved an assay of the extent to which ethnic-group residential segregation was linked to a group's socio-economic class, since Marxist and other American sociologists had suggested that social class was either the principal independent influence in such segregation or, at least, more powerful than ethnicity. Even while American studies have shown that ethnicity as a social influence was independent of social class there (perhaps parallel to it?), questions lingered in Canada. Thus, the results from the Darroch and Marston (1971), Richmond (1972), and Kalbach (1981) studies have become important landmarks in settling whether Canadian ethnic segregation was induced solely by socio-economics. All three reports demonstrated a very definite separate, independent influence on residential patterns arising from ethnicity that could not be attributed to mere social-class effects. Balakrishnan (1978) and Richmond and Kalbach (1980: 194–200) using multiple locations reported the same thing, that there is a definite "ethnic" effect on residential segregation that exists after socio-economic factors have been statistically controlled.

Even with that issue reasonably well settled in favour of "ethnic" power, the residence questions addressed in these works were still focused on the extent to which the various groups differed from some fictitious "average," or from the British, in their patterns of residence. No study had investigated the pattern of ethnic residence of all groups in and of itself, without reference to any criterion group. This was the case, even though maps depicting residential concentration levels within each of many groups were routinely being churned out by Statistics Canada for governments (Multicultural Programme, 1982; Toronto Planning Board, 1972) and by those with access to the Public Use Sample of the census in universities (Richard, 1980; Kalbach, 1980).

To open up this relativistic aspect of ethnic residential patterns, I developed an index of Residential Concentration that is not keyed to the residence patterns of any other single group or collection of ethnicities. This Residential Concentration Index measures precisely the extent to which members of each ethno-racial-religious group resided in each metropolitan census tract at a rate above the percent each group represented of the entire metropolitan population. The theoretical range of this Residential Concentration Index is from 0% (indicative that none of the ethnicity resided in census tracts in which they comprised a proportion of that census tract's residents greater than the group's proportion of the entire metropolitan population) to nearly 100% (indicative that most of the group's members resided in census tracts in which they comprised a proportion of that tract's residents greater than the group's proportion of the entire metropolitan population).

Thus, for every group for which there were tract data (or, before 1951, district or ward data) one can calculate a level of Residential Concentration. The issue of to what group(s) each ethnicity is to be compared is left as an empirical question, ascertained by the pattern of the data. We can decide on which groups are similar to each other *after* the results are in rather than before, a method impossible with "segregation" indices based on the distribution of British or French residences. The ability to compare trends over time both within and between groups, as well as to differentiate at the same point in time is greatly enhanced because this index is not dependent on the residence pattern of any other group or set of groups. All in all, I deem this index of ethnic residential proximity to be superior to any other that is based on comparisons with a criterion ethnicity, or with some hypothetical criterion.

This is not to detract from the excellent work done for over a dozen years on the subject of ethnic residential patterns, especially the work of those who have investigated the relation of urban residence patterns with other ethnic phenomena. In this latter aspect, Kalbach's historical (1980) and cross-ethnic (1981) analyses of the part ethnic residence enclaves have played in ethnic cohesion are of exceptional interest and value. Still, we must take even these works with a modicum of caution, knowing that the residential measure is *not* independent of the pattern in other groups. So, even with such fine work as this, the use of the Residential Concentration Index in this book appears to be the first to elicit totally independent measures of ethnic residential proximity for multiple groups in multiple locales.

Notwithstanding, this index does not as yet provide Canada-wide data. The present data reflect the combined standings for multiple ethno-racial-religious groups in five Census Metropolitan Areas (CMAs): Halifax, Montreal, Toronto, Winnipeg, and Vancouver, representing about one-third of all urban residents of Canada. Thus it is not nearly as inclusive as Balakrishnan's coverage of urban Canada's ethnic residential segregation in 1951, 1961, 1971, and 1981, but it does go beyond that of Balakrishnan or Richmond and Kalbach in years covered, as well as in its application of an ethnically-independent base.

The difference in methodologies, however, may be effective in establishing theoretical purity, but still not produce different results in interethnic comparisons that have already been conducted. When Kalbach (1981: 23) observed that the different measures and perspectives for analysis of ethnic residential patterns had all yielded interethnic differentiation that was "quite consistent...both with respect to levels...in Toronto...and those found in Canada's other major metropolitan areas...," he could just as easily have been describing the general similarities between my own findings and those of others, with perhaps one major exception.

Balakrishnan (1976) said that between 1951 and 1961 the overall level of ethnic residential segregation had declined, but that between 1961 and 1971 there was no apparent continuance of this assimilative trend (Balakrishnan, 1978). My own work yielded somewhat different results. Figure 4.1 showed, in part, that the summary level of Residential Concentration has risen steadily since 1951 (from an average of 24% in 1951 to 29% in 1961, 31% in 1971, and 35% in 1981). So, whatever shifts there have been in ethnic residential patterns, according to my 5-CMA results, they have been increasing, not declining.

Interethnic Residence Patterns

When the individual ethnic trends of Residential Concentration are traced (Figure 6.2 and Table 6.2), considerable ethnic differentiation is revealed, not only between the various ethnicities at any point, but also within each ethnic group over time. Groups that are traceable back to 1881 through 1911 often had a level of Residential Concentration different from that which appears today.

Asians, for instance, seem to have had exceptionally high concentration of residence in 1881 which then declined considerably in the opening decades of the twentieth century. By 1951, it was at about the same level as in 1901 and, despite a lowering between 1951 and 1971, had returned to the 1951 level in 1981. Within the "Asian" group in 1981, though, there was considerable variation. Japanese and Chinese had lower Residential Concentration (40% and 43% respectively); East Indians were at a moderately higher level (51%), while Indochinese held the highest degree of concentration among Asians (67%). The patterns for the other two visible-minority groups are very different: Blacks had a somewhat higher concentration in 1911 than in 1881 and 1901. The next available data is for 1981, when their residential proximity had lowered a great deal compared to a century before. Native Peoples living in the five urban centres covered show, in an incomplete census record, an apparent continuously-declining Residential Concentration.

Other groups had equally varying trends. Italians, except in 1881 and 1951, tended to have high and increasing rates, while Jewish levels of concentration have always been elevated and varied little, reaching their highest level in 1981. Britishers experienced a slightly increasing rate until 1981, when the level of Residential Concentration fell by one-sixth. The French, in contrast, peaked their Residential Concentration in 1901, but the years following the Second World War have been characterized by a moderate upward turn. Scandinavians, Russians, and Dutch have an up-and-down pattern, highest in 1881 and somewhat lower a century later. Germans showed a sharp upward then downward level of concentration between 1881 and 1901, but a very stable and rather low level of residential proximity from 1951 on. The Polish had more elevated concentration, but also a wavering pattern, with the greatest change, one of decline, occuring between 1951 and 1961; 1961 to 1981 was, for the Polish, a period of increasing residential concentration. Ukrainians in the five CMAs studied had lower concentrations in 1961 and 1971, contrasted with higher levels at the beginning of the century and in 1981.

The changes over the past 100 years can be more graphically shown by highlighting those groups with the greatest Residential

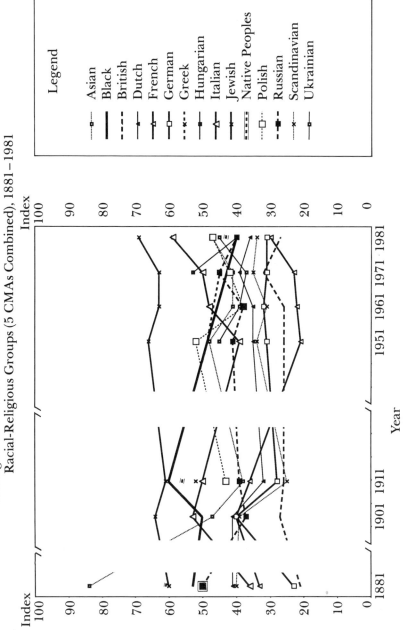

Figure 6.2
Average Residential Concentration within Cities of Canadian Ethno-
Racial-Religious Groups (5 CMAs Combined), 1881–1981

Table 6.2
Average Residential Concentration of Canadian Ethno-
Racial-Religious Groups (over 5 CMAs), 1881, 1901–1911, 1951–1981

Ethnicity	1881	1901	1911	1951	1961	1971	1981
Asian	84	47	38	48	41	41	47
Chinese	*	*	*	*	*	*	43
East Indian	*	*	*	*	*	*	51
Indochinese	*	*	*	*	*	*	67
Japanese	*	*	*	*	*	*	40
Black	53	50	60	*	*	*	40
British	21	27	26	26	26	32	27
Dutch	41	41	32	35	35	29	36
French	33	40	36	21	22	23	30
German	23	40	28	31	32	31	31
Greek	*	*	52	*	*	*	59
Hungarian	*	*	*	*	*	53	40
Italian	36	53	50	39	48	50	59
Jewish	60	64	61	66	63	63	69
Native Peoples	61	*	56	*	*	*	43
Polish	50	*	43	52	38	42	47
Portuguese	*	*	*	*	*	*	62
Russian	50	37	39	41	38	45	40
Scandinavian	40	39	25	34	31	35	34
Spanish	*	*	*	*	*	*	41
Ukrainian	*	*	*	45	39	37	45
All Groups	28	32	32	26	29	32	35

Notes: *No Data.
    The index of Residential Concentration reflects the percent of the group's members that exceeded the "average" percent of members living in each census tract of the city (CMA), based on the percent the group represented of the total city (CMA) population.
Sources: 1881, 1901, 1911, 1951, 1961, 1971, 1981 Censuses of Canada and microfiche records from these censuses maintained by Statistics Canada.

Concentration and those with the least. In 1881, Asians were far-and-away the most residentially concentrated: almost all of their members lived in the same districts. Next were Native Peoples and the Jewish. Lowest in residential proximity a century ago were the British, but the Germans were almost as low, with only about one-fifth of each group's members living in above-average proximity. About one-third of the French were concentrated at an above-average rate.

In 1981, the groups, but not the levels of above-average concentration in residence were different: Jewish were now more residentially concentrated than any other group and more than in 1881 — 69% lived close to each other. The next highest groups were the Indochinese and Portuguese, also above 60%. Also quite high in Residential Concentration were two Mediterranean peoples, Greeks and Italians, whose numbers increased greatly because of immigration over the preceding two to three decades; these two groups were experiencing 1981 averaged concentration of residence over the urban centres at almost a 60% level.

Least concentrated in residence in 1981 were the British, French, and Germans, all at or below a 30% rate. Just above these were Scandinavians (34%) and Dutch (36%). Thus, the major shift among the lowest and highest groups here has been that of the Italians from fourth-lowest a century before to being fourth- or fifth-highest in 1981. In other respects, the groups that were highest in 1881 were still relatively high, and those that, 100 years ago, were low remain so today.

These data put to rest the idea that residential "segregation" understood as involuntary residential seclusion of the visible minorities, has been successful. If the involuntary interpretation of "segregation" is followed, then the visible-minority groups should have shown the highest rates of Residential Concentration every year, and no "white" ethnicity (with the possible exception of the Jewish) should have had a level higher than any visible minority. As can be readily observed from Figure 6.1 and Table 6.2, except for Asians and Native Peoples in 1881 alone, no visible-minority group was highest in Residential Concentration at any time. Thus, if deliberate residential segregation really has been a policy of the "dominant" or "superordinate" ethnic groups, that policy has been increasingly unsuccessful in the twentieth century.

What seems to fit the data patterns much more aptly is a trend of declining discrimination which, after the Second World War, was accellerated by legislation banning discrimination based on ethno-racial-religious origin. The degree to which the Residential Concentration of visible minorities exceeded the 5-CMA average has declined greatly, particularly after 1951. Significantly, this went on at the same time that levels of Residential Concentration among Greeks, Italians, Portuguese, and especially Jewish remained high—and higher in 1981 than most of the visible minority groups.

Not only among the visible minorities have the levels of residential proximity declined from 1881 or 1951 levels; Dutch, German, Hungarian, Polish, Russian, and Ukrainian levels of Residential Concentration also have dropped by about one-third over the past 30 years. While these declines might be attributable to anti-discrimination laws enacted during this time, one could not also claim that discrimination caused the maintenance of recent high concentration rates among Italians, Jewish, and other groups. Certainly, such continuing high and, in some cases, rising rates must, in large part at least, be voluntarily induced as an expression of ethnic enclosure so as to assure ethnocultural survival.

Several conclusions appear manifest from these data: (1) If there was a conspiracy or even an expectation to segregate visible minorities in certain areas of the cities isolated from the superordinate group(s), it has been increasingly unsuccessful since the Second World War; (2) the voluntaristic influences from within the group to develop and maintain ethnic cohesion must be considered as a powerful source of Residential Concentration among certain of the groups covered; (3) both the visible minorities and many of the "white" ethnicities have been experiencing a lowering of Residential Concentration since 1951 or even before; and, finally, (4) it is probably of prime significance that, with the exception of the Jewish, other groups that have had rising or, in 1981, high residential proximity rates are just the groups whose numbers over the past two decades or so have been greatly augmented by immigration, and thereby a revival of ethnocultural forms would not be a surprising process.

Intercity Differences

This consideration of results from data that combined patterns from five different CMAs should not obscure the fact that the levels of Residential Concentration have varied considerably between the different localities, even within the same ethnicity. Indeed, nothing else should be expected. Moreover, this very intercity differentiation over time is of great interest in and of itself, as an indication of the effect of region, size of place, and/or a host of additional factors that might be brought into the causal equation. Important among the other factors likely involved here is the influence of ethnic diversity in the communities; it will be recalled that, over most of this period, ethno-racial-religious diversity in Montreal was declining, while it was increasing in the other four sites (Table 2.2).

Table 6.3
Average Residential Concentration Levels in the 5
Canadian CMAs, 1881, 1901–1911, 1931, 1951–1981

CMA	1881	1901	1911	1931	1951	1961	1971	1981
Halifax	17	15	12	*	22	20	21	24
Montreal	41	43	46	*	25	31	35	32
Toronto	15	25	19	18	23	30	35	40
Winnipeg	*	27	*	33	30	29	38	46
Vancouver	*	*	*	25	21	19	21	25

Note; *No Data.
Sources: 1881, 1901, 1911, 1951–1971: Census of Canada published reports.
1931: Census Bulletin on microfiche; 1981: unpublished Census statistics on microfiche.

The similar pattern of rising ethnic diversity may be associated with somewhat the same change in four of the locales, with Montreal's average Residential Concentration showing a perigee in 1951 (Table 6.3).

Of particular interest are the higher levels of average Residential Concentration earlier in Montreal, the only location covered here with the French as the dominant ethnicity. The individual ethnic-group rates of concentration in Montreal (not included here) also demonstrate a generally higher concentration of ethnic residence than analogous rates in the other, Anglo-dominant, CMAs. Whether this is typical of French Canada, though, should be explored more fully in the future by including other Quebec CMAs in a greatly expanded number of locales, though Richmond and Kalbach's 1980 and Balakrishnan and Kralt's 1987 works show the same results as ours.

The Assimilation Theory Rejected

There is another dimension to the residential proximity issue that should be addressed—the influence of generation in Canada. Assimilation theory would predict that the lowest concentration of ethnic residence should be in the most "assimilated" generation, that is, the third and later generations. When Kalbach (1980; 1981) and Richmond and Kalbach (1980: 192–200) tested this hypothesis, the "assimilation" theory projections were not upheld in any of the CMAs covered. The main departures from the assimilationist-predicted levels were in the third generation. For instance, in

Kalbach's estimable 1981 report (p. 30), the third, + generation in Canada members in 1971 had the *highest* residential "segregation" indices among the Chinese, Greek, Hungarian, Japanese, Portuguese, Scandinavian, and Yugoslav groups in Toronto. Moreover, the immigrant generation was highest only among the French, Irish, Italians, Polish, Scots, and Ukrainians. In the remaining ethnicities (Germans, Dutch, Blacks, Russians, and Jewish) either the second generation members had the greatest residential segregation, or (with Russians, for whom only the immigrant and second generation had enough people to be analyzed) the second generation was higher than the immigrant group.

Of course, we cannot say from this that the same ethnic differentiation existed in the past and that, in many groups, the immigrants had lower or about the same level of residential proximity as that of their children or grandchildren. It may be that in the post-war fervour for things ethnic, the children and grandchildren have been consciously arranging residence in proximity to their ethnic cousins as a planned mode for maintaining (recapturing?) and even strengthening their ethnic culture. Residential proximity, though, may not be of such centrality to immigrants who have, generally, a stronger hold on their "ethnic" culture, the culture of their childhood and often of adult socialization.

If, however, this same phenomenon did exist in the past, then it would help to explain why in groups such as Germans, Dutch, and Italians in 1881—particularly in Montreal and Toronto—Residential Concentration levels were lower than the rates only two or three decades later, and much lower than post-war levels. Since a larger portion of these (in 1881) were immigrants—especially compared to recent times—the perhaps lower need in many groups for immigrants to reside in ethnic enclaves that was evidenced in 1971 was also operative 90 years earlier.

SUMMARY

Residential concentration within ethno-racial-religious groups is multidimensional. First, there is concentration of settlement within the various regions of Canada. Only a few groups have maintained the same regional "home" they had in the closing decades of the nineteenth century. In part, this lack of regional stability in ethnic-group residence was due to the rural-to-urban shift that characterized the internal migration in Canada between 1901 and 1961. Too, the filling of the West led to a shift in immigrant destinations—from farm to city sites—during the twentieth century, especially following the Second World War. And, even among those few groups who, for a long time, have maintained centralization of residence— with the Prairies as the predominant site for this—there still has been some residential drift of ethnic-group members to change residence or, among immigrants, to find first residence in Canada in other, more urban regions.

The greatest regional shift in ethnic residential enclaves has been among the Asians (from British Columbia to Ontario), Blacks (from Nova Scotia to Ontario), and some East-European ethnicities (from the Prairies to Ontario). Greatest stability in region of residence has been among the British, French, Native Peoples, Scandinavians, Ukrainians, and Mennonites and Hutterites.

Shifting to a more microscopic purview, the several measures of within-community proximity of residence by ethnic groups produce ordinal standings that appear about the same. Jewish, Asians (especially the Indochinese), Italians, Greeks, and Portuguese have the highest residential proximity indices. This is so, whether in terms of "segregation" from the reference group used by the researcher(s) (usually the British/French, but sometimes the 3rd, + generation English ethnic group), or "concentration" (the proportion that each ethnicity comprised in each CMA census tract that exceeded the criterion of the percent the group represents in the entire CMA). What is particularly interesting in this is that several "white" ethnicities have had generally higher residential segregation/concentration levels than the visible minorities. Blacks and Native Peoples, for instance, have considerably lower residential proximity rates than Jewish, Italians, Greeks or Portuguese. Some Asian ethnicities are as high as these white ethnicities, but none is higher. At the other end of the residential-proximity continuum are the charter groups and the moderately-to-highly assimilated ethnicities of Germans, Scandinavians, and Dutch after 1945.

Even so, over the last century, there has been considerable change, both in the levels and relative standings of intra-city residential concentration. Also, the assimilation theory does not appear to have any adequate ability to explain residential proximity levels in terms of generation in Canada.

CHAPTER 7

Religious Monopoly

INTRODUCTION: RELIGIOUS MONOPOLY AND ETHNIC-GROUP COHESION

Much has been written about religions and denominations in Canada—Catholicism, Judaism, Hutterites-Mennonites, Doukhobours, United Church, and many others. Growth, change, membership, theology, even architecture are among the dozens of topics concerning religions in Canada that have been analyzed.

By comparison, little has been written about the part religion plays in ethnicity, especially from the perspective of religious affiliation of ethnic-group members. In a small way, this lack of information begins to be corrected here. This is not an altogether straightforward or easy task, however. As the Report of the Royal Commission on Bilingualism and Biculturalism (1970: 96–100) stressed, the relationships between religion and ethnic-group cohesion and religion and ethnic origin are complicated. Some religions comprise the principal or sole basis for ethnic-group identity and thereby become their "ethnicity" in Canada. In some other groups, almost all are of one religious persuasion, while within the remaining ethnicities, membership is spread among many different faiths. Beyond that, within every ethnic group there are people who practise no religion, but who, in the census, may profess one that their parents or even they themselves once practised but later abandoned.

Whether immigrants had taken religion for granted before coming to Canada or had striven against religious oppression in their home country, most asserted their ancestral faith once they arrived here (Harney, 1978). Following the pioneer immigration waves there came the places of worship, especially in the unsettled West— Catholic, Methodist, Anglican, Presbyterian, Lutheran, Greek Orthodox, Jewish and even the Society of Friends (England, 1976).

Many problems confronted immigrants in establishing their churches. Some religions have been much more portable than others: the Mennonites, Hutterites and Doukhobors seem to have had little difficulty in maintaining their forms of worship on the Canadian Prairies, and the Jewish experience was about the same, at least in the cities. Those of other religions were often less fortunate, particularly if they were dependent upon a highly trained priesthood. Often the immigrants did not include priests among their number, and they had little money in the early period to pay priests for their services, let alone construct a building (Royal Commission, 1970: 96). Slowly then, among some groups, but very quickly among others, the parish, the congregation, the shul became the places where immigrants with similar backgrounds and practices regrouped after arriving at their destination. The church or synagogue was a part of the immigrants' heritage, Harney (1978) has emphasized; and, for students of ethnicity, the place of worship was not just a site of religious rites, but also a gathering place for members of one or several ethnic groups.

The clergy often saw their role not only as that of maintaining the faith of the people and ministering to their sacred needs, but also as that of supporting the group's ethnoculture as well. In most groups, the place of worship became the focus of a transplanted ethnic life, and the role of ethnic religion and its ministry in the cultural survival of the group often proved critical. Harney (1978: 3) has suggested that an as yet unexplored aspect of the link between ethnoculture and religion in Canada is the extent to which faith saved language: "A hymn or a sermon in German, Korean, Welsh—a prayer in a mother tongue—carries the same cultural impact...as the more secular use of the mother tongue in a sport's club or a saloon."

Of course, no one among the immigrants was really able to practise the parental faith exactly as in the Old World. The changes were usually subtle and barely discernible to those outside the group, but what had been traditional faith and routine form in the mother country had to be maintained systematically and with care, or else be extinguished. Religious ritual, like all other aspects of folk culture and language is a living thing that borrows from both the environment and the ideas and attitudes of those who enact it. Thus, when environment and the existential phenomenon of life changed, religious ritual and ethnic identity also altered. Linked with the seasons, topography, and moods of the homeland, religious and cultural ritual could not be transplanted unscathed any more than ethnic identity could remain static (Harney, 1978).

The pioneer and/or older immigrants found the inevitable small changes in sacramentals, liturgy, and religious habits—even the accents and manners of the clergy—to be nagging proof of change and of traditions endangered by the ocean's crossing. For those who adjusted to these changes, ethnic churches helped to define and refine their cultural identity in Canada. Very often, the associations in and around the church brought people a far greater awareness of their ethnic culture than they ever had or could have had in the narrowly circumscribed national society they had left (Harney, 1978).

The inevitable interrelation between ethnic religion and ethnic culture was not always one that guaranteed monopolization by the ethnic religion over the sacred elements in the lives of the members of a group. As noted, upon immigration to Canada in most ethnicities, the same religious affiliation was held. The Italians were almost all Roman Catholics; the Japanese, Buddhists; the Ukrainians, either Eastern Orthodox or Ukrainian Catholic. But even among these groups, in Canada, ethnic identity caused ethnoreligious differentiation. The religious within some ethnicities—disturbed by differences in belief, ritual, and language of their traditional religion, and/or when clergy or the religious hierarchy were unsympathetic to ethnoreligious wants—formed Canadian branches of the ethnic religion: Ukrainian Catholic and Polish, Hungarian, German or other "national" Catholic churches in Canada; the Greek, Antiochian, Armenian, Romanian, Serbian, Ukrainian or Russian Orthodox denominations of the Eastern Rite Church; the Dutch Reformed Protestant group—all are instances of the greater fulfilment of ethnic-group compartmentalism through the creation of a "national" church in Canada.

The use of cultural aspects, however, can also be effective in proselytizing members of the ethnicity *away* from the traditional religion. Harney (1978) noted, for example, that the first religious service in Toronto conducted in Italian was Anglican. Inspection of the religious advertisements in the Saturday issue of any metropolitan newspaper will quickly yield the announcements of Pentecostal,

United, Anglican, Baptist or other services in Finnish, Korean, Chinese, Italian, Hungarian, Portuguese, and more. In addition, at least some members of each ethnic group, in a desire to become truly "more Canadian" (whether for purely altruistic reasons or in the pursuit of more pragmatic goals such as social and socio-economic advancement), switch religious loyalties from the traditional ethnic religion to a "Canadian" denomination, for example Anglicanism or the United Church.

Detailed investigations about the ill effects on ethnic identity of membership in a non-traditional religion have yet to be made, but the importance of such research seems obvious. Moreover, in no ethnicity today does one religion have an absolute monopoly. Looked at from a different perspective, Figure 4.1 showed that, over all ethnic groups, about one-half of Canadians were members of religions that held at least a plurality of groups' members. Obviously, in some Canadian ethnicities, the degree to which members belong to the same religion is very high; traditional examples are the French and the Jewish. But other groups are plagued (from the perspective of ethnic cohesion) by great diversity in religious affiliation—the British and Dutch, as we will see, separated by the Catholic-Protestant division, are but two examples.

One can readily hypothesize that the degree of ethnic cohesion is directly related to the degree of Religious Monopoly—the degree to which members of an ethnicity belong to the same religion. Conversely, a low degree of Religious Monopoly would be taken as an indication of a lower level of cohesion, or perhaps a high level of cultural assimilation. Thus, the relevance of Religious Monopoly within Canadian ethnicities is hardly limited to concern for the sacred; it concerns, as well, the foundations of ethnic-group cohesion in Canada.

ETHNIC COMPARISONS IN RELIGIOUS MONOPOLY

As already noted, it is very likely that almost all Central- and South-European immigrants to Canada were Catholic or Jewish in the period before the Second World War; Asians belonged to the several eastern religions. In other groups, however, the extent to which members belonged to the same religion (our definition of Religious Monopoly) was low, being scattered among the Roman or other Catholic or Orthodox faith(s) and one or more of the many Protestant denominations. The British (i.e., the English, Scots, Irish, and Welsh) serve as a good illustration: at one time in the United Kingdom all were Catholic; by Confederation each of the British groups in Canada had members affiliated with Catholic, Presbyterian, Methodist, Anglican or other denominations, mirroring the changed situation in Britain (Table 7.1).

Thus, the meaning in practical terms of Religious *Monopoly* is somewhat inexact when applied to those groups in which a substantial minority belongs to a second religion. The statistics to be presented are based on the highest percent of membership in one religious group within the ethnicity, even if that "highest" percent is well below half of the ethnic membership. Indeed, in a few cases, the "highest" percents earlier versus more recently are for *different* religions/denominations. I could have elected to report the proportion of ethnic members in the *two* most dominant religions in the ethnicity, but this could have eliminated the ability to differentiate between groups with very high exclusivity of ethnic membership in only one religion or denomination. So, what we gain in differentiating ability, we necessarily lose in inclusiveness of empirical coverage. Even so, Table 7.1 reports the two or more religious groups having the highest holds on ethnic members, except when the index of Religious Monopoly is very high.

Some of the percentages reported for religious affiliation are moderate or very low because I wished the reader to know the current rate of membership in religions not prominent now for ethnic groups but which, at one time, possessed a much greater hold on members' religious loyalities. Conversely, some past religious-membership rates reported are low; in these cases we wished the reader to see the beginnings from which religions currently very important had grown.

In all cases of Religious Monopoly below 90%, I also report the percent of ethnic membership professing *no* religion, and/or belonging to a particular "other" religion. The "other" religion, when important in an ethnicity, is identified at the end of Table 7.1. Finally, the "Non-Judaeo-Christian" religions include Baha'i, Buddhism, Hinduism, Islam, Native Peoples' religion, plus other unspecified and numerically small faiths not in the Judaeo-Christian tradition.

Figure 7.1 and Table 7.1 report in graphic and numerical fashions the rates of Religious Monopoly in 1871 for three ethnici-

Table 7.1
Extent of Religious Monopoly (in %) among Canadian Ethno-Racial-
Religious Groups, 1871, 1931-1981

Ethnicity and Year		Religious Denomination									
	Angli-can	Baptist	Eastern Ortho-dox	Luth-eran	Menno-nite /Hut-terite	Presby-terian	Roman Catho-lic	United Church	Non-Judaeo-Chris-tians	Other Reli-gion	No Reli-gion
ARABIC 1981			21				36		32		2
BLACK 1931	18	41					6	21	0*		8
1971	24	18					20	8	3		17
1981	18	16					22	5	7		8
BRITISH 1871	22					25#	19	23			*
1931	28					15	13	33			0*
1941	28					13	14	34			*
1951	27					10	16	35			*
1961	25					9	18	36			*
1971	22					8	20	31			5
1981	20					7	21	29			9
CHINESE 1931						5	2	12	72		8
1941						7	3	14	66		6
1951						11	11	33	*		*
1961						9	7	39	*		*
1971						6	13	18	18		54
1981						3	15	7	6		57
CZECHOSLOVAK 1931				6			80	4			1
1941				6			75	7			*
1951				7			63	10			*
1961				7			59	13			*
1971				6			60	10			7
1981				6			61	8			11
DUTCH 1931	11				25	7	6	32		3	
1941	11				31	6	6	28		3	
1951	10				25	5	9	27		14	
1961	8				14	4	18	24		24	
1971	6				8	5	23	19		33	
1981	4				8	4	22	15		22	

Table 7.1   Continued
Extent of Religious Monopoly (in %) among Canadian Ethno-Racial-
Religious Groups, 1871, 1931-1981

Ethnicity and Year	Anglican	Eastern Ortho-dox	Luth-eran	Men-nonite /Hut-terite	Presby-terian	Roman Catholic	United Church	Non-Judaeo-Christian	No Reli-gion
EAST INDIAN 1981						9		80	3
FILIPINO 1981					84				2
FRENCH 1871						98			
FRENCH 1931						97			
FRENCH 1941						97			
FRENCH 1951						97			
FRENCH 1961						96			
FRENCH 1971						94			
FRENCH 1981						95			
GERMAN 1871	13		18	*		8	31#		
GERMAN 1931	6		36	1		27	18		
GERMAN 1941	5		32	7		25	14		
GERMAN 1951	6		28	7		25	17		
GERMAN 1961	6		28	7		24	18		
GERMAN 1971	5		24	10		26	16		
GERMAN 1981	4		25	10		25	13		
GREEK 1931	11	65				17			
GREEK 1971	1	90				3			
GREEK 1981	1	94				2			
HUNGARIAN 1931					10	73	4		
HUNGARIAN 1941					10	70	8		
HUNGARIAN 1951					12	62	10		
HUNGARIAN 1961					9	61	11		
HUNGARIAN 1971					9	61	10		
HUNGARIAN 1981					9	60	9		
INDO-CHINESE 1981						19		44	26
ITALIAN 1931						93			
ITALIAN 1941						91			
ITALIAN 1951						90			
ITALIAN 1961						93			
ITALIAN 1971						94			
ITALIAN 1981						95			

Table 7.1 Continued
Extent of Religious Monopoly (in %) among Canadian Ethno-Racial-Religious Groups, 1871, 1931-1981

Ethnicity and Year	Angli-can	Eastern Ortho-dox	Jewish	Luth-eran	Roman Catholic	Ukrainian Catholic	United Church	Non-Judaeo-Christian	No Reli-gion
JAPANESE									
1931	6						22	65	3
1951	14						39	41	
1961	13						39	41	
1971	12						30	34	16
1981	8						26	25	28
JEWISH									
1931			99						
1941			99						
1951			98						
1961			97						
1971			93						
1981			94						
NATIVE PEOPLES									
1901	*				*		*	12	*
1911	*				*		*	11	*
1921	*				*		*	6	*
1931	26				52		13	4	0*
1941	29				50		14	1	*
1951	27				53		13	1	*
1961	25				55		12	*	*
1971	19				57		12	*	3
1981	19				51		9	1	7
POLISH									
1931		4	0*	5	85	##	1		0*
1941		3	0*	5	81	##	4		*
1951		5	3	4	70	5	6		*
1961		3	8	3	65	3	8		*
1971		1	*	3	71	2	8		4
1981		1	1	2	75	1	6		6
PORTU-GUESE									
1971					95				1
1981					96				1

Table 7.1   Continued
Extent of Religious Monopoly (in %) among Canadian Ethno-Racial-Religious Groups, 1871, 1931-1981

Ethnicity and Year	Anglican	Eastern Orthodox	Jewish	Lutheran	Mennonite/Hutterite	Roman Catholic	Ukrainian Catholic	United Church	Other Religion	No Religion
RUSSIAN										
1931		10	0*	14	14	28		4	18	1
1941		13	0*	15	9	21		7	22	*
1951		13	14	9	8	15		11	22	*
1961		12	19	20	8	14		13	17	*
1971		16	*	5	5	13		17	20	13
1981		16	4	3	8	8		13	12	20
SCANDINAVIAN										
1931	5				62			12		0*
1941	7				60			17		*
1951	8				47			25		*
1961	9				38			29		*
1971	8				33			27		8
1981	6				34			24		13
SPANISH										
1981	1					81		1		8
UKRAINIAN										
1931		25				69	##	1		0*
1941		29				62	##	3		*
1951		28				42	14	7		*
1961		25				17	33	13		*
1971		20				15	32	14		5
1981		19				17	30	13		8

Notes: * No data.

0* = 0.51%.

For Presbyterian in 1871, includes the Church of Scotland; for United Church of Canada in 1871, combines Methodist and Congrgationalist.

Included in Roman Catholic.

"Other" religion for Dutch is Reformed Church(es), for Russians is Doukhobor.

"Non-Judeao-Christian" religion(s) include Baha'i, Buddhism, Confucianism, Hinduism, Islam, Native Peoples' religion (denoted as "Pagan" before 1981), Sikhism.

Sources: for 1871, G. Darroch and M. Ornstein. "Ethnicity and Occupational Structure.... "*CHR* 61, 3(1980): 305–333. 1931–1981, Censuses of Canada.

ties (based on data from Darroch and Ornstein, 1980) and for these plus others from 1931 through to 1981. Of course, the increasing ethno-racial diversity in Canada since 1951 means that in 1961 or 1971 to 1981, there are several more groups on whom data were specified in the census.

In one way, the overall degree of differentiation between ethnicities over time has changed little in Religious Monopoly. In 1871 or 1931, the range in levels of Religious Monopoly was about the same as in 1981—from well above 90% to under 30%. And, for the most part, the same ethnicities that were highest in Religious Monopoly in 1871 or 1931 were still at that level in 1981; the groups that were lowest in 1871 or 1931 are still at that point today.

Notwithstanding, there has been change in the patterns of Religious Monopoly. First, there has been a greater tendency toward the emergence of strata since the Second World War, so that, in 1981, almost every group could clearly be categorized among high, low or in-between subsets of Monopoly. In 1931, in contrast, there was much less gradation of difference between the high or low sets, compared to the in-between ethnicities. In theory, therefore, it should be easier to develop postulates about causal relationships leading to high/low Religious Monopoly today.

Second, there has been significant change in the level of Religious Monopoly within particular groups. Further to this (although the figure would not depict it, since it is based solely on the highest religious-membership rate within an ethnicity) there have been shifts from the religion having the greatest hold within an ethnicity in 1931 to another religion in 1981. These interreligious changes are reflected in the tabular data and will be stressed below.

In 1931, the Jewish were marginally highest in Religious Monopoly; the French and Italians also had an above-90% Monopoly rate. Exactly these same three ethnicities were among the highest in Religious Monopoly in 1981, though now joined by the Portuguese (who in 1981 were highest) and the Greeks. While it is likely that in 1931, if data were available, the Portuguese also would have been near the top, the same situation did not exist for the Greeks. In 1931, Greeks were somewhat lower in Religious Monopoly (65%), around the middle of all groups. Data covering the years 1941– 1961 are absent, but by 1971 the rate for the Greeks was at 90%, no doubt due in large measure to the sizeable immigration from Greece in the preceding decade.

At the lowest levels of Religious Monopoly 50 years ago were the

Figure 7.1
Religious Monopoly Among Canadian Ethno-Racial-Religious Groups,
1871, 1931–1981

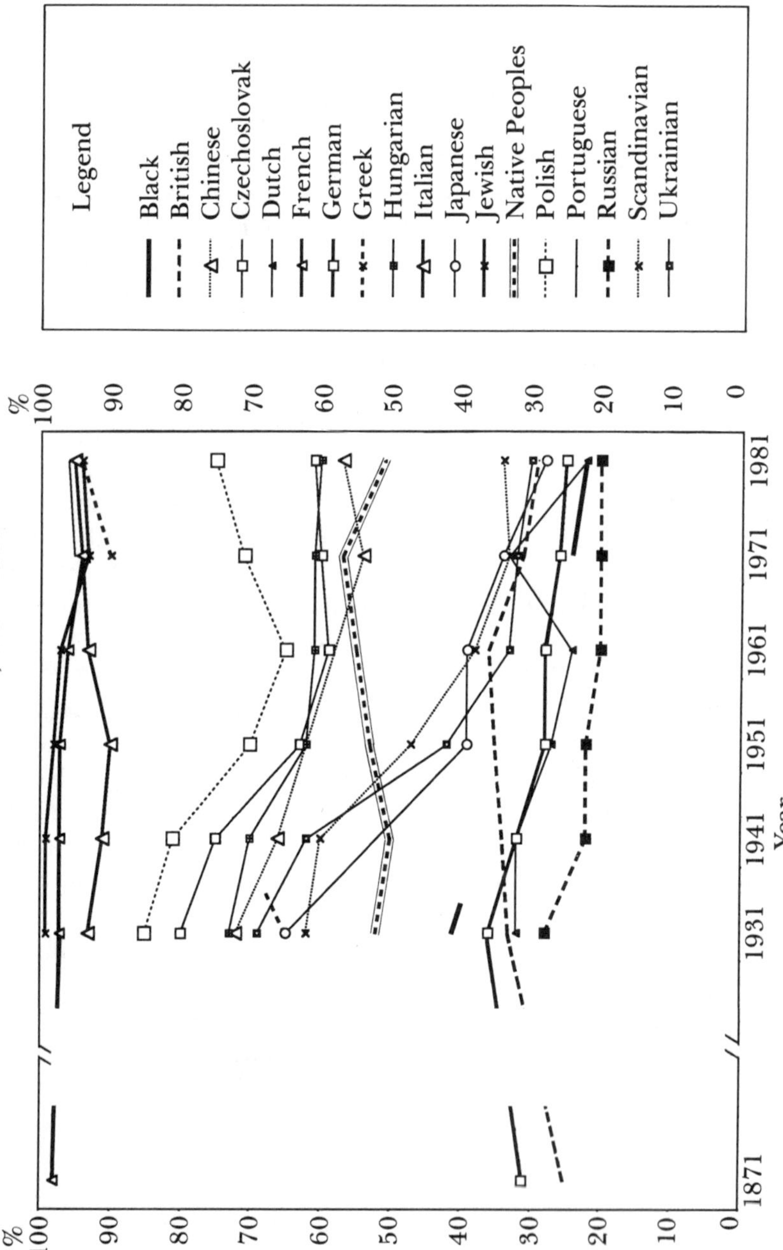

Dutch, Russians, British, Germans, and Blacks, all ranging from just over 30% to just over 40%. Interestingly, in the case of the British and Germans, the 1931 rates were somewhat higher than in 1871. By 1981, in addition to those five ethnicities remaining low, Japanese, Ukrainians, and Scandinavians had joined them in the set of groups with rates of Religious Monopoly below 35%. Lowest of these were the Dutch and Blacks at 22%.

In 1981, there was a clearly-defined intermediate stratum including the Polish, Czechoslovaks, Hungarians, Chinese, and Native Peoples. Fifty years before, these same five ethnic groups occupied this middle ground between the highs and lows of Religious Monopoly. But at that time they were accompanied by the Greeks (who are in the set of ethnicities with very high Monopoly in 1981) and three groups that experienced constantly declining Monopoly rates so that, by 1981, they were among the lowest in Religious Monopoly: Japanese, Scandinavians, and Ukrainians. Thus, it is among these groups that, in 1931, were neither very high nor very low that much of the transitions in Religious Monopoly originated.

It is striking that, except for the Jewish and Chinese, all the other eight ethnicities with either high or intermediate Religious Monopoly in 1981 had that Monopoly within the Catholic/Orthodox axis. In contrast, only two of the eight ethnicities lowest in Religious Monopoly were of that same religious category: Ukrainians and Russians. Five of the six others had their Monopoly within Protestant churches.

The changes and lack of changes, though, are only half the story. The other aspect of Religious Monopoly concerns the specific religious transitions that have occurred within the ethnicities. Thus, each ethnic group covered in Table 7.1 needs to be summarized for any shifts in level and/or category of Religious Monopoly with emphasis placed on the 1981 pattern.

Arabic: Arabs in Canada, first of all, differ in geographic origins. The 1981 census noted that there were both "Asian Arabs" and "North African Arabs," the former being more numerous. The appellation of "Asian" here means only a place of origin somewhat to the east of North Africa, probably because Lebanon and Syria were, at one time, listed in the census under the "Asian" rubric, along with Chinese, Japanese, and other ethnicities.

The myth in Canada is that "Arabs" are also, by definition, Muslims. However, Arabs see themselves as an *ethnic* or ethnolinguistic group, different from their non-Arabic (and non-Arabic-speaking) neighbours, many of whom *are* Muslim. Another little-known aspect is that a substantial portion of the "Asian Arabs" consider themselves to be "Palestinians," over and above their Arabic origins (Abu-Laban, 1980: 21–23, 129–144; Elkas, 1987: 2, 14–16; Helewa, 1982).

For Arabs, the only available data on Religious Monopoly is that of 1981, but these likely also reflect much the same situation as existed with the much smaller number of Arabic Canadians a decade before. Far from being wholly Islamic, as myth would have it, less than one-third of the Arabs in Canada are Muslim. The largest proportion, in fact, are Roman Catholic (36%) with another one-fifth belonging to the Eastern Orthodox Church. Only a tiny fraction of Arabs in Canada profess no religious association.

Blacks: Once more, information from only selected years is available. Moreover, Blacks are another example of an ethnic category that includes a wide variety of peoples: Atlantic and Ontario Blacks who are descendants of free or slave Loyalists fleeing the United States two centuries ago, descendants of those escaping slavery via the Canadian terminus of the "Underground Railroad," American Blacks who immigrated to Canada in the twentieth century, African Blacks of relatively recent arrival, and especially Caribbean Blacks, themselves comprised of over a half-dozen differing cultures. Thus, we should expect to note sharp differences between early and recent distributions of religious memberships among Blacks in Canada.

In 1931, the largest portion (41%) of Canadian Blacks were Baptists, with half that percent in the United Church and fewer still within the Anglican church. Forty years later, less than half the percent for 1931 were Baptists or United Church members. In 1931, these two denominations accounted together for nearly two-thirds of all Blacks; in 1971, only a touch over one-quarter of Blacks were in these churches. Counterbalancing these shifts was the more than 300% increase in Black membership in the Roman Catholic Church and the slight rise within the Anglican Church. In 1981, the percent of Blacks who were Anglicans had slipped back to its 1931 level, and the percentages in the Baptists and United churches were below the 1971 rates. The proportion of Blacks who were Roman Catholics rose, to become the highest religious-group representation among Canadian Blacks in 1981. In that year also, a small but distinct percent of Blacks reported non-Judaeo-Christian religions, predominantly Islam. Incidentally, the proportion of Blacks who were Rastafarians was tiny, contrary to the impression projected by some of the sensationalist media. An additional small fraction claimed no religious association, about the same percent as in 1931, but half that of 1971.

So, the general trends over the five decades were: first, away from the Baptist group, largest in 1931, to third in 1981; second, equally away from the United Church; third, no change in Anglican percents in 1981 compared to 1931; fourth, a better than 300% increase in the fraction of Blacks who were Roman Catholics, so that this church held the plurality of Black Canadians. Finally, affiliation by Canadian Blacks in non-Judaeo-Christian religions (mainly Islam) was non-existent in 1931, but noticeable in 1981.

British: For this charter ethnicity, there is over a century of statistics. Even so, it must be recognized that "British" includes four or more separate and distinct ethnic-origin groups whose relative representations within the British designation have altered considerably over the years (see Table 2.1). Notwithstanding, the United Church and its predecessor member denominations were prominent among the British. Anglicanism was more popular in the years immediately preceding and following the Second World War than it was in either 1871 or 1971–1981. Possibly because of the decline in the percent Scots make up of the British, the portion of British who were Presbyterians (originally, the Church of Scotland in Canada) has fallen by nearly three-quarters, from being the largest religious segment in 1871 to one of the smaller ones today. Roman Catholic membership among the British was lower in the 1931–1941 decade than in either 1871 or 1971 and 1981. Finally, although virtually all British reported some church membership in 1871, nearly one-tenth of British Canadians today claim no religious affiliation. In broad group and time perspectives, Presbyterians comprised one large British religious body in 1871, but since the formation of the United Church of Canada, it has held the greatest portion of British from 1931 to the present. Anglicanism is another important church in the ethnicity(ies) and has always been so, apparently, as is also the case for Roman Catholicism. Thus, there is very low Religious Monopoly among the British, mirroring the structure of religion among residents of the United Kingdom over a century ago, just after Confederation.

Chinese: In 1931 and 1941, about two-thirds of the Chinese were affiliated with either Buddhism or Confucianism. By 1941, however, about one-seventh of the Chinese had become members of the United Church of Canada, and this association increased over the next 20 years, peaking in 1961, when nearly four out of every ten Chinese belonged to the United Church. The fraction of Chinese who declared no religion was under 10% in the period 1931–1941. Although specific figures are not available for the 1951–1961 period, the combined percent for Oriental religions and no religious affiliation declined from 80% in 1931 to 44% in 1951 and 39% in 1961.

With the 1960s, however, and increased immigration, primarily from Hong Kong, the religious pattern in Canadian Chinese altered radically so that, in both 1971 and 1981, the category claiming a majority of Chinese was "no" religion! Correspondingly, the relative size of membership by Chinese in the United Church as well as the eastern religions declined markedly; neither of these amounted to more than 10% of Chinese Canadians in 1981.

Another shift in religious membership among the Chinese recently brought Roman Catholicism into greater prominence, claiming the second highest religious connection among the Chinese, greater now than the combined weight of the United Church and Oriental religions. The only other religion claiming anything beyond a tiny fraction of Chinese over the past half-century was the Presbyterian Church, but even at its height in 1951, it accounted for only 11% of this group.

Thus, the Chinese do not show a simple pattern of change in Religious Monopoly. Originally associated primarily with their traditional Oriental religions, today's much larger Chinese community has moved—since the Second World War and the emergence of a Communist state on China's mainland—to being generally of no religious affiliation. Complementarily, a somewhat smaller part of the Chinese in Canada today are members of various Christian denominations (20%) than was the case in 1931 (28%).

Czechoslovaks: Today, as in 1931, Roman Catholicism dominates among the Czechoslovaks, despite its decline from 80% in 1931 to 61% in 1981. Interestingly, though, the 1981 rate represents a slight increment from the 1961 rate. This slight decline followed by a rise was complemented by a slight rise followed by a decline in United Church membership among Czechoslovaks during the 50 years following 1931. The increase in the percent of Czechoslovaks who said they had no religion (from 1% to 11% over the same period) is, immense by comparison. Finally, a small but consistent fraction of Czechoslovaks have been Lutherans.

Dutch: A different pattern of change in the degree of Religious Monopoly exists for the Dutch: post-war growth among Dutch Canadians in the two traditional religions of Holland. In 1931, the Dutch in Canada were committed primarily to the United Church, the Mennonite-Hutterite groups, or the Anglican Church. Following the Second World War and the great immigration of Dutch from the Netherlands to Canada, the participation of Dutch Canadians shifted toward the Dutch Reformed Church in Canada (under "Other" in Table 7.1) and to Roman Catholicism. This very marked shift was at the expense of proportional membership in the Anglican, Mennonite-Hutterite, and United churches.

Whereas these latter three churches counted well over 66% of Canadian Dutch among their congregations in 1931, by 1981 this had shrunk to a mere 17%. For Roman Catholicism and the Canadian Dutch Reformed Church, the 1931 membership of less than 10% of the Dutch swelled to 44% in 1981. Again, the implications of the date for the beginning of the shifts is that immigration was directly responsible, but further research is necessary to verify this.

East Indian: Data on Indo-Pakistanis are available only for 1981. The great majority of East Indians in Canada belong to the four traditional religions of the Indo-Pakistani-Bangladeshi subcontinent: Buddhism, Hinduism, Islam, and Sikhism. Roman Catholicism claims just under one-tenth of East Indians. A natural question arising from the Christian religious affiliation for 17% of East Indians is the extent to which these Christian East Indians are second- or later-generation Canadians.

Filipino: Only 1981 figures are available, and these show that the Filipinos are predominantly Roman Catholic. Being a group quite new to Canada, the Filipinos may be another ethnicity that will, at some time, experience a decline in Religious Monopoly, depending on whether immigration from the Philippines continues through the present decade at the same rate as earlier.

French: The French in Canada present a very stalwart situation: great Religious Monopoly at least since 1871, with only minor drifting away. In 1981, nearly all the French were Roman Catholics.

Germans: Germans are the third group for whom 1871 information is available, plus the data from 1931 to 1981. What is most interesting about this earliest date is that the German Canadians of that era seem to have been much more assimilated to "Canadian" religions than was to be the case over a century later. In 1871, the greatest portion of German people belonged to the Methodist or Congregationalist denominations (grouped under United Church after 1921); the next largest group, 18%, were Lutherans, and about one-seventh of Germans in 1871 were Anglicans.

The extent of membership in those religions was quite different in 1931. United Church membership was much lower, less than one-fifth of Germans, and the percent of who were Anglican had declined by one-half. Instead, the greatest extent of Religious Monopoly among Germans in 1931 was with Lutherans, who had doubled their representation in the ethnicity over the intervening 60 years to more than one-third. Almost as large a portion of Germans were Roman Catholics in 1931, this reflecting a quadrupling of the percent of German membership. Finally, a tiny fraction were in the Mennonite-Hutterite faith.

For German Lutherans and Roman Catholics, 1931 marked the apex for proportional affiliation. Over the following 50 years, the Religious Monopoly of those denominations declined somewhat, more for Lutheranism than for Catholicism. United Church membership also declined thereafter, recovering by 1961, but falling again over the next 20 years. The only religion to show a marked increase in its presence among German Canadians was the Mennonite-Hutterite one, rising to include 10% of the ethnicity in both 1971 and 1981.

Thus, while Mennonite-Hutterite Germans have become more prominent, the Lutheran and Roman Catholic churches remain as the ones with greatest percent of Germans in Canada, albeit lower than in 1931. In 1931, 81% of Germans were in the three religions with the highest percent of Germans; the top three groups in 1981 represented 63% of Germans, so what has remained stable is the variety of religious groups holding the loyalty of the German ethnicity, and what has changed are the levels of affiliation—downward mostly.

Greeks: Greeks in 1931 appear to have been religiously "Canadianized" to a moderate extent. Fifty years ago, just over one-tenth of Greeks were Anglicans, and another one-sixth were Roman Catholics. Even so, the largest portion, nearly two-thirds were members of the Greek (Eastern) Orthodox Church in Canada. As has been discussed before, the 1960s witnessed the beginning of extensive Greek immigration to Canada. As part of their cultural apparel, they brought membership in the Orthodox Church, so that, in 1971, that church's hold on Canadian Greeks had climbed to 90%. With continued immigration during the 1970s, the rate of Orthodox affiliation also increased—to 94% in 1981. That high a Religious Monopoly makes the Greeks one of only five ethnicities to have had a Monopoly level about 90% in 1981—the others being the French, Italians, Jewish, and Portuguese.

Attending the sizeable increment in the Eastern Orthodox Church membership among Greek Canadians was the very much lowered membership rate of Greeks in the Anglican and Roman Catholic churches—down to 2% or less in 1981. Since Greek immigration to Canada had already begun to decline in the latter 1970s, and more so in the 1980s to date, it will be interesting to see, in the 1991 census, whether the rate of Greek Religious Monopoly reflects that decline.

Hungarians: Hungarians in Canada, like the Czechoslovaks, have always had primary religious association with Roman Catholicism. And, as with the Czechoslovaks, the level of Catholic Religious Monopoly has been slowly declining. Fifty years ago, it embraced almost 75% of all Hungarians in Canada, but following the Second World War, the rate rapidly dropped to about 60%, where it has remained.

In 1931, the only other church to have a sizeable Hungarian membership was the Presbyterian, with 10%; another 4% were in the United Church. Now, given the decline in the Catholic monopoly after 1931, a reasonable hypothesis would be that one part of the share lost from Catholicism would go to enlarge the membership in the two Protestant groups that had a small hold in 1931. However, the data reveal that, after 1951, the proportion of Hungarians who were Presbyterians actually became less than at any time in the 1931–1951 era. The prospect above for movement to the United Church, though, is upheld: in the period 1941–1981, more than twice the percent of Hungarians were in United Church congregations than was the case in 1931.

Since the total percent in the three above-mentioned churches in 1931 amounted to 87%, compared to 78% in 1981, it seems there has also been a slow drift to other religious bodies in Canada as the consequence of lowered rates for the Catholic Church. None of these other groups, however, showed enough of a rise to warrant being detailed.

Indochinese: Again, only 1981 data are available. Another problem in interpreting the Religious Monopoly figures here is the diversity of ethnicities/nationalities included in this largely immigrant group: Vietnamese, Thais, Cambodians, and Laotians. Within this combined category, the greatest number follow eastern faiths, primarily Buddhism, while a sizeable minority professes no religion. About one-third of Indochinese are Christians, and most prominent among these is the almost one-fifth of the group that is Roman Catholic.

Italians: Italians are another group whose degree of Religious Monopoly in Canada has always been high. There is, however, a special variation on the high Monopoly theme. From 1931 through 1951, the level of religious exclusivity had been slowly going down, so that, in 1951, it was down three points from the 1931 rate, to 90%. The 1950s, of course, was the decade in which more than 250 000 Italians came to Canada. With that there came also a rededication to Catholicism. In ten years, the degree of Religious Monopoly climbed three points—back to the 1931 level. It continued to rise over the following twenty years, so that, in 1981, it stood at 95%, the highest level ever recorded since data have been kept on this matter.

In this way, the Italians are like the Dutch, Greeks, and Hungarians; their post-war immigration either stemmed a decline or actually increased the rate of Religious Monopoly in the traditional ethnic religion.

Japanese: The religious loyalties of Japanese Canadians have been charted for each census since 1931, except, significantly, 1941. A half-century and more ago, nearly two-thirds of the Japanese in Canada were, for the most part, members of the Buddhist-Taoist or Shinto religions. Back then, just over 20% of Japanese Canadians were in the United Church. Overall, under one-third of Japanese in 1931 were Christian.

Then, shortly after the 1941 census information had been collected, came Pearl Harbor and with it the swift and intemperate "internment" of Japanese Canadians, lasting much too long after the war had been concluded. In 1976, Adachi forwarded the theory that to expiate the crime of disloyalty implied by the internment, the Japanese remaining in Canada consciously repudiated their ethnic cultural forms so as to assimilate culturally and structurally. By this cultural suicide—by taking on the culture of their jailors—the Japanese, Adachi suggested, would prove they were loyal and worthy Canadians. That this social hara-kiri involved religious association, the data here make very clear.

By the time the war had been over a few years, the Japanese had begun their religious shift, first to Christian churches, then to non-association. In 1951 and 1961, the proportion of Japanese Canadians within their traditional religions had dropped by well over one-third, and the proportion that was Christian had risen by nearly one-half to 59%. The largest Christian membership among the Japanese was in the United Church, which held nearly as many Japanese as did all the eastern religions in 1951 and 1961. Another one-seventh of Japanese were Anglicans, about the same proportion as over both 1951 and 1961.

By 1971, however, and continuing to 1981, a different shift occurred: greater withdrawal from religious association, both eastern and Christian. The proportion of Japanese who declared no religion in 1971 was one-sixth of all Japanese, over five times that in 1931; by 1981 this had jumped to almost one-third of Japanese Canadians. Concomitantly, Christian affiliation fell from 59% in 1961 to 47% in 1981, and both of the leading Christian bodies—the Anglican and United churches—have suffered sharp declines over the past two decades among the Japanese.

One cannot help but wonder whether the horrific experiences of the Japanese between 1941 and 1946 had so burned the cultural soul of the Japanese Canadians that the rise in the proportion of Japanese without religious membership—now the largest portion of Japanese, compared to other religious categories within the Japanese ethnicity—represents the demise of the Japanese-Canadian cultural core. The alternative explanation, carrying quite different implications for the cultural life of the Japanese-Canadian community, is that this increment in "no" religious association is similar to that experienced among the Chinese and many other Canadian groups. This question, in all likelihood, will be answered, not from further detailed census-data analysis, but from original data collected specifically for this purpose from a wide sample of Japanese Canadians.

Jewish: The Jewish are the only group in Canada to have an extremely high rate of Religious Monopoly which is not in an Eastern- or Western-rite Catholic denomination. Now, some may see nothing particularly spectacular in the fact that more than 90% of those who report a Jewish ethnicity are also Jewish in the matter of religion. Yet, is this any less remarkable than the Catholicism of Italians, French, Portuguese, and other groups, or the Orthodox fealty of Greeks? The central issue here is not how expected such instances of high Religious Monopoly may be, but that it maintains in an adopted country and has assuredly done so for well over a century.

In any event, since the first reports in the census, the Religious Monopoly of ethnic Jewish Canadians has been very great. The other side of this empirical coin is that, between 1931 and 1961, Jewish religious loyalty declined a mere two points from the 1931 rate of 99%. Thereafter, though, the decline was more abrupt, apparently: a 4% drop between 1961 and 1971. This, however, is likely due to statistical artifact: in the 1971 census, all those who listed Judaism as their religion were also counted as "ethnically" Jewish, disregarding any other ethnic identification they may have listed (Kalbach and McVey, 1979: 200, 219). Thus, for 1971, the denominator figure for the number of people of Jewish ethnicity would have been artificially inflated, yielding a lower percent of Religious Monopoly than if this procedure had not been applied. It is more likely that a figure more comparable with the rates calculated for all other years was, in 1971, something between 97% and 93%—say 95%. Unless the statistical sidestep in the 1971 data can be returned to the same basis as in past and more recent years, then we will probably never know the "true" rate.

The artificiality of the 1971 figures notwithstanding, it is without question that the extent of Religious Monopoly among the ethnically Jewish is well above 90%. This brings the Jewish into that exclusive circle of five ethnic groups with rates above 90% in 1981.

Native Peoples: The religious associations of Native Peoples reported since 1931 are demonstrative of the degree of their religious assimilation to their colonizers' beliefs and do not at all reflect the original religions of the Indians or Inuit.

According to the best information now available, the religion of Canada's Native Peoples was very different in values, structure, process, and content from any of the Christian faiths. The Natives' religion placed them within a web of interacting spirits; the basic doctrine throughout Canada before European control was the kinship of the Native Peoples with all aspects of nature. Natives made no distinction between themselves and animals, or even between themselves and inanimate nature. To the Native Peoples, all nature was bound together—the rocks on the hillside, trees, animals, rain, winds, and stars—all were endowed with different outward forms, but all possessed personalities similar to the peoples. Thus, the universe of the Native Peoples was filled with spiritual entities, all of which, according to their religion, claimed the Natives as their kin (Jenness, 1976).

What religious leaders they had were priests or priest-shamans who devised rituals to protect their people from evil spirits. Among some tribes the function of religious leadership was separate from that of the medicine man. "Keepers of the Faith" supervised religious matters and called upon their Great Spirit to protect, support, and aid them (Nixon, 1984). According to a late nineteenth-century white, Christian, observer, the Native religion was—in terms of structure—"at variance, in many things, with the Christian religion. . . . (T)here is the belief in a God—a Great Spirit. . .—but there are also inferior deities" (McLean, 1889: 300).

The lesser deities to which McLean referred were generally given the names of eminently important aspects of nature as perceived by that tribe, such names as, "rulers of the four quarters of the sky"; there were, as well, subdeities resident in the sea, or the mountains, or the sky, plus those of the sun and moon. Above all these, was their Supreme Being, who was not the Great Creator, or the ultimate source of all power, but, instead, the most powerful of all the spirits, with the remaining power distributed among other parts of nature, including the Native Peoples.

Another major difference between the Europeans' religions and that of the Native Peoples was their notion of the source of evil. In Christianity, God is the fount of all power and thereby the source of all goodness. Evil is the result of humans acting improperly or of the Divinity withholding its supreme power from humans for some divine reason. Among the Native Peoples, in contrast, there was a duality in the universe that included the Supreme Deity as well as a power of evil (or sometimes only trickery), with less power than the Supreme Deity, but still with power over the Natives and many other elements of nature. Most Natives accepted without question the existence of evil and concerned themselves with avoiding it, hence part of the role of priests and shamans (Jenness, 1976).

McLean (1970 [1889]) not infrequently took special note of the "the intense devotion of the people to their own religion" and their often equally-intense opposition and antagonism toward the European religions. By the closing decades of the nineteenth century:

> The Indians tribes of our western country are the possessors of a civilization that is fast decaying, and the followers of the mountain, prairie and forest gods...no longer sway the minds and hearts of these red men as in the days of yore.
>
> In their transition state, between losing faith in their native religion and accepting Christianity and civilization, they rapidly decrease. Despondency takes possession of their hearts. The oppressive feeling that they are a conquered race pressed heavily upon them, and, like the wild caged birds, they sicken and die.
>
> Polygamy has ceased to be practiced among the tribes who have fully embraced the Gospel. The medicine man's incantations, the death song...the native burial customs...have, to a great degree, come to an end. Christianity has...suppressed many of the tribal laws.... Native customs have become subject to Christ, the social life of the camps have become more uniform and refined, and the domestic relations of the people have been changed to accord with the views of the great teachers of life [the missionaries].... The hunter has become a farmer or mechanic, the breech-cloth and blanket have been replaced with tweed and broadcloth garments, made by a fashionable tailor; and the wild fruits of the forest no longer exercise exclusive sway over the red man's palate and table (McLean, 1970 [1889]: 289–290).

Thus was extinguished the religion and way of life of many of Canada's Native Peoples, "the ancient lords of Canada, who owned the land which has become our heritage..." (ibid.: 289). By the opening of the twentieth century, the process of religious assimilation begun, according to McLean (1889: 329–337), in 1614 by the Roman Catholic Church and continued with equal zeal by the Anglican Church, as well as by missionaries of the Presbyterian,

Moravian, Methodist and other churches, was very close to complete. Using ethnic- and religious-group population figures from the censuses, a reasonably good estimate of the extent of Native Peoples' remaining affiliation with their native religion can be drawn.

In 1901, probably only about one-eighth of the Native Peoples were practising the religion of their ancestors. This low rate decayed continuously, so that, by 1921, the likely rate was less than 10%, and never more than 5% thereafter. From 1951 to today, the rate likely has been about 1%. Every once in a while another story surfaces about the slow rediscovery or re-creation of their traditional religion(s) by Canada's Native Peoples, but this has yet to be reflected in census figures.

In 1931, the earliest date for which precise figures on Native Religious Monopoly are available, a majority of the Native Peoples claimed association with Roman Catholicism. This rate fell from 52% in 1931 to 50% a decade later, but then began an increase that lasted until 1971 when it registered 57%. In 1981, it had dropped to 51%. Ordinarily, one of the other religions prominent within an ethnicity would show a pattern of rate compensation for the upward and downward trends, but there is nothing like this for the Native Peoples, with the possible exception of those who profess no religion. This designation, all but absent among Native Peoples in 1931, counted for 3% of Natives in 1971 and 7% in 1981.

The denomination second to Catholicism among Native Peoples is Anglicanism, holding more than one-quarter of Natives between 1931 and 1951. In 1941, however, it was apparent there was a decline in Anglican membership among Native Peoples, and this continues through today when just under one-fifth of Natives belong to that church. As might be expected, the United Church also has Native affiliation, but it too was considerably greater earlier in the century than in 1981 when only 9% of Native Peoples claimed membership.

In 1931, the Native religion and the three main Christian groups claimed the loyalty of nearly all (95%) of the Native Peoples; today, the comparable figure is 80%, which, along with the 7% who claim no religion, still leaves about 8% of Native Peoples with a different religious affiliation than in 1931—other Christian churches, mostly Protestant. The 1981 figures indicate that many of these Natives seem to have joined the rapidly-growing, actively-proselytizing denominations such as, the Pentecostals and Seventh Day Adventists.

There is, finally, more than a hint that religious patterns among Canada's Native Peoples are shifting more now than at any previous time. With the exception of Anglican membership and the traditional Native religion, religious association levels altered abruptly between 1971 and 1981. It seems likely that a pattern different from that of 1971 will emerge in 1991.

Polish: Like Czechoslovaks and Hungarians, the Poles in Canada have been experiencing a slippage away from their traditional religion. A half-century ago, only one-seventh of the Polish were *not* members of the Roman Catholic Church, whereas, by 1961, this had markedly intensified to the point where just over one-third were not among Roman Catholic congregations. This occurred despite (or because of?) the more than 700 000 Polish immigrants to come to Canada during the previous 20 years, mainly in the 15 years after the conclusion of the war. However, as has been the case with many other groups with a significant proportion of their membership in the Catholic Church, the degree of affiliation within the group increased during the following two decades to the point where, in 1981, only one-quarter of Polish Canadians were not adherents of that faith.

One explanation for the decline in Catholic hegemony among the Polish is the small, but increased and thus important, number who had joined the United Church since 1931. Some others, about 5% in 1971 and 1981, acknowledge no religion, and this also represents a considerable increment over the past half-century or more. Interestingly, however, Poles in the Eastern Orthodox and Lutheran churches, together accounting for up to 9% of this group between 1931 and 1951, have today lost even that hold, so that jointly they included only 3% of Polish Canadians in 1981.

Comparing the Roman Catholic and United Churches, plus those who say they had no religious membership, the 1931 subtotal of Poles was 86%, whereas in 1981 it was 81%. The loss in Polish Religious Monopoly can be partially explained by the probability that at least some of the immigrants from Communist Poland over the past 30 or more years would not, in Canada, bind themselves to any religion. This could have combined with a tendency in many other groups that could well be present also among the Poles—a degree of religious absorption of ethnic-group members by the United Church of Canada.

Yet, the contrary pattern in the Orthodox and Lutheran churches works against the ready acceptance of any facile explanation. One way, though, of interpreting the departure of some Poles from the Eastern Orthodox Church is that the formation, some decades ago, of the Polish National Catholic Church in Canada may have had the dual effect of drawing Poles from the Orthodox Church and Protestant denominations increasing the Religious Monopoly of Catholicism. In any case, the civil disorder of the early 1980s in Poland in which Roman Catholics—laity and clergy—were heavily involved, has led to a new wave of immigration from Poland to Canada. Because of the deep Catholic commitment on the part of most of these immigrants, it is not unreasonable to forecast that this, combined with the great empathy with which Polish Canadians have viewed the events in Poland, will bring on a continued augmentation of Catholic Religious Monopoly among Polish during the next few decades.

Portuguese: The last of that exclusive aggregation of ethnicities with a rate of Religious Monopoly over 90% is the Portuguese. Like other ethnicities whose membership is made up of recent immigrants, conformity to their traditional culture includes a high degree of participation in the ethnic religion and is, therefore, a principal element of Portuguese ethnic cohesion in Canada. Given the nearly universal adherence of Portuguese Canadians to Roman Catholicism, there seems little probability of a strong decline in this religious fealty over the next 10 to 20 years.

Russians: In contrast to the very solidary groups just discussed, the Russians present an image of great diversity and even, possibly, divisiveness in religious membership. As the data well demonstrate, *all* of the six religious categories that have played a prominent role among the Russian Canadians since 1931 have experienced radical fluctuations in membership rates. In 1931, for instance, four religions were important among Russians: Roman Catholicism, Lutheranism, the Mennonite-Hutterites, and an "other" (Doukhobor) religion. However, each of the four religious groups over the next 50 years tended to lose significance within the Russian community: the four accounted for 74% of Russians in 1931, but only 31% in 1981.

The proportion of Russians who held to no religion in this period rose from 1% to 20%. In the same period, a considerably smaller increment in the rate of United Church membership has taken place, rising from only 4% in 1931 to between 13 and 17% between 1961 and 1981. The last religion of major relevance to Russian Religious Monopoly is the Eastern Orthodox Church, which initially was the Greek Orthodox Church, in 1931. Increasingly since, however, the Russian Orthodox Church has been supplanting the Greek Church among Russians in Canada. The Eastern Orthodox churches together claimed only 10% of Russians 50 years ago, but more than half-again that percent in 1981.

This being so, the Eastern Orthodox churches can be said either to represent the source of greatest Russian Religious Monopoly, or to reflect the great diversity/divisiveness in the religious sphere among Russians in Canada. Whichever way one decides to characterize this situation, there is no question that the level of Religious Monopoly among the Russians is extremely low, particularly when compared to the French, Greeks, Jewish, and Portuguese in Canada. Moreover, there is little, if any, reason to expect that the degree of religious exclusivity will rise much among the Russians.

Scandinavians: Of all the European ethnicities, Scandinavians show the greatest decline in the degree of Religious Monopoly over the past 50 years. Nearly two-thirds of Scandinavians in Canada were members of the Lutheran church in 1931; today, Lutheranism is the religious home for just one-third. In the same period, the United Church has doubled its share of Scandinavians from one-eighth to one-quarter. As well, the percent of the ethnicity that reported having no religion mushroomed from nil to 13%. Finally, the Anglican Church has had a small, stable portion of Scandinavians.

Thus, in this dimension of ethnic cohesion as well as in others, Scandinavians in Canada have assimilated, by leaving their traditional Lutheran affiliation for either the United Church or for no religion at all. Moreover, there is a second stage of religious reduction among Scandinavians in that the peak in their United Church membership occurred in 1961. Since then, there has been a fall of about one-sixth the rate. Many of these probably profess "no" religion, but others have drifted to other Protestant faiths.

All in all, if high Religious Monopoly is deemed a desirable ethnic-group property, then Scandinavians are exceptionally unlikely to improve this aspect of their ethnic cohesion, particularly in the fact of the very low Scandinavian immigration levels of recent years.

Spanish: The sole figures for this ethnicity are from 1981. In 1981, Spanish Canadians were quite high in possessing Religious Monopoly: 81% were Roman Catholics. The largest portion of the other Hispanics in Canada denied any religious affiliation.

Ukrainian: In some ways, the Religious Monopoly experiences of the Ukrainians are similar to those of the Scandinavians, but, in other ways, the two groups are entirely different. They are similar in that there has been a steady shrinkage in the extent of Ukrainian participation in both the Eastern Orthodox and Roman Catholic Churches. Some of those who left the Eastern and Roman churches joined the United Church of Canada: the proportional Ukrainian participation has multiplied thirteenfold over the 50 years of the decline in the Orthodox/Roman churches membership.

Of much greater significance, however, was the emergence of the Ukrainian Catholic Church in Canada as the principal locus of religious allegiance. In 1951, only one-seventh of Ukrainians were members of this denomination, but ten years later this had more than doubled to one-third, though there has since been a slight contraction either to rejection of all religions, or to religions other than the two other Eastern- and Western-rite denominations. This is evident when we contrast the situation of 1931 with that of today. In 1931, 94% of Ukrainians were counted as either Roman Catholic or Eastern Orthodox; today, these two churches combined with the Ukrainian Catholic Church embrace only 67%, the United Church another 13%, and "no" religion a further 7%. The total for all of these is 87% leaving, in 1981, a small portion of Ukrainians who had turned to other religious associations.

This remainder may be small, but it is nevertheless, significant. Since 1961, all four of the principal Christian religious denominations have either been stable in their Ukrainian membership (Roman Catholic and United Church) or have become less important among Ukrainians (Eastern Orthodox and Ukrainian Catholic). Thus, while the "leakage" from both the main traditional faiths and the principal Canadianized religion was small in 1981, it either promises to increase, which means, at the worst, a further deterioration in Ukrainian Religious Monopoly or, at best, a maintenance of the status quo which would prevent any improvement in the group's Religious Monopoly.

Thus, from 1951 to 1961, the Ukrainians seemed well on the way to increased Religious Monopoly in their national church. This transformation, however, stalled and now appears to be blocked at a level of moderately-low religious exclusivity, with not much chance for any change upward.

Summary: There are four—or, more accurately, four and one-half—distinctive patterns that emerge from the transition in Religious Monopoly. First, there is the pattern of the largest category of ethnicities, those who have experienced either a renewed degree of Monopoly or a constantly maintained exclusivity of one religion at a rate of at least 75% of the ethnicity's members; some groups are included here on the basis of only recent data. (Table 7.2): Portuguese (96% in 1981), French and Italians (both 95%), Greeks and Jewish (both 94%), Filipinos (84%), Spanish (81%), East Indians (80%), and Polish (75%). It is of considerable significance that seven of this group of nine ethnicities have their Religious Monopoly within Roman Catholicism or Greek Orthodoxy.

A second pattern is represented by the two ethnicities in which religious primacy was held by Roman Catholicism and which experienced some decline in exclusivity of membership until 1960 and which have, since then, been either stable or augmented in their Roman Catholic Monopoly: Czechoslovaks and Hungarians—both at 60–61% in 1981. A third group fully- or half-following this pattern is the Native Peoples, who had an increase in Catholic primacy through 1971 followed by a slight decline.

The third distinctive pattern is represented by the seven ethnicities whose Religious Monopoly relfects either increasing assimilation away from the traditional ethnic religion or a low, but stable, level of Religious Monopoly, also indicative of cultural assimilation accompanied by great diversity in religious membership: Indochinese (44% in 1981), Scandinavians (34%), Ukrainians (30%), British (29%), Germans (25%), and Blacks and Dutch (22% each). Among these ethnic groups, it is noteworthy that, with the exception of the Ukrainians, none of these seven ethnicities had Roman Catholicism/Eastern Orthodoxy as their main traditional ethnic religion.

The final pattern to emerge is that of three ethnic groups which,

Table 7.2
Highest Level (in %) of Religious Monopoly in Canadian Ethno-Racial-
Religious Groups, 1871, 1931–1981

Year	Arabic	Black#	British#	Chinese	Czechoslovak	Dutch#
			Ethno-Racial-Religious Group			
1871	*	*	25	*	*	*
1931	*	41	33	72	80	32
1941	*	*	34	66	75	32
1951	*	*	35	*	63	27
1961	*	*	36	*	59	24
1971	*	24	31	54**	60	33
1981	36	22	29	57**	61	22

	East Indian	French	Filipino	German#	Greek	Hungarian	Indochinese
1871	*	98	*	31	*	*	*
1931	*	97	*	36	65	73	*
1941	*	97	*	32	*	70	*
1951	*	97	*	28	*	62	*
1961	*	96	*	28	*	61	*
1971	*	94	*	26	90	61	*
1981	80##	95	84	25	94	60	44##

	Italian	Japanese#	Jewish	Native Peoples	Polish
1931	93	65##	99	52	85
1941	91	*	99	50	81
1951	90	39	98	53	70
1961	93	39	97	55	65
1971	94	34##	93	57	71
1981	95	28**	94	51	75

	Portuguese	Russian#	Scandinavian	Spanish	Ukrainian#
1931	*	28	62	*	69
1941	*	22	60	*	62
1951	*	22	47	*	42
1961	*	20	38	*	33
1971	95	20	33	*	32
1981	96	20**	34	81	30

Notes: * No data.
    # Religious category with highest % different over the years covered.
    ** Category with the highest % was "No Religion."
    ## % is for a combination of more than one non-Judaeo-Christian religions.
Source: Table 7.1 (above).

in 1981, had a plurality of members professing no religion: Chinese (57%), Japanese (28%), Russians (20%). Among the Russians this has been a minor factor which has recently increased. For the Chinese and Japanese, this is also a relatively recent phenomenon, occurring within the past 20 years. It surely is *not* due to any Communist association among the Japanese, whose fealty to the Shinto and Taoist faiths remains strong in Japan. The Communist connection, likely among Russians, is only somewhat plausible among the Chinese (most of whom are immigrants from Hong Kong).

If there is any underlying similarity it is that of higher rates of Religious Monopoly associated with pre-Reformation religions: the Roman Catholic and Orthodox Churches, Judaism, Hinduism, Sikhism and Islam (Table 7.3). Nevertheless, the diversity of levels and patterns of transition from one level to another (especially within those groups maintaining Roman Catholicism) is greater than the similarities between groups. Moreover, knowing the level of religious cohesion or pattern of change in one of the groups with a high 1931 Monopoly within Catholicism still does not accurately "predict" to 1981 for other groups with high percentages of Catholic cohesion. These dissimilarities are sufficient evidence, I think, to once again emphasize the principle of ethnic relativity: to understand ethnic cohesion phenomena in something like the way the members of each group understand and live them.

GENDER VARIATIONS

We saw earlier that there have always been differentiations between and within groups in Canada in the degree to which women comprised ethnic-group membership. This difference is expressed here by the Gender Ratio. Within each ethnicity, the male rate of Religious Monopoly was divided by the female rate (then multiplied by 100) to calculate the Gender Ratio of ethnic Religious Monopoly for that religion. (The figures, though, are not presented here.)

First, in general trends, the Gender Ratios over most of the comparisons do not vary much from 100, indicating about equal gender rates of participation in the same religion(s) within the ethnicities. Second, and notwithstanding the above, in some ethnic groups the Gender Ratio is rather elevated within a traditional ethnic religion, suggesting a greater male participation rate than

Table 7.3
Rankings for Religious Monopoly among Canadian Ethno-Racial-Religious Groups, 1931, 1951–1981

Ethno-Racial-Religious Group

Year (# Ranks)	Arabic	Black	British	Chinese	Czechoslovak	Dutch	East Indian	Filipino	French	German	Greek	Hungarian
1931 (17)	*	13	15.5	10	5	17	*	*	2	14	9	6
1951 (15)	*	*	12	9	5	14	*	*	2	13	*	6
1961 (15)	*	*	11	9	6	14	*	*	2	13	*	5
1971 (18)	*	18	16	10	8	13	*	*	2.5	17	5	7
1981 (23)	15	22.5	19.5	12	10	22.5	8	6	2.5	21	4.5	11

Year (# Ranks)	Indochinese	Italian	Japanese	Jewish	Native Peoples	Polish	Portuguese	Russian	Scandinavian	Spanish	Ukrainian
1931 (17)	*	3	8	1	12	4	*	15.5	11	*	7
1951 (15)	*	3	10.5	1	7	4	*	15	8	*	10.5
1961 (15)	*	3	8	1	7	4	*	15	10	*	12
1971 (18)	*	2.5	11	4	9	6	1	13	13	*	15
1981 (23)	14	2.5	19.5	4.5	13	9	1	17	16	7	18

Notes: Rank 1 was assigned to the group with the highest % of Religious Monopoly; the group with the lowest % of Religious Monopoly was assigned the rank with the highest number
* No data

Sources: Tables 7.1, 7.2 (above).

for ethnic females. Conforming to this pattern are British Presbyterians between 1931 and 1961, British Anglicans early in this period, German Lutherans and Catholics through 1961, Greeks in Orthodoxy through 1981, Russian Catholics and Orthodox through 1961, Scandinavian Lutherans throughout the entire period, and Ukrainian Orthodox and national Catholic denominations after the separation from the Roman Church 1951. In addition, many of the groups for whom Roman Catholicism was the traditional ethnic faith also exhibited the same higher male religious cohesion in that church until 1971 or 1981: Czechoslovaks, Hungarians, and Poles. Also, from the fragmentary data available, it seems that until the post-war years, this male supremacy in the traditional religions also existed among the Chinese and Japanese in Canada.

A third gender pattern found was the lower ratio (often much under parity) in some ethnicities for group members in "Canadian" or, at least, non-traditional faiths. Usually, French, German, Polish, Russian, Scandinavian, and Ukrainian women have far outnumbered their male counterparts in the Anglican, Presbyterian, and United churches. This gender variation has increasingly been the case, and gender ratios usually were lowest in 1981. Thus, religious assimilation seems to have been more a female than a male ethnic phenomenon. This is a direct corollary of the greater male Religious Monopoly rates in the traditional ethnic religions.

URBAN-RURAL VARIATIONS

Just as urban residence influenced the degree of ethnic-language maintenance in a fashion different from that of rural residence, so too should urban/rural locations affect the degree of Religious Monopoly in the ethnicities (E. Herberg, 1986). Theoretically, in at least some groups, rural residence should have led to a stronger adherence to the traditional ethnic religion, while living in the urban centres should have led to a pattern of assimilation. This would be because, in those particular ethnic groups, residence was primarily on farms or their rural environs. This would make ethnic enclosure almost coterminous with residential concentration, and the two would jointly maintain the old religion as an integral part of maintaining the rural ethnic culture. The principal dynamic behind the hypothesis that rural residence would have benefited Religious Monopoly in some ethnic groups is that the members of those groups would have been protected from the twin assimila-tionist influences of the urban-technological culture in the cities and the competing temptations of the many other religions concen-trated in the urban locales. This "protectionist" hypothesis would apply especially for those Canadian ethnicities who were predom-inantly or, at least, "above average" in being farm-rural residents.

For other groups whose principal places of residence have been in the cities, their traditional religions should have been best maintained in the urban locales. In this situation, urban residence would mean high concentration and geographic proximity of resi-dence. Rural members of such groups, in contrast, may have been less able to sustain their ethnic religion under conditions of lower membership and lack of residential concentration.

Finally, it should be recognized that even if one of the urban-centric or rural-dominant models was apparently explanatory of early patterns of Religious Monopoly within an ethnicity, there is the possibility that the locus of higher Religious Monopoly will have changed since 1931, what with the internal migration to the cities in Canada, the Great Depression, the Second World War, and the post-war immigration and ethnic diversification.

So, in large part, the data presented below is in the way of a test of the conventional models of ethnic enclosure combined with the particular locale of principal residence, urban versus rural. Increas-ingly, however, it would be expected that the level of rural Reli-gious Monopoly will have declined with the move to urban sites and that at least some assimilation to "Canadian" religions will have ensued.

In contrast, for those ethnicities whose principal residence has been in the urban centres of the country, Religious Monopoly should, in 1931, have been greater in these urban places, compared to that of rural residents. Theory would dictate also, that, as Canada became more urban, these groups' degree of religious exclusivity would not have lessened much or could, in fact, even have increased slightly, especially during the post-war decades.

Testing these hypotheses, Table 7.4's rank-correlation statistics (the Rho coefficient) provide a clear-cut differentiation. In Table 7.4, the Rho correlations for the *rankings* of the percent urban residence in each ethnicity compared to the *rankings* in degree of Religious Monopoly over the five dates beginning with 1931 are recorded. For three of these dates, and for all dates combined, there were considerably lower degrees of Religious

Table 7.4
Rho Correlations Between Rankings of Canadian Ethno-Racial-
Religious Groups on Percent Urban Residence and Percent Religious
Monopoly in the Group, 1931, 1951–1981

	1931	1951	1961	1971	1981	All Years
Rho Correlation	.430	.509	.429	.576	.490	.496
(p =)	(NS)	(.05)	(NS)	(.025)	(.05)	(.001)

Note: NS = Not Significant

Monopoly for groups that were lowest in urban residence (= highest in rural location).

The lack of contribution from rural residence was particularly significant for the Dutch, Germans, Native Peoples, Russians, and Scandinavians, who had among the highest degrees of rural residence but were very low-ranking in religious cohesion. The reverse—very great urban residence in a group tied to a high degree of Religious Monopoly—was exemplified in the East-Indian, Greek, Italian, Jewish, and Portuguese ethnicities. The large portion of recent immigrants in all of these ethnicities but the Jewish may have influenced the urban religious-cohesion phenomenon. The Jewish have been urbanites for centuries, if not millenia, a tradition essential in the maintenance of Judaism wherever they have resided. Moreover, it is worth noting that every group showing a rural-low Religious Monopoly are ethnicities that were well-established in Canada before the First World War, (and by the turn of the century or before, for many) opposite to the recent immigration influence amongst many groups who were urban and had high religious cohesion.

There is a further analysis of Religious Monopoly that can be done, one I call a "concordance" analysis. The concordance is by Religious Monopoly with the extent to which the ethnic group was above or below the national average for percent of urban residence. A scale was constructed of five points, ranging from very much above the national average (10 or more percentage points above average in urban residence), to moderately above (5–9 points above), to average (+4 to −4 percentage points for which there were no cases), to moderately below (5–9 points below average) and, finally, to very much below (10 or more points below average). Each group for each date was categorized. Then in each ethnicity for each date, it was ascertained whether urban or rural residents in the group had higher Religious Monopoly and how great the percentage difference was. The "concordance" between the prediction of where religious cohesion would be tested based on percent of urban residence was then recorded. Groups whose urban residence was much above average were "predicted" to have much higher religious cohesion among their urban residents. If the categorizations for urban residence and Religious Monopoly perfectly corresponded a "++" symbol was assigned. At the other extreme, great dissonance between Religious Monopoly and urban residence received an "=" symbol, with corresponding symbols for moderate concurrence or lack of concurrence.

Tables 7.5 and 7.6 contain the results from this concordance analysis, using the symbols summarized above as the tables' "data." (For complete explication of the symbols, see the note at the bottom of Table 7.5.) Of all 19 ethnic groups compared in Table 7.5, only four possessed a perfectly concordant pattern over all dates: Italians, Jewish, Scandinavians, and Ukrainians. Another five groups, though, were mostly concordant over the five dates compared: Dutch, French, Hungarians, Native Peoples and Russians. Not one ethnicity showed an entirely non-concordant pattern over all dates, but five ethnicities did have more instances of non-concordance than the predicted outcomes of higher religious cohesion: Black (only two dates for comparison, but dissonant at both), British, Czechoslovakian, German and Polish.

Another pattern emerging from this concordance analysis of Religious Monopoly was either a shift from concordance to non-concordance between 1931 and 1981 (French, Germans, Japanese), or the reverse, a transformation to concordance from non-concordance (British, Chinese, Dutch, Greeks, Poles, and Russians).

Moving to a more numerical form of summarization in the concordance analysis, we find that, in 67% of the total 75 comparisons, there was moderate to high concordance of the degree of urban residence with the site of residence that held higher religious cohesion. More detailed inspection of concordance within urban-dominant groups versus rural-dominant groups reveals a temporal difference between urban and rural residence locales in the extent of concordance with Religious Monopoly (Table 7.6). Among

Table 7.5

Degree and Direction of Concordance by Religious Monopoly Among Canadian Ethno-Racial-Religious Groups with the Degree and Direction of Variation in Urban-Residence Rate from the National Average, 1931, 1951–1981

Year	Black	British	Chinese	Czechoslovak	Dutch	Indian	French	German	Greek	Hungarian
						Ethno-Racial-Religious Group East				
1931	=	-	=	+	-	*	+	+	-	+
1951	*	=	*	+	+	*	+	+	*	+
1961	*	=	*	-	+	*	+	-	*	-
1971	*	=	*	-	+	*	-	-	*	+
1981	=	+	+	+	+	+	-	-	++	+

Year	Italian	Japanese	Jewish	Native Peoples	Polish	Portuguese	Russian	Scandinavian	Ukrainian
1931	+	+	+	+	-	*	=	++	*
1951	+	*	++	+	-	*	++	++	++
1961	++	*	++	++	-	*	+	++	++
1971	++	=	++	-	+	*	+	+	+
1981	+	-	++	+	+	+	+	+	+

Notes: ++ = Concordance was based on at least 10 points difference in urban-rural extents of Religious Monopoly.
+ = Concordance was based on 5–9 points difference.
- = Non-Concordance was based on 5–9 points difference.
= = Non-concordance was based on at least 10 points difference.
* = no data

Source: calculations on data reported in Censuses of Canada.

Table 7.6
Synthesis of the Concordance Analysis, by Urban or Rural Residence
Pattern Among Canadian Ethno-Racial-Religious Groups, 1931,
1951–1981

Year	Above-Average Rural Residence # Concordant /Total # Comparisons	Percent Concordant	Above-Average Urban Residence # Concordant /Total # Comparisons	Percent Concordant
1931	2/9	56	2/6	33
1951	9/9	100	2/4	50
1961	6/7	86	2/6	33
1971	4/6	67	4/6	67
1981	5/7	71	9/11	82

Source: Table 7.5 (above)

groups with an above-average degree of rural residence, the level of concordance was highly variable over the five dates. But, among those ethnicities that had above-average rates of urban residence, there seems to have been an increasing extent of concordance with higher religious cohesion in urban sites, especially between 1961 and 1981.

SUMMARY

Several major lines of variation have emerged from this chapter's investigation of ethnic Religious Monopoly. First, it is evident that there are marked differences in the extent of Religious Monopoly, primarily between ethnicities, but not limited to that dimension. Further, almost all of the groups have experienced sizeable *within-ethnicity* shifts in their rates of religious exclusivity, and these have not always been downward.

Generally, the highest degree of Religious Monopoly has attached to those ethnicities whose traditional religion has been Roman Catholicism or Eastern Orthodoxy, Judaism, Hinduism or Islam. But there is also a moderately high degree of inter- and intra-ethnic differentiation even in these particular groups. Beyond this, there are two other major influences on the extent of ethnic Religious Monopoly: gender and urban/rural residence. The very highest level of Religious Monopoly has been found among male members of ethnities with a long history of urban residence and who belong to their traditional ethnic religions.

Lowest Religious Monopoly attends: Blacks, the British, Dutch, Germans, Russians, Scandinavians, and Ukrainians, who have a long history of religious diversity in Canada (and even, for some groups, in the country of origin). To these should be added the Japanese, whose culture was drained out of them by a wartime internment and its post-war sequelae. In addition, women were shown to have a greater tendency to join Canadian "assimilating" religions.

It must be remembered, however, that, by and large, those ethnicities that much earlier in this century had high Religious Monopoly still tend to do so. Relatedly, despite the very real differences caused by gender or rural/urban residence, the greatest source of differentiation in Religious Monopoly was interethnic: ethnicities vary all the way from those having two or even three different faiths important in their group which jointly incorporate less than 75% of the group's members (e.g., Dutch, German, Russian and Scandinavians), to those with one religion monopolizing more than 90% of the whole ethnicity (e.g., French, Greek, Italian, Jewish, Portuguese) in 1981. Thus, there is no "Typical" ethnicity, nor even any "average" aggregate with regard to Religious Monopoly.

CHAPTER 8

Ethnic Family Aspects— Endogamy and Fertility

INTRODUCTION: ETHNIC FAMILY AND ETHNIC-GROUP COHESION

Ethnic-group cohesion can be considered to both begin and end in ethnic families. Most of the people that make up the membership of an ethnic community entered that community via the family in Canada; thus, it is they with whom the analyses of ethnic-group cohesion are ultimately concerned. In addition, ethnic behaviour, both of individuals within families and the families' collective attitudes toward and utilization of the ethnic community resources comprise the social foundation upon which ethnic cohesion rests. While the latter facets are the specific content of ethnic cohesion, the addition of new members via reproduction lies at the root of much ethnic cohesion. The formation and products of ethnic families are the twin concerns here relating to ethnic-group cohesion.

The Canadian censuses have never collected any information concerning the attitudes or behaviours of ethnic family members that could be considered to reflect ethnic-cohesion outcomes, with the possible exceptions of the extent of ethnic language use in the home (= family), which was addressed in Chapter 5, and endogamy and fertility, which are taken up in this chapter. However, two excellent reports from the Toronto Ethnic Pluralism Study by Isajiw (1981) and Isajiw and Makabe (1982), do provide details about the kind of family-based ethnic-group behaviour in which students of ethnic cohesion are most interested. Notwithstanding, the sort of ethnic family content dealt with in this chapter is more basic than that covered by Isajiw; here, we inspect ethnic-group endogamy and fertility, the founts of ethnic-group affiliation and cohesion.

ETHNIC-GROUP ENDOGAMY

"Endogamy" as analyzed here means marriage within the same ethnic group. Expressed as a percentage rate, this rate has a theoretical range from 100% to 0%. Practically, though, the continuum ranges from close to 100% to about 20% of the married people in an ethnicity. The degree to which endogamous marriages exist within an ethnic group reflects the potential power of the ethnic heritage to hold sway and of the ability of the mutually-reinforcing influences of this and the other cohesion forces to create the next generation of the ethnic community. The exchange benefits from identical linguistic, residential, and religious cohesion to continued cultural vigour are powerful and of long duration, given the foundation of endogamous marriages. With low endogamy, theory dictates, the future of the group's cultural cohesion becomes bleak. Ethnic endogamy can thus be likened to the glue binding the other cohesion factors together in one of the major arenas in which ethnic community cohesion is sustained.

Intra-group marriage was one of several ethnic-group cohesion factors that first emerged in census analyses in the two "monograph" volumes (12 and 13) of the 1931 census reports that, in effect, established the base for empirical elaboration of ethnic-group cohesion. Other elements covered at that time were the rate of heritage-language retention, group residential patterns, and ethno-religious affiliations. What is studied today about these topics is, in large measure, merely a continuation of the work begun then. With respect to Endogamy, Hurd's (1942) monograph (using data from the 1921 and 1931 censuses) opened the investigation of "intermarriage" dynamics and rates. The best source for statistics covering the 1941, 1951 and 1961 dates is Book 4 of the Report of the Royal Commission on Bilingualism and Biculturalism

(1970: 92–94, 279–281, 300). While basic endogamy data was contained in the 1971 published census reports, Kalbach and McVey (1979: 320–323) have a more detailed treatment of the 1961 and 1971 rates, focusing particularly on endogamy levels of "native-born" heads of families in multiple ethnic categories.

At time of publication, separate 1981 gender rates of Endogamy could be obtained only for the British, French, and Jewish groups. For the other groups on which data were available, the rates are for combined male and female married members of the respective groups, as obtained from the Public Use Sample at the Population Research unit of Erindale College, the University of Toronto (kind thanks to Warren Kalbach and Madeline Richard). Given the fall of the data, it seems very likely that the gender trends of past years continued and that the separate gender rates would be just above and below the joint rate cited in Figure 8.1 and Table 8.1.

It should be noted that there are, conceptually, two forms of endogamy which we could investigate: ethnic endogamy, which we have been discussing, and religious endogamy—marriage within the same religion or denomination. Unfortunately, there have never been religious-endogamy data generated from the censuses on more than a few distinct religious categories, and, apparently, none at all before the 1981 figures, which are inadequate for the elaboration of any detailed patterns. Nonetheless, there are excellent statistics covering endogamy *at time of marriage* in the published reports of Canadian vital statistics covering the 60 years following 1921. As fine as these data are, the patterns that emerge from the analysis of these vital statistics point only to the degree of endogamy among newly-married adults in that calendar year. Ignored, therefore, are all previous marriages, so that, if we assume a declining rate of religious endogamy over the decades, then analysis of the vital statistics yields a severe underestimate of total religious endogamy. When better figures from the census are available, we will be able, of course, to ascertain exactly the variation between "at-marriage" and total religious endogamy. In any case, partly because of the conceptual defect represented by the vital statistics reference and also because of space limitations, detailed analyses of purely religious cohesion components are not included in this book.

Table 8.1
Endogamy Rates among Canadian Ethno-Racial-Religious Groups, by Gender, 1921–1981 (in %)

Year & Gender		Asian	British	Ethno-Racial-Religious Group Czechoslovak	Dutch	French	German	Greek	Hungarian
1921:	Male	*	*	*	*	*	71	*	*
1931:	Male	*	*	79	53	*	72	74	90
	Female	*	*	80	56	*	70	88	88
1941:	Male	83	59#	62	53	93	58	50	68
1951:	Male	75	85	*	43	90	52	*	*
	Female	87	86	*	43	88	52	*	*
1961:	Male	80	81	*	55	88	52	*	*
	Female	86	82	*	56	86	51	*	*
1971:	Male	81	81	*	52	86	49	*	*
	Female	86	80	*	56	84	51	*	*
1981:	Male	93	80	*	52	87	50	*	*
	Female		78			86			

Year & Gender		Italian	Jewish	Native Peoples	Polish	Russian	Scandinavian	Ukrainian	All Groups
1921:	Male	78	*	*	*	*	57	85	*
1931:	Male	77	97	95	79	71	46	91	*
	Female	91	91	90	73	80	48	86	*
1941:	Male	55	95	95	51	56	*	80	*
1951:	Male	*	93	94	57	*	37	75	80
	Female	*	96	89	57	*	39	71	
1961:	Male	77	91	*	49	48	31	62	77
	Female	82	93	*	53	48	33	61	
1971:	Male	76	91	79	43	*	27	54	76
	Female	83	94	70	46	*	29	54	76
1981:	Male	84	90	*	49	*	17	49	75
	Female		92						

Notes: *No data.
Rate is for the "English."
1981 "Asian" rate is for the Chinese.
With the exception of rates for the British, French and Jewish, 1981 rates are for combined male and female members of the group.
Sources: 1941, Royal Commission (1978, p. 300); 1921–1931, 1951–1971, and British, French and Jewish in 1981, Censuses of Canada; all other 1981 rates from the Public Use Sample, Population Research Unit, Erindale College, University of Toronto.

Figure 8.1
Male Ethnic Endogamy Rates, 1931–1981

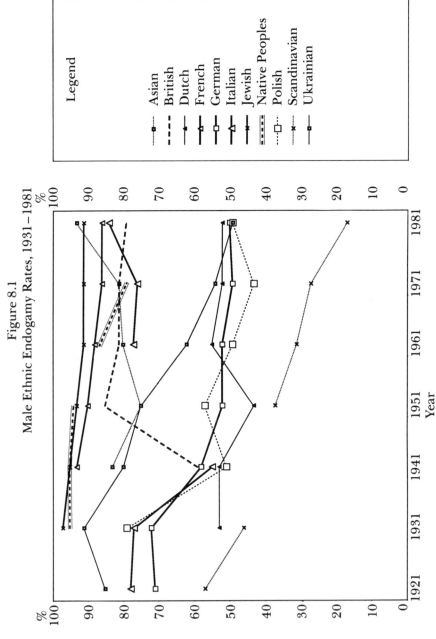

Source: Table 9.1; 1981 data for joint rates, except for British, French and Jewish

Longitudinal Patterns of Ethnic Endogamy

In 1931, all but one of the groups for whom data were available had over 50% Male Endogamy (Figure 8.1), the exception being the Scandinavians. A decade earlier, even that ethnic group had been above 50% by a comfortable margin (Table 8.1). Even in 1941, all but the Scandinavians remained above that bench-mark level in Endogamy, despite a sharp decline during the previous decade by the Poles, Italians, and Germans from between 72% to 79% in 1931 to between 51% to 58%. With few exceptions, that 1931–1941 decline in those groups established the pattern of Endogamy differentiation that would persist through 1981.

Looked at differently, in 1931, all but the Dutch and Scandinavians had Endogamy rates of at least 70%, comprising either two or three aggregate categories: the three ethnicities for whom there are 1931 data with above 90% rates (Jewish, Native Peoples, and Ukrainians) and likely the French and even the British as well, had figures on them been published; the three groups with Endogamy rates between 80% and 70% (Polish, Italian and, Germans); and the two lowest groups (Dutch and Scandinavians), or all ethnic groups with Endogamy below 80%. In 1941 this differentiation pattern was even clearer and, for most groups, persisted thereafter. Forty years later, there was still one set of ethnicities with very high levels of Endogamy: the Asians (Chinese in 1981), Jewish, French, Italians, and British (and in 1971, the Native Peoples*)—all above the 75% mark. All of the other ethnicities were under the 55% level, comprising either one category or two, if the very low Scandinavian rate could be considered to constitute a separate category, the Endogamy rate being more than 30 points lower in 1981 than those of the nearest ethnic groups, the Poles and Ukrainians, both at 49%

Overall, most groups experienced a considerable decline in Endogamy over the 40 or 50 years between 1931/1941 and 1981. Among the charter ethnicities, plus the Jewish (and perhaps the Native Peoples, based on the 1971 statistics), however, this decline was relatively minute. But for the Ukrainians, Germans, and Scandinavians, the decrease was substantial, amounting to at least one-third to under one-half of the 1931 rate; Endogamy fell among these ethnic groups from a joint (male and female) rate of well over

---

*No 1981 data for Native Peoples

three-quarters to about one-half. For this aggregate of groups, such a drop in Endogamy probably dooms the members to either marital assimilation into other groups at worst, or, at best, to the further decline in ethnic-group cohesion because of the failure of the Endogamy mechanism to bind members to the group in the 1980s and beyond.

There are ethnicities that bucked the general trend of lowered Endogamy levels. The Italians in 1941 seemed destined for marital assimilation or disbursement, having fallen from 78% in 1921 and 77% in 1931 to only 55% by 1941. Unaccountably, there was no Italian figure for 1951, but by 1961 the male Endogamy level had risen back to the 1931 level of 77%, no doubt riding the crest of post-war Italian immigration. In 1981 the Italian Endogamy had risen beyond the 1961 and 1971 rates, to exceed the highest previous rate recorded, that of 1931. In miniature, the same sort of transition characterizes the Asian condition. In 1951, the rate for the Asians (who always have been comprised more of Chinese than any other ethnicity) had lessened one-tenth, down to a still-comfortable 75%. Ten years later, though, the 1941–1951 loss had almost been made up, and in 1961 and 1971 male Asian Endogamy hovered around 80%. If the joint Chinese datum for 1981 represents the general Asian situation, it would appear that the heavy immigration of the post-1968 years among the Asians-Chinese has greatly benefited their Endogamy, which was likely above the rate recorded in 1941. The Dutch experience replicated that of the Italians and Asians/Chinese, but not to the same degree. Falling to a 1951 low of 43%, the Dutch Endogamy increased to 55% in 1961, above even the 1931 and 1941 level of 53%. The 1971 male Endogamy of 52% and the 1981 joint rate of 52% probably represent a continuing but very slow decline related, no doubt, to the small immigration of Dutch to Canada.

Rankings in Recent Endogamy Levels

The relative standings between the various ethno-racial groups in 1981 were very similar to those of 1931. Jewish remained high in Endogamy, though perhaps no longer the highest of all groups, 90% of their members being married to other Jews. The Asians/Chinese may well be the group with the highest Endogamy rate today. Not all ethnicities within the Asian rubric have as high an Endogamy rate as the Chinese, however. Limited data on the situation of Toronto Japanese (or at least those who are members of the Toronto Japanese Canadian Cultural Centre (JCCC)), indicate that about 67% of the Japanese there have endogamous marriages (JCCC Newsletter, 1984). The French continue to maintain their long-standing record for being second- or third-highest in Endogamy (87% in 1981). In that year, the fourth- and fifth-highest were the Italians and the British, the former being more maritally cohesive, apparently, than at any other time. The 1971 rate for the Native Peoples shows a slide from highest in Endogamy in 1951 (94%) to their lowest point ever in 1971 (79%).

The 1971 rate for Native Peoples and the higher British level in 1981 mark the lower boundary for those pre-eminent in Endogamy. From there, it is a nearly 30-point drop to the 52% mark for the Dutch, who set off the margin of those groups "lower" in Endogamy. The exceptionally steep decline among the Ukrainians, from 91% in 1931 to 49% in 1981, leads to questions of how well Ukrainians can withstand other culturally assimilative tendencies without the internal strength flowing from ethnic Endogamy. The same pattern and questions loom also for the Germans and the Poles, with Endogamy of 79% to 72% in 1931 declining to about 50% in 1981. The Dutch, who have remained around the 50% rate since 1931, with the sole exception of a 1951 decline, appear to be stabilized in Endogamy. Between those ethnicities "lower" in Endogamy, it was still a relatively huge decline of 32 points down to the Scandinavians, with the lowest rate of Endogamy, a minuscule 17%.

Averaged over all ethnicities for which there were data between 1951 and 1981, Endogamy lessened only slightly, from 80% in 1951 to 75% in 1981, but undoubtedly more over the period 1931–1981, about a 15- to 20-point decline. Thus, Endogamy has declined only slightly, even from the overall 1931 level, mainly because of the continuing high levels of Endogamy within the charter groups. Given recent trend lines, both of decline and of stability or even increase, it is likely that the 1970s and 1980s may come to be recognized as representing a major alteration in the pattern for ethnic Endogamy, a kind of cultural watershed. Indeed, given the omnipresence of the ideology of multiculturalism, it is likely that only the Scandinavians, Ukrainians, and perhaps the Native Peoples will continue to suffer further cultural destitution from the trauma of declining ethnic Endogamy.

What is not yet revealed by data are the rates for ethno-racial groups which in 1971 and in 1981 were subsumed under the Asian rubric—so new to Canada in substantial numbers that their Endogamy levels were not calculated: Arabs, Blacks, East Indians, Filipinos, Greeks, Indochinese (or more accurately, Cambodians, Laotians and Vietnamese), Japanese, Koreans, Latin Americans, Portuguese, and others. A first-time elaboration of the Endogamy levels for these groups is essential to filling out the present-day picture of ethnic-group Endogamy in Canada.

Gender Patterns in Ethnic Endogamy

Gender-differentiated rates of ethnic Endogamy were calculable for most groups over the entire period from 1931 to 1971 and three groups in 1981, excepting 1941 when statistics regarding only male rates were published. Using Table 8.1 figures, Gender Ratios for the rates of Endogamy were determined and are set out in Table 8.2. Several things can produce gender differentials in rates of Endogamy. An imbalance in the number of adolescent or younger males compared to females can readily lead to the gender with the smaller number later having a higher Endogamy rate, because the gender with the larger number will have an insufficient "supply" to enter into endogamous marriages. Of even greater import, probably, has been the gender variance within immigrants, especially unmarried immigrants. In the past, Canada's immigrants have had a greater number of males than females, but beginning in the 1960s, the trend has been increasingly toward gender parity, or even a surplus of females in the immigration flow. Another powerful influence would be from the culture of the particular group, especially concerning which of the parents is primarily or mostly responsible for inculcating and retaining ethnocultural principles and practices; this question has been researched little. Finally, some groups trace their ancestral lines principally through the female side (e.g., the Jewish); others trace them jointly through both parents (e.g., Spanish and Latinos); most ethnicities however, trace the lines back through the father.

In any case, for the periods 1931–1971 or 1951–1981, the figures in Table 8.2 indicate that of the dozen ethnicities for which there were at least two temporal data-points, five experienced a moderate to marked decline in gender ratios in Endogamy: Dutch, Germans, Jewish, Polish, and Ukrainians. The greatest shifts went from much higher male rates of Endogamy (gender ratios of 107–

Table 8.2
Gender Ratios of Ethnic Endogamy Rates, 1931, 1951–1981

Year	Asian	British	Czechoslovak	Dutch	French	German	Greek	Hungarian
				Ethno-Racial-Religious Group				
1931	*	*	99	95	*	103	84	102
1951	86	99	*	100	102	100	*	*
1961	93	99	*	98	102	102	*	*
1971	94	101	*	93	102	96	*	*
1981	*	102	*	*	102	*	*	*

Year	Italian	Jewish	Native Peoples	Polish	Russian	Scandinavian	Ukrainian
1931	85	107	106	108	89	96	106
1951	*	97	106	100	*	95	106
1961	94	98	*	92	100	94	102
1971	92	97	113	93	*	93	100
1981	*	97	*	*	*	*	*

Notes: *No data.
Source: Table 8.1 (above)

108) to decided female superiority in Endogamy (gender ratios of 93–97), representing a decline of from 10 to 15 points in the gender ratio: Jewish and Polish. Another four ethnic groups (Asians, Italians, Native Peoples, and Russians) evidence the reverse transition, i.e., to increased male Endogamy. The Asians are greatest in this, but even so, the rise in the gender ratio is toward gender parity. Only the Native Peoples had an upward trend that began at a rate above 100. The remaining three ethnic groups had a pattern either of stability in the gender ratios of Endogamy (French, continuously at 102), or a diminutive shift upwards (British) or downwards (Scandinavians).

In 1931, the Polish, Jewish, Native Peoples, and Ukrainians all evidenced a considerably higher male rate of Endogamy, while at that same date or in 1951, the Asians, Greeks, Italians, and Russians yielded a much greater female Endogamy. In 1971 or 1981, the same degree of gender variation in Endogamy existed only among the Native Peoples, who thereby possessed the highest gender ratio (113)—the greatest degree of male superiority in Endogamy. The next highest incidence of an above-100 ratio was among the British and French, just above gender equality. Ukrainians had gender parity, and the Jewish (97) and Germans (96) had a slightly higher degree of female Endogamy. Next in order were Asians, Dutch, Poles, and Scandinavians (gender ratios of either 94 or 93), with Italians having the lowest ratio (92).

ETHNIC-GROUP FERTILITY

"Fertility" within ethnic groups means the average number of children—born either to women in the ethnicity (1931, 1941 census definitions) or to married women in the ethnic group (1971 and 1981 definitions). True fertility data were not published in the 1951 census reports, and the nearest approximation is the number of children living in the family home at the time of the 1951 census.

As with Endogamy, a 1931 census monograph was the primary source for Canadian demographic investigation into differential fertility rates between ethnoracial groups. In one section of an exhaustive exploration into the fertility of the Canadian population, Tracey (1942: 292–307) reported data for the years 1926 through 1936 on multiple ethnicities, including three of the British ethnicities. Since then, there have been occasional ventures into further exploration of ethnic fertility, prominent among them

Henripin (1968), Kalbach and McVey (1979: 109–110), and Trovato and Burch (1980). All in all, ethnic-group fertility is a topic that has received relatively little academic attention, and no previous work has compared long-time trends within and between multiple ethnicities.

One of the possible reasons for this was alluded to earlier: though there are comparable figures for 1931, 1941, 1971, and 1981, the data for 1951 focuses on a rather different aspect that vaguely reflects fertility, but is not fertility itself. Further, there is no data at all that we could find even indirectly referring to fertility for 1961, which is particularly unfortunate because, as we have seen, the 1951–1971 period was one containing important shifts in ethnocultural phenomena. Because of the lack of comparability, the 1951 figures on number of children in the home are not contained in Figure 8.2, but do appear in Table 8.3, for reasons to be explained later.

The interpretations of the 1931 and 1941 data versus the 1971 and 1981 sets are much less problematic because the differences are much slighter. The base concept of "number of children ever born" remains identical. What did vary was the criterion used by the census technicians to determine mothers' eligibility for inclusion in the "count"—only women who were ever married are included in 1971 and 1981. Mothers who reported in 1971 or 1981 that they had never been married were excluded. Notwithstanding, in real terms, the actual marital status of mothers in 1931 and 1941 was probably very much like the "ever-married" status of mothers included in the 1971 and 1981 censuses because, in those earlier decades, there were likely fewer instances of children born to never-married women than is the case today.

Fertility indices are important to ethnic cohesion because they point to intergroup differentials in the potential to maintain the culture through natural increment. Groups with higher fertility, then, could be forecast to have a greater opportunity to maintain their culture than groups whose membership could increase less or even shrink because of lower fertility levels. It would be imprudent to overstate the significance of ethnic-group fertility for the future of group cultural cohesion, but neither should its importance be underestimated.

Figure 8.2 and Table 8.3 contain the relevant information. In recent decades, only the Native Peoples have maintained fertility levels at approximately the same level as those of 1931 and 1941.

Figure 8.2
Ethnic Family Indicators: Number of Children
Ever Born, 1931–1941, 1971–1981

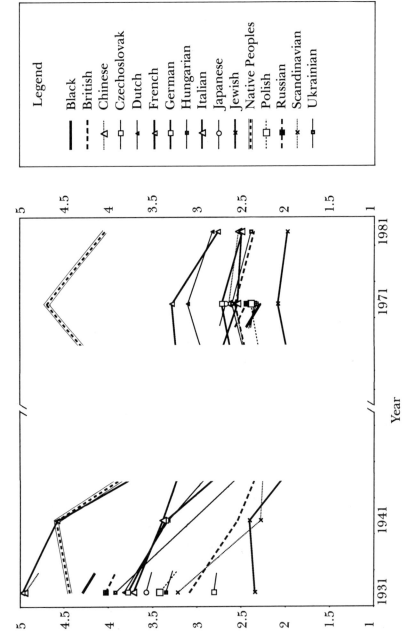

Table 8.3
Fertility Indices for Canadian Ethno-Racial-Religious Groups,
1931–1951, 1971–1981

Year and Index	Asian	Chinese	Japanese	Black	British	Czechoslovak	Dutch	French	German	All Canadians
1931: $\overline{X}$ # children born	*	4.95	3.57	4.29	3.08	2.80	3.82	4.97	3.78	3.92
1941: $\overline{X}$ # children born	3.44	*	*	*	2.54	*	3.32	4.57	3.35	3.20
1951: $\overline{X}$ # children home #	2.48	*	*	*	2.20	*	2.61	3.13	2.40	2.49
1971: $\overline{X}$ # children born **	2.28	2.63	2.67	2.28	2.56	2.35	3.10	3.28	2.71	2.77
1981: $\overline{X}$ # children born **	*	2.53	*	*	2.35	*	2.82	2.76	2.48	2.49

Year and Index	Greek	Hungarian	Italian	Jewish	Native Peoples	Polish	Russian	Scandinavian	Ukrainian
1931: $\overline{X}$ # children born	3.01	3.35	3.71	2.34	4.43	3.42	4.03	3.21	3.92
1941: $\overline{X}$ # children born	*	*	3.38	2.40	4.58	*	*	2.28	*
1951: $\overline{X}$ # children home #	*	*	*	1.76	3.32	2.10	*	2.23	2.19
1971: $\overline{X}$ # children born **	2.32	2.32	2.54	2.08	4.69	2.38	2.44	2.56	2.60
1981: $\overline{X}$ # children born **	*	*	2.49	1.97	4.04	*	*	*	2.38

Notes: * No data.

** To ever-married women.

Comparable only between groups, not to index in other years.

Sources: 1931–1951, 1981, Censuses of Canada; 1971, adapted from A.H. Richmond and W.E. Kalbach. *Factors in the Adjustment of Immigrants and Their Descendants.* (Ottawa: Statistics Canada, 1980), p. 223.

Indeed, they were one of only two groups to have higher fertility in 1941 than in 1931, the other being the Jewish, but at a level of fertility about half that of the Native Peoples. The general trend was a major decline in fertility within all other groups during the years of the Great Depression and the Second World War. Fertility was slightly higher in 1971 and, thereafter, again declined in every ethnicity, including the Native Peoples.

In 1931, there were no sharp demarcations between the ethnicity with the highest childbearing rate and that with the lowest. That is, the 16 ethnicities depicted in Figure 8.2 were rather evenly distributed between the range from lowest to highest fertility. In 1941, the pattern had shifted to the existence of three categories of ethnicities: those two groups high in fertility (the Native Peoples and the French with nearly, or above 4.5 children ever born); an intermediate group (fertility level of about 3.2–3.3 children (Dutch, Germans, and Italians); and three ethnicities with much lower fertility (British, Jewish and Scandinavians). Unfortunately, eight of the 17 groups on whom there were 1931 data were not shown in the 1941 census reports on fertility, so this threefold division of fertility levels may be more apparent than real.

There is some internal evidence, however, from Figure 8.2 that this division was real: the continued downward shift in fertility levels and the formation of perhaps four strata, albeit again with fewer 1981 ethnicities than in either 1931 or 1971. But in both 1971 and 1981, the Native Peoples comprised a category of their own by dint of their exceptionally high fertility. There was a high(er)-intermediate category made up of the French and the Dutch and a low(er)-intermediate aggregate containing a majority of the ethnicities: Blacks, British, Chinese, Czechoslovaks, Germans, Hungarians, Italians, Japanese, Poles, Russians, Scandinavians, and Ukrainians. At the bottom of the fertility continuum, considerably below every other ethnic group, were the Jewish.

In explanation of the ethnic-group differentials in fertility, Trovato and Bruch (1980: 14) offered the hypotheses of "minority status" leading to group insecurity and at least partial cultural assimilation versus a subcultural ethnic-group effect on "family size" (number of children ever born to ever-married women in the ethnic group). Analyzing 1971 census data on eight ethnic groups, Trovato and Bruch revealed that the assimilation thesis accounted well for the fertility levels of the French, German and Italian groups, but that the ethnic-group effect hypothesis held for the other ethnicities, the Dutch, Jewish, Native Peoples, Poles, and Ukrainians. Their interpretation was that the ethnic-group effect served to

> enhance the fertility of Native Indians and Dutch minorities while for Jewish, Polish and Ukrainian groups it acts to lower their respective family sizes...the predicted differentials of the French, Germans and Italians (from the British) warrant the acceptance of the...assimilation hypothesis.

These variations existed for both the assimilation-effect ethnicities as well as the ethnic-group effect ethnicities, despite the wide differences in the absolute levels of fertility in each of the conceptual categories used by Trovato and Bruch.

Looking at the Figure 8.2 and Table 8.3 results in a more comparative fashion, it is obvious that the Native Peoples have continued to have extremely high levels of fertility, especially over the past two decades. In contrast, there are the Chinese (and "Asians," of whom the Chinese have always been the largest single component), Blacks, French, Hungarians, and Ukrainians whose declines in fertility were significantly more than those of other groups and much more than the national average. The British, Hungarians, and probably the Czechoslovaks seem to have experienced a somewhat lesser decrease in fertility than the other groups depicted here. Finally, only the Scandinavians (along with the Native Peoples) actually increased their level of fertility by a substantial degree; the Scandinavians did have a very sharp decline in fertility between 1931 and 1941, but it had rebounded by 1971 (Table 8.3).

Rankings in Ethnic-Group Fertility

Rankings between groups in a particular census year are much less susceptible to differences in comparability of data than contrasting the absolute values of the statistics. Thus, the slight differences in the empirical measures between the 1931–1941 versus the 1971–1981 fertility data and even the altogether different measure for the 1951 data are transformed into much more validly comparable phenomena by focusing only on the ordinal rank in fertility level during that particular year. These ranking statistics are contained in Table 8.4 and permit a better tracing of persistencies and shifts in relative fertility levels over the half-century covered by the figures.

Of first importance here is the continued prominence of the French and Native Peoples in the fertility standings, occupying two of the top three levels in every one of the five dates. Another pattern that emerged is the reverse: the Jewish were, in every year, lowest or second-lowest in fertility. A third trend is the move by the Dutch in the rankings from being intermediate in the childbearing rate at the beginning of the period covered, to the second-highest position in 1981. The opposite of this, however, characterized more groups; going from higher to relatively much lower in fertility positions were: the Chinese, (*cum* the Asian category), Japanese, Blacks, Scandinavians, and Ukrainians. The other groups showed only slight alterations in their fertility ranks, and these were all within the intermediate aggregate of ethnicities.

Relatedly, the argument exists that there is an "assimilation" transition involved in the decline of fertility rates. That is, ethnicities that are dominated demographically and culturally by their high proportion of immigrants have been thought to have higher rates of childbearing than "older" ethnicities whose members are predominantly Canadian-born. Accordingly, those groups comprised largely by third, +-generation members would be forecast to have the lowest fertility. This assimilation transition, however, is not supported by the data: the three groups with the highest fertility rates in 1971 and 1981 are at, or near, the bottom in terms of the proportion of immigrants in their generational composition, directly opposite, therefore, to this assimilation transition hypothesis. Moreover, in 1971 and 1981, the groups with the highest proportion of immigrants (Chinese, Blacks, and Italians) are close to or well below the middle levels in the childbearing hierarchy illustrated in Table 8.4.

While it is possible that when more complete analyses of the 1971 and 1981 census data can be made, focusing on other groups recently appearing in Canada in large numbers—East Indians, Indochinese, Koreans, Latin Americans, and Portuguese—the rejection of the assimilation transition thesis may not be so forthcoming. Even so, not even data on other groups not covered in Table 8.4 can invalidate the fact that childbearing among the groups with the relatively fewest immigrants in Canada is highest of all Canadian groups that we currently know about, and will remain so even when figures for additional ethnicities are included in the future.

Table 8.4

Rankings in Fertility Indices for Canadian Ethno-Racial-Religious Groups, 1931–1951, 1971–1981

Year (# Ranks)	Asian	Chinese	Japanese	Black	British	Czechoslovak	Dutch	French	German
1931 (of 17)	–	2	10	4	14	16	7	1	8
1941 (of 9)	3	–	–	–	8	–	6	2	5
1951 (of 10)	4	–	–	–	7	–	3	2	5
1971 (of 16)	–	6	5	15	8.5	13	3	2	4
1981 (of 9)	–	4	–	–	8	–	2	3	6

Year (# Ranks)	Greek	Hungarian	Italian	Jewish	Native Peoples	Polish	Russian	Scandinavian	Ukrainian
1931 (of 17)	15	12	9	17	3	11	5	13	6
1941 (of 9)	–	–	4	9	1	–	–	7	–
1951 (of 10)	–	–	–	10	1	9	–	6	8
1971 (of 16)	–	14	10	16	1	12	11	8.5	7
1981 (of 9)	–	–	5	9	1	–	–	–	7

Notes: Rank 1 = Highest fertility.
– Not available.
Source: Table 8.3 (above)

202 / Ethno-Cultural Maintenance in Canada

Generation in Canada

There is a general presumption (or hypothesis, if you will) that generation in Canada inversely influences the level of fertility over all ethnic groups; immigrants should have the highest fertility and third,+ generations the lowest. Regrettably, the 1981 census did not include a question on the birthplace of the respondent's parents; it is impossible, therefore, to mount a test of this using that census' data. Fortunately though, the 1971 census did include the question, and Richmond and Kalbach (1980: 223) did examine this aspect; their data are reported in Table 8.5, and the within-generation rankings based on these figures are in Table 8.6. First, only among the Chinese, Dutch, Italians, Scandinavians, and Ukrainians did the first generation (immigrant) mothers have higher fertility than their Canadian-born counterparts. Indeed, of the 16 ethnicities analyzed, five groups had highest fertility within the oldest generations (third and later): Blacks, British, Czechoslovaks, French, and Native Peoples. And, among the Blacks, Czechs and Native Peoples, there is a direct linear relation with generation in Canada— the fertility level of second-generation mothers was higher than in the immigrant generation, and the fertility of the third,+ generations was highest of all, completely opposite to the commonly-stated hypothesis. Further, even of those groups that did have highest fertility among immigrant mothers, only the Italians, Scandinavians, and Ukrainians had a linearly inverse correlation of fertility to generation—immigrants highest, third,+ generations lowest. So, while the Richmond and Kalbach investigation shows that there is an extremely diverse association between ethnic groups studied and generations with highest fertility, it is clear the "assimilation" transition in fertility does not hold in most ethnicities.

Turning our attention now to the between-ethnicity rankings (calculated separatedly for each of the three generation categories, Table 8.6), we see again that there is little regularity between ethnicities, suggesting great diversity in the attitudinal aspects and cultural prescriptions within many ethnicities regarding fertility. If this were not so, then both the fertility levels and/or the rankings would be similar. Only the French and the Jewish possess similitude between the generations in both absolute levels of childbearing and the respective within-generation rankings. And only the British had approximately the same levels of fertility in all three generational

Table 8.5
Number of Children Ever Born (to Ever-Married Women) by Generation
for Ethno-Racial-Religious Groups, 1971

Generation in Canada	Ethno-Racial-Religious Group							
	Chinese	Japanese	Black	British	Czechoslovak	Dutch	French	German
Immigrant	2.73	2.65	1.77	2.42	1.15	3.30	3.14	2.70
Second	1.84	2.82	2.14	2.53	1.57	2.81	3.05	2.96
Third,+	2.58	1.20	4.52	2.63	2.57	2.87	3.29	2.52

Generation in Canada	Hungarian	Italian	Jewish	Native Peoples	Polish	Russian	Scandinavian	Ukrainian	All Canadians
Immigrant	2.25	2.58	2.10	2.37	2.35	1.89	2.87	3.18	2.52
Second	2.77	2.53	2.13	4.37	2.50	3.06	2.61	2.59	2.61
Third,+	1.50	2.04	1.85	4.81	2.19	1.94	2.04	1.97	2.92

Source: A.H. Richmond and W.E. Kalbach. *Factors in the Adjustment of Immigrants and Their Descendants*. (Ottawa: Statistics Canada, 1980), p. 223.

Table 8.6
Rankings in Fertility for Canadian Ethno-Racial-Religious Groups,
by Generation in Canada, 1971

Generation in Canada	Ethno-Racial-Religious Group							
	Chinese	Japanese	Black	British	Czechoslovak	Dutch	French	German
Immigrant	5	7	16	9	13	1	3	6
Second	16	5	14	11.5	10	6	3	4
Third,+	6	16	2	5	7	4	3	8
	Hungarian	Italian	Jewish	Native Peoples	Polish	Russian	Scandinavian	Ukrainian
Immigrant	12	8	14	10	11	15	4	2
Second	7	11.5	15	1	13	2	8	9
Third,+	15	10.5	14	1	9	13	10.5	12

Note: Rank = 1 highest fertility; Rank 16 = lowest fertility.
Source: Table 8.5 (above)

categories, while no group possessed similar between-generation rankings, without dissimilarity in the actual degree of fertility.

More characteristic of these ethnicities was a sharp contrast between generations in the rankings for fertility. The greatest of these was within the Native Peoples (Canadian-born generations having much higher ranks than for the immigrants); Blacks, British, and possibly Czechoslovaks (the third,+ generations possessing a much higher ranking); the Chinese (second-generation mothers had a much higher ranking than the other two generation categories).

Corresponding to the linearity of the association with the actual fertility rates noted for the Blacks, Czechs and Native Peoples (Table 8.5), there is the same direct trend for fertility rankings in Table 8.6. The reverse is true, or nearly so, for the Italians, Scandinavians, and Ukrainians, who also had an inverse correlation between generation and fertility levels. Thus, only three of the sixteen ethnic groups in 1971 could be characterized as possessing an "assimilationist" pattern of fertility being highest in the immigrant and lowest in the third,+ generations. If any generalization can be made about the various groups, it is that the groups vary both between generations and between groups in a way that could be conceptualized as "ethnic relativity."

SUMMARY

Endogamy—marriage within the ethno-racial-religious group—is the glue that binds other ethnic-cohesion mechanisms together; ethnic culture becomes a family affair, a collective practice and celebration of cultural heritage. And, if Endogamy is a powerful cohesion influence, then ethnic-group fertility can be seen as the progenitor of the ethnic group itself, a *sine qua non* of ethnic-group cultural maintenance. Both of these essential factors linked to ethnic cultural retention were considered under the rubric of the ethnic family, a critical arena for ethnic-group cohesion. Endogamy marks the initiation of the family, and fertility represents its fulfilment as, in part, the agent of cultural adherence.

Ethnic-group Endogamy appears to be superior in group cohesion to Language Retention and perhaps even Residential Concentration, at least in several ethnicities. In six of the eleven ethnicities on which data have consistently been made available, there has been either a resurgence in Endogamy to a level existing in 1931, or a decline so slight as to still ensure that three-quarters of married Canadians have spouses from the same ethnicity as their own. Given the trend through 1981, it appears that only the Scandinavians have become maritally assimilated into other ethnic groups. In addition to the five or six groups that continue to maintain high Endogamy, the rate of decline in all other groups but the Ukrainians has either slowed, or reversed to increased Endogamy. So, all but two or three of the ethnicities covered will probably maintain Endogamy at a rate above or close to the psychosocially symbolic criterion of 50%.

Gender ratios of the rates of Endogamy have been declining in the majority of ethnicities; these are characterized by ratios well below gender equality (100), indicating that male rates of endogamy are lower than those of females in those ethnicities; only the Native Peoples have a gender ratio of Endogamy rates markedly above 100.

Conforming to the general Canadian pattern over the past half-century, fertility levels within most ethnic groups had sharply declined by 1981 to levels at or below one-half of their 1931 magnitudes. Only three ethnicities showed a differing pattern: the Native Peoples, again, who have continued to maintain an exceeding elevated childbearing rate; the Jewish, who have had very low fertility over the entire half-century; and the Scandinavians, who experienced a fertility increase between 1941 and 1971 (the two dates for which comparable data are present). The fertility of the Jewish, who have the lowest rate among these ethnicities, is under one-half the rate for the Native Peoples, who have the highest. Most of the other ethnic groups are close to each other in fertility levels.

The "assimilation transition" thesis was tested in two ways and rejected both times. Trovato and Burch (1980), however, suggest that fertility levels among the French, Germans, and Italians in Canada are due to an assimilationist process. First, highest childbearing rates are within groups with very low proportions of immigrant members and within groups dominated numerically by immigrants who had low or intermediate levels of fertility in the period 1971–1981. Second, intergenerational data from the 1971 census by Richmond and Kalbach (1980) overwhelmingly disproved the assimilation thesis of immigrants having the highest fertility rate and third,+ generations the lowest. Only three of the sixteen ethnicities studied possessed this pattern, and more groups than that had highest fertility in the third,+ generations. Only the British and the Jewish had approximately the same rate of child-bearing in all three generation categories. Lastly, many groups were characterized by marked variation in fertility levels between their generations.

CHAPTER 9

Institutional Completeness

INTRODUCTION: IMPORTANCE OF INSTITUTIONAL COMPLETENESS

In the previous chapters, we have inspected the degree of ethnic cohesion existing in the entire national population: language retention and use, residential concentration, religious monopoly, and endogamy and family. In 1964, one of the earliest and most important explorations of the contributory forces in Canadian ethno-racial-religious cohesion was produced by Raymon Breton. Breton, then (as now) interested in the makeup of ethnic groups' social infrastructures, looked, not to the individualistic and family-based phenomena of language use or residential proximity, but, instead, to a facet of the social life of industrialized nations that is their hallmark—formal organizations. What Breton examined almost 25 years ago, he termed *Institutional Completeness*, and he cast this concept of ethnic development as a continuum, ranging from ethnicities virtually without any such organizations to those groups whose organizations represent every possible sphere of ethnic-group life.

Institutional Completeness, as a dimension of ethnic solidarity, loyalty, and/or cohesion can be defined as the extent to which an ethnic group in a particular locale possesses organizations developed by or for members of that ethnoculture. Generally, these organizations will parallel those of the wider extra-ethnic community that serve the public at large; Breton offered the examples of parallel educational structures, one serving youth and adults from all segments of the city or region, the other developed and controlled by members of a particular ethnicity and oriented toward the teaching of ethnic content—language, history, culture, and such.

From the standpoint of the members of the ethnicity(ies) involved, the formation and use of ethnically-specific organizations help define the boundaries of possible enclosure. While it is important to have a multiplicity of organizations serving the same ethnic function in some cases, Breton stressed that diversity of organizations was more important than sheer numbers for maintaining ethnic cohesion in a group. Furthermore, Breton indicated his belief that the diversity of organizations was also of greater significance to ethnic cohesion than whether particular kinds of organizations existed under ethnic auspices. Thus, developing the entire spectrum of organizations to meet any and all needs of ethnic-group members would assure that the members' daily lives could be monopolized within the ethnic enclosure, thus avoiding interaction with members of the other ethno-racial-religious groups. Given this idealization, the degree of Institutional Completeness for an ethnicity can readily by seen to: (1) be geographically limited; (2) exist parallel to the extra-ethnic organizations; (3) represent a diversity of social-life functions, while simultaneously (4) reflecting a degree of completeness on a theoretical scale from none to totality.

We use the term *Institutional* completeness rather than, say, *organizational* completeness partly because of its connotations: the vital aspects of social life; and the potential for complete enclosure of every life process and function within ethnic-group boundaries, so that individuals might live out their entire lives within such ethnic enclaves (Reitz, 1980: 218).

Obviously, the emergence of ethnic organizations was a development of the first sizeable wave of immigration into a particular part of Canada. The development of ethnic organizations was important, especially for non-English/non-French immigrants whose ethnic and/or secular culture differed markedly from the dominant culture in their area. Many immigrants had had little experience with such voluntary (i.e., private, non-tax-supported) organizations other than the church, upon their arrival in Canada. The family, kin network, and church had provided the social structures in their homelands. In Canada, settlers in rural areas seem to have established few organizations because farming generally required few resources outside of the personal efforts of oneself and one's family, supplemented by occasional exchanges with companies for seed, equipment, foodstuffs, cloth, and the like. Immigrants living in towns and cities, however, usually created a variety of organizations, either to fill traditional wants or to meet the new needs created either by immigration or residence in an unfamiliar place (Royal Commission, 1970: 107).

Ethnic organizations were established to meet those wants and needs shared with fellow group members (but not necessarily with all the city's residents) or to meet universal wants in ways traditional to the ethnicity. Different types of ethnic organizations have emerged at different periods because of the varying types of immigrants coming to Canada in each era and because of the different levels of development in the places of settlement (Royal Commission, 1970: 107–108).

Apparently, mutual-benefit associations emerged first. Faced with few resources in a frontier society, new immigrants banded together to provide the kinds of assistance supplied by family and kin in the homeland. Sometimes these mutual-aid societies flourished and expanded into long-standing prosperous businesses. Often, they were short-lived because their functions were only temporarily required (Royal Commission, 1970: 108). After a successful settling in, immigrants' attention could then turn to a variety of other needs and wants—provision for the maintenance of the ethnic culture in their new home. This involved many and varied institutions: principal among them, the ethnic religion.

According to the *Report of the Royal Commission on Bilingualism and Biculturalism* (1970: 109), the period between the two world wars was, in part, marked by the emergence of ethnic associations representing members of the ethnicity to other Canadians, to the federal and provincial governments, and to the new governments in the homeland. Following the Second World War, groups possessing many ethnic associations—with the competition and ineffectiveness that goes along with such multiplicity—established, or tried to establish, overarching bodies to co-ordinate these organizations. Virtually all of these, the Royal Commission noted (1970: 110), were founded in the 1940s or later. Since both the co-ordinating bodies and the other ethnic associations were composed largely of immigrants, it is not certain whether they will continue, since they have not usually been successful in recruiting Canadian-born members to their service.

Relatedly, Breton's (1964) work on Institutional Completeness dealt with the influence of such organizational development on immigrants. But, of course, there is ample evidence that institutional development is not of benefit merely to the immigrant members of a group; they also help Canadian-born members and even, in certain instances, non-group people. Further, some of the ethnic organizations, like the mutual-aid societies developed by the immigrants may ultimately be of no further use, and so they either disincorporate or shift their services to alternative or multipurpose functions. This decommissioning of some ethnic organizations has occurred when their newly-immigrant clients have overcome their linguistic and/or socio-economic problems (Reitz, 1980: 219). However, other ethnic organizations started by the first immigrants continue, fulfilling purposes beyond the particular ones of the settling-in period and serving both earlier-wave immigrants and new arrivals, as well as second- and later-generation members.

In this way, ethnic organizations of all types directly contribute to the level of ethnic cohesion enjoyed by a group in a particular locale. The ethnic-cohesion function of such organizations is readily appreciated by those members of the group who are actively involved in the activities of the ethnic institutional network. But, as Reitz has alluded (1980: 219), ethnic organizations can also be important in fostering ethnic cohesion with regard to people who identify with the ethnicity, but do not yet interact much with the group. Such nominal group members can be drawn into a state of greater self-identification with the group and into more active participation through the informal interaction that takes place when they make use of ethnic organizations. In short, the ethnic organizations promote ethnic cohesion by generating in-group networks of interaction and by increasing the salience of ethnic identity and culture among both the active and latent members.

What may not be as readily evident is that ethnic groups with high institutional completeness have the potential for contributing to the group's vitality even through the utilization of ethnic organizations by non-group members. By contributing to the economic or social success of the ethnic organizations, the non-group clients/consumers unconsciously help assure the continuation and even the expansion of ethnic institutional services. Anyone who is not Chinese but who regularly eats in Chinese restaurants or frequently makes purchases from the food stores or bakeries of the various Chinatowns in Canada's cities indirectly aids the cohesion of that city's Chinese community. As another example, the thousands of non-group members who year after year visit many of the scores of ethnic "pavillions" in Toronto's annual multiethnic Caravan or in similar celebrations elsewhere aid ethnic cohesion in many groups in two ways. First, the visits to the ethnic pavillions confer both a social and economic legitimation on the ethnocultures of these groups. This assures that the maintenance of the culture will be more readily accepted and respected in the future. Second, the human and material resources required to put on such cultural displays draws on the organizational resources within the ethnic communities and (usually) helps to improve the institutional co-ordination among the ethnic organizations, if only on an informal level.

In myriad ways, therefore, the degree of Institutional Completeness possessed by an ethnic community in each locale can be seen as contributing to the group's cohesion. While most students of ethnicity in Canada would readily admit this generalization as valid, I go further to assert that the extent of institutional development in an ethnic community is becoming increasingly the single most important factor upon which the survival of a group's cohesion and culture depends. In part, this conclusion is based on the lowering language-retention rates and the, perhaps, less-rapid diminishment in the other individualistic and family-based spheres of ethnic cohesion.

Although ethnic organizations in Canada were started by the first sizeable wave of immigrants, the growth of Institutional Completeness has by no means been limited to that era. The immense growth in the number and elaboration of ethnic organizations in the cities of Canada was based only partially in either the original or subsequent immigrants. That is, the increase in the number and specialization of ethnic institutional organizations cannot logically be correlated with a decline in linguistic retention and the other forms of ethnic cohesion, in that loss of cultural attributes would not ordinarily be inversely related to the diversity and vitality of the ethnic organizations.

Instead, I reach a different conclusion: the growth of ethnic organizations parallelling those in the entire city had been slow through to the 1960s. Thereafter, in the 1970s and 1980s, it increased dramatically, first as a stage in the transition experienced by each ethnicity or its subgroup from initial arrival in Canada through adaptation in the constantly-altering situation of the group *in Canada*, to the present time. In short, the expansion and increasing elaboration in institutional development in Canada's ethnic groups is, primarily, a stage—perhaps an inevitable stage—in the adaptation of the ethnocultures to the unique values, structures, processes, and contents of recent Canadian societal life.

Further, I maintain that ethnic Institutional Completeness is the most essential influence on a group's cohesion because it includes all of the physical and formal arenas within which ethnic culture must be utilized and applied if it is to survive as anything more than a set of beliefs and behaviours peculiar to some particular individuals or families. That is to say, ethnic culture must be practised in public situations, be relevant to these public and "formal" interactions, and even be necessary for their conduct as something more than arbitrary personal norms if ethnoculture is to survive in Canada.

Finally, I see Institutional Completeness as being the most critical of the factors affecting ethnic cohesion because it provides a middle-range venue for the practise of ethnoculture. Certainly, the major site of utilizing ethnic cultural attributes or of having interactions on the basis of these is in the innumerable instances of primary relationships between two or more members of the group. By "primary" I mean face-to-face interactions in which the relationship between the participants is one based on kinship, friendship, or some other uniquely ethnic trait (common geographic origin of parents or grandparents, for instance), in which the objective of the interaction is purely personal enjoyment or satisfaction.

The opposite arena of possible interaction among persons of the same ethnicity is in the performance of a role within a formal organization. In this context, ethnoculture is usually irrelevant or ruled out as a consideration influencing the interaction. People whose roles are to represent or/and perform in such formal organizations (place of work, or other "public" roles) are urged to be "objective" regarding ethnicity, that is, to ignore the particularistic feelings and actions connected to the ethnicity of the client, or to use "ethnic" character only in such a way as to serve the client in the manner prescribed by the formal organization. Under such conditions, which make up a considerable portion of people's days, the ethnic cultural prescription for variant ideation and behaviour is contrary to mainstream formal organizational role performance.

Ethnic organizations, however, comprise a middle ground in which ethnoculture is of special salience, even within a "formal" organizational structure. In this intermediate arena of behaviour, part of the reason for the client/consumer presence is ethnic identity and the goal (even if not conscious) of participation in ethnocultural behaviour. And, this ethnic interaction is conducted within the context of a formal organization, with all of the high potential for meeting the varied expectations of people that formal organizations possess because of their "formal" resource and administrative foundation.

Thus, in the ethnic organization(s) the most favourable set of circumstances exists for assuring ethnic cohesion and cultural maintenance. The ethnic culture is the "script" for interactions, and a formal structure enables the responsiveness, permanence, and sufficiency of service that is demanded. Usually, antithetical kinds of ethnic resources are combined and operate in a mutually reinforcing fashion.

As well as being a significant instrument for adults to use and preserve their heritage, ethnic institutions are also important in developing ethnic cohesion among the young, who are much more susceptible to a tendency to reject their parents' culture or to be assimilated away from it. As Reitz (1980: 223) has inferred, parental participation in ethnic organizations would serve as a socialization model for the young. Language retention would be encouraged, along with participation in the ethnic religion. And also, perhaps, ethnic group members would be encouraged to reside close to the sites of multiple ethnic organizations (or these institutions would spring up in proximity to residential concentrations of ethnic group members). High institutional completeness in an ethnic community, therefore, can create the context within which the ethnoculture becomes relevant in all facets of life. Since "private" primary-relationship utilization of the ethnic culture carries only a small portion of this great social potential for sustaining ethnoculture, the formal organizations collectively should be considered as having the most important influence on the cultural survival of ethnic groups in every part of Canada.

RESEARCH

The above assertion, i.e., that of all the media of ethnic cohesion Institutional Completeness is the most important, is based on theoretical and personal estimation of the ethnic scene as observed in Metropolitan Toronto and, more directly, in the research reports of University of Toronto students on many ethnic groups in the Toronto CMA. Ideally, analytical judgments are based on comprehensive research by seasoned investigators, but to my knowledge, there have been very few studies of Institutional Completeness in Canada.

The first, of course, was Breton's (1964) study on Montreal's ethnic groups in the latter 1950s. Breton's data indicated that certain groups could be ranked empirically as having a high degree of institutional development: Greeks, Germans, French, Italians, and Ukrainians, among others. The Danish, English, Portuguese, Swedish, and West Indian communities earned a low ranking. However, since ethnic schools and voluntary organizations were not included and because these findings reflect the situation nearly three decades ago, they must be received with caution. Montreal and its ethnic groups have changed considerably, especially because of the later extensive Asian, Haitian, and Portuguese immigration. Then, too, one must consider that Montreal is a unique metropolis.

Interestingly, however, Driedger and Church's (1974) report utilizing 1961 census data on Winnipeg ethnic groups and original information on their ethnic institutional development and activities, yielded results that parallelled Breton's rankings. In addition, Driedger's (1975; 1976) data from University of Manitoba students in 1971 on their own ethnic-group behaviour led to essentially the same conclusions as Breton's about the extent of Institutional Completeness—despite the differences in date and locale.

To my knowledge, these are the only Canadian studies to have been conducted on the broad range of ethnic organizations in and of themselves. There have been a few studies which require inferences about Institutional Completeness because they each focus on respondents' participation in or utilization of ethnic institutions. The first of these is in an exceptionally competent and interesting book by Reitz (1980: 215–225). If we can accept the inference that the use of ethnic institutions accurately reflects their existence, then Reitz's national data is informative. Participation in ethnic institutions was highest among the Southern Europeans of Reitz's sample, with an average of nearly one-third being quite highly involved in some way. Next came the Chinese; more than one-quarter were highly participant. About one-sixth of Eastern Europeans and less than one-tenth of Northern Europeans were as highly involved. The charter ethnicities were excluded from the study.

Thus, Reitz's results could be interpreted as demonstrating marked differences between these four ethnic categories. Unfortunately, this potentially valuable source of information on ethnic structure did not include anything concerning the Jewish, visible minorities other than the Chinese, or, as noted, the charter groups. Despite that, comprehensive correlational analysis established the importance of (participation in) ethnic organizations for respondents' within-group interaction and their sense of ethnic identity; the institutional participation was more important, in fact, than generation/years in Canada, years of education, and ethnic workplace combined (Reitz, 1980: 224).

Isajiw's (1981) report on ethnic identity retention among eight ethnic groups in Metropolitan Toronto provided a rather different perspective on institutional development, if one is willing to infer institutional topography from reported frequencies of use of certain ethnic community resources. Four particular aspects from Isajiw's much longer ethnic identity list are of interest here: (1) attendance at ethnic-group functions such as parties, picnics, dances, rallies, lectures, and concerts; (2) use of ethnic-group sponsored vacation facilities such as, resorts or summer camps; (3) tuning in to ethnic radio or TV programs; and (4) reading ethnic newspapers, magazines and so on. The data were analyzed by generation in Canada; there were three groups (Blacks, Chinese, and Portuguese) in which data were only on the immigrant generation. Isajiw's findings have been reproduced here, his information reorganized, and averages calculated over the four kinds of institutional activity (Table 9.1).

If we attend to the levels within the immigrant generation as, first of all, imputing to the degree of institutional development, we discern extreme interethnic differentiation, with equally great intra-ethnicity variation between the four institutional activities. In every ethnicity here, one of the institutional practices is either much higher or much lower than the others. Whether this differentiation pattern reflects actual variations in the degree of institutional development among the various ethnic groups in Toronto or differing degrees of utilization of what exists is not completely clear. However, judging from the variations within the two Canadian-born generations, which tend to be a more extreme set of departures from the immigrant members of the groups, I suspect that Isajiw's data is more about degree of utilization than degree of institutional development within each of the ethnic communities. In the absence of other, let alone better, data, though, Isajiw's figures are both interesting and instructive.

Table 9.1
Isajiw's Findings (in %) Concerning Ethnic Institutional Practices in Toronto, by Generation in Canada

Ethnicity & Generation		% Utilization of Institutional Resource				
		Ethgroup Functions	Ethgroup Facilities	Ethnic Radio-TV	Print Media	Average
BLACK	1st	65	4	66	68	51
BRITISH	1st	22	39	71	40	43
	2nd	24	13	56	21	28
	3rd,+	24	6	33	18	20
CHINESE	1st	22	2	49	69	35
GERMAN	1st	19	1	49	42	28
	2nd	16	1	5	3	6
	3rd,+	1	1	1	1	1
ITALIAN	1st	72	17	89	73	62
	2nd	35	4	25	14	29
	3rd,+	8	2	20	2	8
JEWISH	1st	54	21	40	66	45
	2nd	50	27	29	60	41
	3rd,+	41	34	30	52	32
PORTUGUESE	1st	45	50	35	23	38
UKRAINIAN	1st	71	47	54	64	59
	2nd	58	16	34	23	33
	3rd,+	36	2	4	1	11

Source: W.W. Isajiw. *Ethnic Identity Retention*. (Toronto: University of Toronto Centre for Urban and Community Studies, 1981), pp. 26–35.

In addition, Kalbach's fascinating (1981) analysis of the correlation of residential segregation in the groups in the Toronto Ethnic Pluralism Study with ethnic behaviour, if imputationally interpreted, builds a solid relationship between residential and institutional patterns (pp. 54–61). Even with these three recent studies by Reitz, Isajiw, and Kalbach, there is still a very scant basis for determining the degree of ethnic Institutional Completeness throughout Canada or even in any one urban site today. Breton's original work suggested both a method for recording data and several of the various kinds of ethnic institutions that can exist in Canada, but he specifically emphasized the rather severe limitations of his work. However, a complete model for conducting such investigations does not, to my knowledge, exist; and it is this deficiency that will first be addressed before going on to any further data on specific ethnic institutions.*

---

*Rather than await interminably for someone else to publish the directions for conducting such study, to provide my students with a procedure by which they could conceptualize their own ethnic community's institutions more completely, I long ago devised an outline of the various kinds of ethnic institutions and presented the information in lectures. In response, both of the first two years I did this, several students sought my aid in conducting their course research on the degree of Institutional Completeness in their ethnic communities. Thus, to the outline of institutions, I added several factors that they and I believed were central to any research about the topic.

This set of institutions, variables to describe each institution's nature, and a method to collect such data—which I over-dignify here with the term of "model"—has been utilized by hundreds of students from over two dozen specific ethno-racial-religious groups (e.g., Croatian, Lebanese Palestinian, Guyanese, Goan, Filipino, Welsh (and all the other three main British ethnicities), various kinds of Chinese (e.g., Singaporean, Malaysian, Hong Kong, West Indian Canadian-born), Sikh, Sephardic Jewish, Azorean Portuguese, Maltese, Slovenian, etc., etc.) plus all the other more major ethnic identities one finds in such an ethnically diverse place like Toronto.

Having been applied for several years now, with quite good results—as judged by their verbal and written comments and their completed studies—my "model" would seem to offer decided advantages to those interested in the study of Institutional Completeness especially in comparison to the lack of any other recent guidelines for investigating this topic. Some such methodology is required, of course, because the Canadian Census collects no information at all relating to this most central of ethnic topics. While Statistics Canada and some other federal or provincial agencies may collect some kinds of relevant information, with perhaps two exceptions (to be considered later in this chapter), I have not seen reference to such in any of the Canadian literature on ethnicity.

So, we do seem to need something like my model.

A MODEL FOR RESEARCH INTO ETHNIC INSTITUTIONAL COMPLETENESS

This model has three parts: (1) a listing of the institutions any Canadian ethnic group potentially can develop, (2) a few central dimensions (variables) relevant to each ethnic institution, and (3) a methodology by which such research can be conducted. They will be dealt with here in the reverse order.

Methodology for Information Collection

The best methods for collecting material about any group's institutional development should be generally intelligible and capable of execution by people who are not necessarily skilled academicians. Indeed, the simpler the methods are, the greater and better will be the information elicited.

For anyone interested in collecting data (i.e., any kind of information) on one's own ethnic group in his or her locale, the task begins with a listing of the institutions or ethnic organizations with which that person has had personal experience. Also to be recorded at this earliest stage are potential contact persons with whom to discuss each institution, again drawn from one's own knowledge and experience. Parents and relatives who reside in the same geographic area are valuable initial informants who can amplify the researcher's own experiences.

The basic technique thereafter is one that survey researchers call "snowballing": the procedure whereby one collects more information from each later source, depending on earlier sources to point one toward these other informants. Beginning with the information dredged from one's own and kin's or neighbours' knowledge and experiences, the researcher asks (him/herself and others) who would be a good informant on one or more of the organizations or entire institutions already known. Using the variables listed below to inquire about as many of the institutions about which this second-stage informant is knowledgeable, the investigator at some point seeks to identify third-stage informants to go to next.

By the time the researchers have gotten around to the second-stage informants, they should also have checked the telephone books (white and yellow pages), other secular directories, and any existing ethnic-group directory for the names, locations, and phone numbers of ethnic organizations of which they, their relatives and neighbours were unaware or which they had not remembered.

This amplified list of ethnic organizations provides the basis for later questioning in two ways: first, informants at each later stage are asked about ethnic organizations on the list in their institutional sector. Data should be collected on each organization on the central list of each informant, until the investigator deems that sufficient information has been collected on a particular organization; second, each informant should be asked about any defunct or currently operating organizations not on the list.

From the second stage through to the completion of the data-collection process, the same basic procedures are followed: eliciting from informants (1) data on organizations already known to the researcher, (2) the names of and information about ethnic organizations not yet known to the researcher, and (3) other informants to whom the researcher can go. Of course, the executives or other officers of ethnic organizations should be interviewed and will often prove to be among the most valuable informants.

For the investigator interested in the institutional development within two or more ethnic groups, the procedures are essentially the same as those for studying only one ethnicity, except that they must be repeated for each group studied. Ideally, the researcher will have fellow investigators for this multi-ethnic study, drawn from the respective ethnicities being studied. The process then is simply that described above for one ethnic investigation, carried out simultaneously for each of the different groups.

The object, whether one or many groups are being studied, is to obtain as complete a list of past and present ethnic organizations as is possible by interviewing as many persons as possible and using as informants those people suggested by prior informants. Through carefully planned interviews, a great wealth of explicit information can be collected, especially when one is prepared and able to follow up adventitious leads given by informants.

Research Dimensions for Ethnic Institutional Sectors

Most people interested in an ethnic group's institutional development will want to detail far more than a mere list of organizations in each institutional sector. The objective of the dimensions discussed below is to provide both a sense of the temporal shifts in institutional development within the group and an elaboration of existing ethnic organizations. (Table 9.2).

Diversity

Within each institutional sector, one interest is in the extent of current and past diversity in that sector. First, there is what might be termed *demographic diversity* within the institution, in terms of use or development by different generations (i.e., youth-adults-seniors; immigrant, second, third and later), periods of immigration, gender, income levels, religion, language, and so on. Second, there is diversity in *identity*, ideology, or focus of the different organizations that make up the institution (e.g., different religions, alliances with the home country, information versus action).

Number of Organizations

Among the most important variables is the *number* of discrete organizations that, in toto, make up each particular institutional sector. The number can vary from none or only one of a particular type, to literally hundreds in a community (e.g., ethnic funeral homes, retail grocery stores). Unless there are only a relative few organizations of a particular sort, the most precise information available may be only of an approximate nature (i.e., "between 15 and 20," "about 30," "at least 150").

Participation in the Institution/Organization

Another very necessary kind of information concerns the degree of participation, especially with respect to the resources available in the organization or entire institutional sector. The first aspect deals with as accurate an estimate as possible of the *percent of* the ethnicity's *members* in the area that *use* or belong to the organization (or institution). Sometimes actual membership figures are available, but, usually, estimates of the number or proportion of ethnic-group members can be obtained.

Second, the *membership* or utilization numbers should be *related to the amount of resources* possessed by the organization or institution. Again, the best characterization will often be an ordinal approximation. A recommended continuum of resource utilization is one beginning with "very much underutilized" through "good match

Table 9.2
Model for Analysis of Ethnic-Group Institutional Completeness

Time and Analytical Dimension		Institutional Sector								
		Religious	Educational	Economic	Social & Recreational	Media	Arts & Cultural	Governance	Health & Social Service	Political
Past	Founded									
	Other Historical									
Present	Diversity									
	Number of Organizations									
	Functions									
	Financing									
	Stage of Organizational Evolution									
Future	Trendline									
	Desirable Outcomes									

Ethnic Group: _____

between clients and resources" and "utilized to limit of resources," to "resources stretched beyond reasonable limits" or "more resources very much required."

Function(s) of the Organization/Institution

Central to the study of any organization or institutional sector of an ethnic group is the nature of its function, over and above being part of a general social form of activity. First in mind here is the extent to which an organization's function is exceptionally *specialized* (supplying one particular service) or, at the other end of the continuum, exceptionally broad (conducting many, quite varied activities within the same organization/institution).

There is another, very different, element that should also be considered: whether the function of the organization is *solely intra-ethnic*: only members of the ethnic group are addressed or permitted to utilize the organization (this can be characterized as "centripetal"); a *combination* of intra- and extra-ethnic; *or solely extra-ethnic:* the organization's function is to explain the ethnicity to non-group members, or to adapt the ethnicity to external conditions (this can be characterized as "centrifugal").

Financing

Obviously, financing of an ethnic organization is critical to that organization and to its constituency. Even so, financial information is often among the most difficult to obtain, and this applies to more than just dollar amounts. Nevertheless, there are two dimensions about which informants are likely to have some knowledge.

The first of these is the *number and identity of financial sources* for the organization/institution. Obviously, the number of income sources can move upward beyond two or three to over a dozen, perhaps. Sources can also be as individually-based as voluntary contributions; membership fees; fees for service (e.g., counselling, training, daycare); or can be from very complex formal sources, such as The United Way, government grants or contracts, corporation payments for services rendered, and the like.

The other factor that should be considered is the extent to which *income* is *sufficient to meet the costs* of existing services and, beyond that, to start up new services demanded by the organization's clients/consumers.

Stage of Organizational Evolution

By "organizational evolution" I mean something akin to, but more than, *life-stage* of the organization. The kind of datum appropriate to this variable is location of the organization (or institution) on a continuum that extends from "new, just developing" through such characterizations as "mature," "wide-ranging," "active," and/or "vital," to "defunct," "moribund," "obsolete," and so on. Obviously, what this variable aims to assess is the the point in the life of an organization that seems apt to describe its current social foundations and level of functioning, in addition to the organization's life-stage.

Temporal Perspective

We readily recognize that, while it can be difficult to elicit information about the current nature and operations of ethnic organizations and institutional sectors, it is considerably more difficult to collect data about the same or similar organizations in the past. Yet, the historical dimension ranging from the group's origins in Canada or the particular location of interest through to the future is implicit in any work aiming to understand the change and adaptation of Canadian ethnic groups. We cannot escape the social fact that any extant ethnic organization or institution is, in a very real way, merely the existential reflection of an entity in a time-space field that stretches back in years and ahead to future history.

Looking to the *past* of an organization or institutional sector, one should, first of all, find out the exact or approximate date of foundation. This can also be related to the group's history of immigration or to the particular locale of interest. Second, one should then inquire into the history of each of the other variables described above. Quite often, the most helpful informants are those especially knowledgeable about the organization's (institution's) history.*

The *present* status of ethnic organizations or an entire institutional sector has already been covered above. This description is intended as no more than an outline of the most central aspects. While I naturally hope that others will use this scheme, investigators ought also adapt the scheme for their own use—excluding some aspects, adding others.*

---

*As a personal note, I would be exceptionally interested in learning about experiences others have had in researching Institutional Completeness, either using my model or another scheme.

It is difficult to gather sufficient, pertinent information to present an adequate history of the past, but it is unquestionably more of a problem to predict the *future* of an ethnic organization or institution. Mainly because, to do so, one must have the ethnic group's own perspective on itself and its institutions firmly in mind. At the same time, the investigator must also be able to take the detailed information collected about the past and future possibilities and apply the "objective" theoretical framework implied in this kind of data-collection, to interpret the reasons for the founding and later experience of the organization (or institution).

Given that, the group's phenomenological (i.e., its own particular) perspective on its past and present organizational life must be melded with the "objective" research perspective on the group. That accomplished, this combined summary of the past leading to the present must be extended to draw a picture of the future. This task is obviously more easily and accurately accomplished if a member of the ethnic group being studied has participated closely in the research. Moreover, it could be of immense benefit for the investigator to take advantage of the interpretive and predictive sensibilities of several people from the ethnicity.

In addition to these considerations, there are two more regarding the prediction of the future for the ethnicity's Institutional Completeness in its various sectors. The first might be described as projecting the existing pattern into the future, using both the ethnic-phenomenological and "objective" perspectives.

The second manner of prediction is more complex. It requires, first of all, ascertaining the objectives desired by the ethnic group (or subsets of it, as well as non-group members?) of its institutional network. Such goals should be carefully identified in as much detail as possible. Then, the investigator (and ethnic colleagues) can analyze what must be changed, if anything, in the operation of the ethnic institutions to achieve the goals determined earlier. This latter process is akin to corporate and government planning procedures that attempt to match goals to organizational structure and processes. It also seems to be similar to the model applied by most royal commissions, although the emphasis here on the importance of the ethnic perspective in formulating ethnic-group ends/means formulae derives directly from my belief in an ethnic-relativistic approach to analyzing Canadian ethnic groups, rather than from any inclination to follow the procedures of government commissions.

The steps involved in applying an ethnic-group perspective are: (1) identification of desirable future institutional patterns and objectives; (2) determination of exactly how such future patterns and goals represent differences from the current patterns of institutional operations; (3) deciding who (persons, subsets of the ethnicity, particular organizations, etc.) must do what and when they must do it, to achieve the altered patterns or goals; and (4) a reasonable estimate, if possible, on the likelihood of effecting the changes necessary to achieve the desired outcomes. Alternative strategy determination can also be built into the future-shifting process as a kind of "feedback" tactic.

Underlying this latter action-oriented process of estimating and altering the future, is the conviction that members of ethnic groups cannot merely await the future, but must take an active role in shaping it to their particular wants and needs. This perspective suggests that the future does *not* unfold as it should, but, instead, that ethnic-group visions for their future and the willingness to mobilize members to alter the shape and direction of change are the true desiderata of ethnic institutional life in Canada. Indeed, this perspective on the future of ethnic Institutional Completeness must be at the fount of ethnic transitions in this country from an immigrant to a made-in-Canada ethnoculture.

Ethnic Institutional Sectors

This discussion of ethnic institutional sectors is founded on the definition of Institutional Completeness as the existence of organizations and institutions developed by and for the ethnic group and operating parallel to the usual social institutions for the entire population of a nation, province, region or city. This, goes far beyond the variety of "institutions" studied by Breton, Driedger (either alone or with colleagues), Isajiw, Kalbach or, I believe, anyone else in Canada who has written about or studied the network of ethnic institutions.

The only institutions that are excluded from this analysis of ethnic institutions are the family and marriage, and other primary-group attachments that make up family and neighbourhood life. These are, however, covered in earlier portions of this book, under Residential Concentration (as implying ethnic neighbourhoods) and Endogamy (relating to the institution of the family).

As I have developed it over the years, the "Institutional Completeness" of an ethnic group in Canada involves nine distinct institutions. Each will be described briefly and particular analytic elements will be pointed to. Table 9.2 provides a prototype data-collection form, combining the various institutions with the several variables listed in the left margin of Table 9.2 and discussed above.

Religious

Harney (1978) has characterized the religious institution of an ethnic group as "a series of rings—circles of activity and organization" surrounding the functions of pastoral and ritual services. At the core is a house of religion as a physical presence and a moral and theological entity. Around this core are rings of diverse activities: educational, social, and cultural and those which affect work, housing, and businesses. From the house of religion there may emerge a credit union, the perception of a need for ethnic undertakers, florists, printers, and so on. Under its auspices, ethnic theatre, language and cultural education, ethnic media (Harney, 1978), and even political rallies may take place. Thus, a central point of interest in the religious institution is in the variety of functions carried out under its aegis and the degree to which this institution overlaps with others in the ethnic community.

Another obvious focal point is the number of different religions represented within the entire institutional sector and the relative importance of each therein. As is obvious from the patterns of Religious Monopoly, there are tides of religious affiliation within Canadian ethnicities, and these have direct bearing on the stage of organizational (and institutional) evolution, as well as on financing and participation, and temporal trends and outcomes (i.e., concern with secular-social needs in addition to the sacred).

Educational

As indicated in the discussion about the religious sector, the educational institution in an ethnic group can overlap with another institution: religious, social/recreational, arts/cultural among others. Moreover, ethnic educational services today are in part conducted by the tax-supported "public" schools (including the "separate" schools in Ontario and elsewhere). Five provinces permit heritage-language courses in the tax-supported schools, some, like Alberta, permit these during the regular school hours, but others, like Ontario, only in "After-4" hours. Alberta, in fact, has over a ten-year history of bilingual education programs in languages other than French/English (primarily German/English and Ukrainian/English). In these programs the unofficial language is used as the language of instruction over half the day, unlike those of Ontario in which instruction in an unofficial language is prohibited. But even in Ontario's After-4 Heritage-Language Programme, it is obvious that, while the language is being taught, various ethnic cultural and historical data are also conveyed within the secular (non-ethnic) educational system.

This is certainly quite different from what existed for past generations of ethnic youth, whose only source of linguistic and cultural education was from an ethnic educational institution. Thus, the temporal patterns here may be of principal concern, although it will be important to collect information about the remaining variables.

Economic

There are two distinct lines of analysis that should be followed in delineating the parameters of the ethnic economy. The first is the extent to which an "ethnic sub-economy" or "ethnic economic concentration" may exist in an ethnic community. Reitz (1980: 154–156; 1981) calls this "ethnic job segregation," meaning the concentration of ethnic-group members in one occupational or industrial sector. Reitz would have us consider such economic concentration as having invidious status distinctions for the ethnic-group jobholders so concentrated, even though he himself pointed to the distinct benefits from this for Italians and Jewish (1981: 59–63). In any case, this first aspect centres on this kind of occupational/industrial concentration, e.g., Italians in construction and Jewish in the professions.

The second line of analysis to be followed in delineating the parameters of the ethnic economy is the diversity of economic organizations and businesses that exist for the ethnic group's members. This includes, in part: ethnic banking and credit-union services, import-export services, retail outlets (grocery, furniture, books, bakery, clothing, hardware, etc.), insurance, real estate, construction/renovation companies, personal services, and the myriad other kinds of business services that are possible. In

Toronto, and other places, several ethnic communities annually publish directories of their very many economic outlets and services, indicative of the very great diversification and specialization in ethnic economies.

Social and Recreational

In this institutional sector are the various services, organizations, and companies that parallel the recreation industry for the total regional or city population. This includes such things as ethnic restaurants, ethnic performing arts (theatre, motion pictures, and music), ethnic fine arts, voluntary clubs (card-playing, crafts, cultural, sports), community centres, and the like.

To some extent, several of the organizations in the social and recreational institution overlap with the economic and/or arts and cultural institutional sectors. This can produce analytic problems; nevertheless, this is the way things are; economics or culture are often inseparable elements. In some ethnic communities, moreover, both institutions are essential to an enterprise. For other ethnic groups, the perspective may be to carefully categorize something as either economic, or social and recreational; whereas in still others, the cultural identification or combined cultural-economic (or cultural-social and recreational) will have primacy. These kinds of ethnic semantics are of much less concern from a research perspective than the adequate identification and analysis of the disparate parts of what a particular ethnic community in a locale will define as being within its social and recreational institution.

Media

To be covered within the ethnic media rubric are: print, radio, and television. Considering only print, the indices of frequency of issue (daily, weekly, etc.), financial sources, and circulation are of particular analytic concern. With respect to radio and TV, the number of different programs, hours per week, and whether programs are carried on the "free" stations, or on cable are of concern. In Toronto, for instance, many groups have programs on the free radio and TV stations, while many of the same ethnicities and others produce programs that are carried on Channel 10, the "community-service" channel of the cable company, and/or on the subscription-only pay channels (e.g., Chinavision, Latinovision). In addition, the Greek community, for one, has a radio cable medium that serves Greek businesses and restaurants for about 18 hours a day.

Relating to both the print and the radio/TV media are the analytic factors of: the language(s) employed, the extent of the "centripetal" versus "centrifugal" focus of content—that is, the extent to which the media content addresses the ethnicity in the city/province/Canada/country of origin alone, versus the degree to which an interethnic perspective is communicated. Within the internally-directed (centripetal) focus, we can differentiate between content that addresses the homeland alone versus content on the ethnic group in Canada.

Perhaps because of federal supervision of at least a part of the ethnic media, statistical information on the media is the only hard data on ethnic institutions available for at least one province (Ontario, in this case), let alone the nation. There is good early information from the Royal Commission on Bilingualism and Biculturalism on AM radio (the commonest kind) broadcasts in unofficial languages for 1966 in Ontario (Table 9.3). Tables 9.4 and 9.5 furnish information first on the radio and TV ethnic programming (in both the official and unofficial languages) in 1981 (again for Ontario alone); and a comparison of ethnic radio programming changes from 1966 to 1981 within Ontario. The information is suggestive, more than definitive, providing an indication of change in one province. While it is limited in temporal and geographic coverage, it does offer some answer to the question about the magnitude of change that has taken place in the use of the airwaves by ethnic groups.

It should be noted that there were a dozen ethno-racial-religious groups (Table 9.4) who had radio programming in Ontario in 1981, but none in 1966. Thus, in the 15 years following 1966, about one-third of the groups gained radio programming probably for the first time. And, as Table 9.5 shows, only Finnish, Hungarian, and Ukrainian airtime decreased during that 15-year period in Ontario. At the other end of the spectrum, Asian, Croatian, Greek, Macedonian, and Spanish-Portuguese programming hours expanded over five magnitudes in this period, largely reflecting the immense increase in membership in most of these groups during the post-1971 period. What these data do not convey is information about the content of these ethnic media.

Table 9.3
Number of Program Hours Broadcast in Unofficial Languages
on Ontario AM Radio Stations, by Ethnic-Group Language, 1966

Ethnic Language

	Arabic	Croatian	Czech/Slov	Dutch	Finnish	German	Greek
Hours	0	2.02	.25	2.42	3.75	27.55	9.5

	Hungarian	Italian	Japanese	Lithuanian	Macedonian	Polish	Spanish & Portuguese
Hours	1.92	61.25	.5	0	1.0	1.05	2.17

	Russian	Serbian	Scandinavian	Ukrainian	Yiddish & Hebrew	All Groups
Hours	0	1.5	0	8.2	0	125.57

Note: Groups not listed had no broadcast time in Ontario
Source: Royal Commission on Bilingualism and Biculturalism. *Report: Book 4* (Ottawa: Information Canada, 1970), pp. 344–345.

Table 9.4

Ethnic Non-English/French Broadcasting in Ontario, 1981 (in Hours/Week)

Ethno-Racial-Religious Group

Medium	Arabic	Armenian	Asian	Cambodian	Chinese	East Indian	Japanese	Korean	Vietnamese
Radio	4.50	1.00	27.25	0.00	2.00	24.25	.50	.50	0.00
TV	1.00	1.00	18.50	1.00	4.00	10.00**	1.00	1.00	1.00
Total	5.50	2.00	45.75	1.00	6.00	34.25**	1.50	1.50	1.00

	Austrian	Belgian	Black ##	Bulgarian	Celtic	Croatian	Czechoslovak	Dutch	Filipino
Radio	1.00	.92	0.00	2.08	5.00	14.00	1.00	6.50	.75
TV	1.00	0.00	3.00	1.50	.50	2.25	3.75	2.00	2.00 #
Total	2.00	.92	3.00	3.58	5.50	16.25	4.75	8.50	2.75 #

	Finnish	German	Greek	Hungarian	Italian	Islamic	Jewish	Lebanese	Lithuanian
Radio	2.50	54.92	188.00	1.42	114.83	0.00	5.17	.50	.50
TV	2.50**	5.25	9.50**	1.00	22.00**#	.50	4.50 #	0.00**	0.00**
Total	5.00**	60.17	197.50**	2.42	136.83**#	.50	9.67 #	50**	.50**

	Macedonian	Maltese	Native Peoples	Polish	Portuguese	Romanian	Russian	Scandinavian
Radio	2.75	.50	12.67	11.50	129.50	2.00	1.50	0.00
TV	2.00	2.50	1.00 #	6.00 #	17.50**	1.75	.50	2.50
Total	4.75	3.00	13.67 #	17.50 #	147.00**	3.75	2.00	2.50

	Spanish	Swiss	Turkish	Ukrainian	West Indian	Yugoslav	All Non-Eng/French Groups
Radio	6.50	0.00 #	2.00	7.83	6.50	7.50	623.09#
TV	2.50	0.00 #	0.00 #	5.50 #	1.50	1.50	128.75**#
Total	9.00	0.00 #	2.00 #	13.33 #	8.00	9.00	791.84**#

Notes: "non-English/French" refers to ethno-cultural, *not* language of broadcast; Totals include time for "South Asian" and "Lutheran" programs.
** Plus "occasional" programming on other stations.
# Plus unspecified hours of programming per week by other TV companies.
Does not include West Indian programming.
Source: Multicultural Programme: *Broadcasting Guide to Programmes for Ethnocultural Communities in Ontario*. (Toronto: Ontario Ministry of Culture and Recreation, 1981).

The shifts among ethnic newspapers have also been charted, fortunately for almost a century (Table 9.6). Not surprisingly, the largest increases in the number of ethnic newspapers have been over the past two decades and for the Chinese, Greeks, Italians, and probably, the Portuguese (for whom there is only fragmentary evidence). Some groups—Germans, Hungarians, and Scandinavians—actually declined in the number of newspapers after 1965, probably reflecting their cultural paths due to lowered immigration during this period and/or a declining ethnic cohesion.

However, the number of newspapers and the hours of broadcasting constitute only two of the many more variables that are necessary to describe adequately the nature of the ethnic media in Canada.*

Arts and Cultural

Once more, this institutional sector may be perceived as overlapping with the social and recreational institution or the ethnic economy—indeed, in some groups it is likely they will be subsumed under one or the other. Be that as it may, this sector does, from an "objective" comparative perspective, warrant attention equal to any other institutional area.

In this sector are categorized the performing and fine arts, both in terms of the content itself and in the ethnic organizations that bring their culture to the group's members (and often to those in other ethnicities as well). Other kinds of organizations in this sector are the culturally-edifying societies named after ethnic illuminati: the Goethe Society, the Dante Society, the Copernican Association, and so on, whose functions are akin to those of the Royal Society of Canada or the Learned Societies—to sponsor reports about significant elements of the Canadian society.

The analytic dimensions—other than the number of each type of arts and cultural organizations—are the nature of the functions, the frequency of productions for their ethnic constituencies, and the degree of participation by members of the ethnicity.*

---

*Additional perspectives on the analysis of one aspect of ethnic arts and culture can be drawn from *Polyphony* 5 (Fall-Winter, 1983): 2, on ethnic theatre in Canada.

Table 9.5

Longitudinal Change Indices between 1966 and 1981 In Ethnic Program
Hours Broadcast on Ontario Radio Stations, by Ethnic-Group Language

Ethnic Group

Change Index	Asian	Japanese	Croatian	Czech/Slov	Dutch	Finnish	German
# Hours	26.75	0	11.98	.75	4.08	-1.25	27.37
Ratio: 1981/1966	5450	100	693	400	268	67	199

	Greek	Hungarian	Italian	Macedonian	Spanish & Portuguese	Ukrainian	All Groups
# Hours	178.50	-.5	53.58	1.75	133.83	-.37	497.52
Ratio: 1981/1966	1979	74	187	275	6267	95	496

Note: to the the extent the 1981/1966 Ratio exceeds 100, the 1981 hours of programming exceeded the 1966 hours; to the extent the 1981–1966 ratio was below 100, the 1981 hours of programming were less than the 1966 hours.

Source: Tables 9.3 and 9.4 (above)

Table 9.6

Number of Ethnic Newspapers Among Canadian Ethno-Racial-Religious Groups, 1892–1981

Ethnicity	1892	1905	1911	1921	1931	1941	1951	1959	1965	1981
Baltic groups**	*	*	*	*	*	*	1	10	8	8
Chinese	*	*	1	1	2	2	2	5	6	9
Dutch	*	*	*	*	*	*	*	12	10	10
German	13	11	14	4	8	6	5	20	12	17
Greek	*	*	*	*	*	*	*	2	5	11
Hungarian	*	*	1	1	2	1	1	6	9	6
Italian	*	*	2	5	3	3	*	8	11	23
Japanese	*	*	2	2	1	1	*	2	3	5
Jewish	*	*	2	3	9	11	12	12	15	19
Polish	*	1	1	2	2	3	3	4	6	5
Portuguese	*	*	*	*	*	*	*	1	3	*
Russian	*	*	*	*	1	1	1	2	3	*
Scandinavian	2	9	13	9	10	7	6	7	8	6
Spanish	*	*	*	*	*	*	*	*	*	4
Ukrainian	*	1	1	6	7	9	8	36	32	20
Other groups	0	0	9	9	20	21	22	62	75	108
Total	18	22	37	34	49	48	43	148	155	251

Notes: * No Data.

** Includes Estonian, Latvian and Lithuanian.

Totals undoubtedly represent an undercount.

Sources: Royal Commission on Bilingualism and Biculturalism. *Report: Book 4* (Ottawa: Information Canada, 1970), p. 342; S. Zybala. Problems of Survival for the Ethnic Press in Canada. *Polyphony* 4,1: 27.

Governance

By "governance" is meant the organization(s) or other form of structure that claims to provide leadership for the ethnic community, to establish its policies and "laws", and to aid in the administration of the ethnicity. The nearest secular (extra-ethnic) analogy is that of elected government, whether municipal, provincial or federal.

Of particular importance in this institution are: (1) the diversity of leaders in terms of their occupational identities, organizational origins and/or constituencies; (2) the degree of solidarity among the various participants in governance of the ethnic group; (3) the degree of democratic processes underlying the actual governance practices (e.g., oligarchy or dictatorship versus election by the grass-roots membership of the group). Breton (1981) illuminated many of these aspects with survey data from the Toronto Ethnic Pluralism Study.

Perhaps also within the scope of ethnic governance (but likely also in the purview of ethnic health and social services) is the policy-planning and implementation function. Some ethnic groups in particular locations have developed a special organization or committee to determine group policy and programs, and the strategies by which these can be achieved. Sometimes this function is clearly separate from the governors of the group; at other times it is a constituent part of that assembly.

A final aspect of governance is whether the governance of the ethnic membership is formed by the federation of the various other ethnic organizations—a member from the directorial board of each of the ethnic organizations being formally assigned to represent the particular organization in a separate governance association. This is a somewhat critical issue in ethnic-group governance because it is usually such a governing body (or several such bodies if it is the semi-misfortune of the group to have more than one governing source) that makes representations to governmental and funding agencies, upon which ethnic-group institutions are becoming increasingly dependent.

If there is governance within a group by self-appointed, often competing persons or organizations, this has definite implications for the likelihood of success in achieving desired outcomes within the ethnicity. Thus, the several aspects of structure and process in ethnic governance deserve close and careful assessment.

Health and Social Services

Undoubtedly, the origin of ethnic health and social services is found in the mutual-benefit societies developed to serve the first large waves of immigrants into Canada. Harney (1979) has noted that, although the creation of these societies by members of the ethnic group answered socio-economic and ritual problems first (funeral costs, sickness or accident insurance, then home loans and credit), they also spoke to the dignity and morale of both individual immigrants and the ethnic group collectively. Apparently begun in the late nineteenth and early twentieth centuries, these mutual-benefit societies had goals as varying as the ethnicities and locales; however, some groups seem never to have instituted such an organization (Harney, 1979).*

To meet changing needs, the ethnic mutual-aid society was founded to assist members of the group in those aspects of life in which family, church or the host society did not, could not or would not provide help. Today, the spirit of these first ethnic social-service agencies has expanded to comprise the rationale for many different kinds of potential services. Included in this institution are ethnic physicians whose practice is wholly or partly of the ethnicity; attorneys, dentists, and other professionals—of the group and serving the group.

At a more formal level of structure, other possible health and social services can include ethnic health clinics (e.g., pre-natal and post-partum, well-baby and family-health clinics, herbal or other traditional health care); individual or family counselling agencies; senior-citizen services or residences; immigrant-aid agencies; income-supplement services; translation-interpreter services; vocational counselling and/or occupational education services. At a still higher level of function there may be a community development agency, or agencies, whose purpose is to enhance the linguistic, cultural or other aspects of the group's social well-being, or the integration of the ethnicity more adequately into the city or region as a whole.

Of special concern here may well be something other than the existence of a particular kind of service—its absence. Another kind

---

*Further historical observations on eleven groups and their societies in different places are contained in a special issue of *Polyphony* 2 (Winter, 1979): 1.

of interest is the extent of overlap or duplication of services to the group membership and, relatedly, the degree of co-ordination among al the existing health and social services, especially those provided by an ethnic planning agency.

Political

Because ethnic groups in Canada are a subset of the population, the political institution in an ethnic community does not overlap as much with the governance sector as it would for the entire populace of a city, province or the nation. Perforce, political institutional forms are somewhat different within an ethnic group in a particular locale.

What is included here are political partly alliances within the ethnic group, whether formal, as in an essentially ethnic-group riding association in an area of high ethnic Residential Concentration or unorganized, as in the major loyalty of the ethnic membership being to one political party. The 1984 federal elections provided excellent examples of both the formal and unorganized links that comprise part of the ethnic political institution. Another portion of this issue is the efforts by ethnic-group members—both individually and collectively—to force the attention of politicians and candidates onto the particular concerns of the ethnic group (e.g., immigration levels and rules, legislation and programs to stimulate linguistic and cultural maintenance). One aspect that is definitely related, but in a way that is difficult to specify, is the extent to which members of the ethnic group become candidates for and/or are elected to serve as local, provincial or federal representatives, or officials in riding associations or political parties.

A quite different side of the political institution of an ethnic group is the set of arrangements that can exist between the ethnicity in Canada and official or semi-official organs of the homeland government. Members of many ethnic groups in Canada, for instance, retain voting rights and/or citizenship even after becoming Canadian citizens. Not infrequently in such ethnicities, there is some form of formal or quasi-formal organization in the ethnic community that aims to orchestrate the influence of the homeland government on the Canadian (provincial/city) membership of the group and vice versa. This facet involving off-shore concerns, in fact, can often assume greater importance to the members of some ethnicities in some places than toward Canadian political activities.

SUMMARY

In this chapter, the constituent parts of ethnic institutions have been explicated, along with the major social dimensions along which they can be analyzed. With all this, the boundaries of (1) an institution of an "ethnic group" as opposed to that of the entire area population, and (2) whether a specific organization or activity belongs to one particular ethnic institution or another (or whether it is a shared component of both), remain somewhat vague.

Compartmentalizing ethnic objectives, activities, and organizations into a variety of institutions for social analysis—especially with the intent of comparing institutions of one group with those of another ethnicity, or a particular ethnicity in one location with the same one elsewhere—is rather like attempting to construct a box out of string. Theoretically the task can be accomplished, given caveats as to what constitutes a "box," but its stability of form will hardly approach the ideal. Yet, extending the analogy to its extreme, there may be an advantage to using string for this ethnic box: you can with certainty carry specific kinds of things in it, while also being able to inspect the contents whenever you wish and from whichever perspective you desire, without your view being seriously blocked.

Now, I recognize that the "string-box" analogy is a rather ridiculous one. Instead, consider the imagery of fusing the perspective of the ethnic group with that of the social researchers to ascertain the cultural size, weight and contents of each institution, to discover what links the various institutions together, and how they are kept together.

In addition, these are not just idle, speculative questions. It has already been suggested that, of all the dimensions of ethno-cultural life in Canada, Institutional Completeness is the most critical of the factors affecting ethnic-group cohesion. Further, the long history of decline in many other indicators of ethnic cultural and community maintenance contrasted with the continuing—even increasing!—vitality of the institutional component of almost every ethno-racial-religious group in virtually all locales, makes the study of ethnic Institutional Completeness all but a *sine qua non*. We have relatively precise knowledge about language or religious maintenance, but this is far from the case in regard to ethnic Institutional Completeness.

The model presented here, involving the entire spectrum of

ethno-racial-religious groups in Canada, provides a pioneer per-spective for the analysis of ethnic groups' Institutional Complete-ness. It is a primitive tool, and not in any sense polished, but it does offer a beginning taxonomy and methodology.

## PART 3

THE ADAPTATIONS OF ETHNIC GROUPS IN CANADA

INTRODUCTION

The final part of this book is an analysis of the adaptations of Canadian ethnic groups. Ideally, this would combine data on actual alterations in the values, structures, processes, and content of the ethnicities with explanatory theory or theories. By now, however, the absence of complete empirical information ought to be apparent. Thus, this section can inform on only selected aspects of the cultural transitions of ethno-racial-religious groups in Canada. Nonetheless, this section represents what may well be a precedent-setting analysis of ethnic-group adaptations in this country.

The analysis begins with a synthesis of many theories concerning the process and/or content of group adaptation, differentiating these theories between two-stage conceptions and three-or-more-stage conceptions. This delineation is probably among the first to summarize and compare the many conceptualizations of how and why ethnic groups do, or are forced to, adapt (Chapter 10). The second part of this foray into group-cultural change (Chapter 11) is an entirely original conceptualization of the ethnic-group adaptation process, prepared by Dorothy Chave Herberg. She has been pre-eminent in the exposition of ethnic-group process and structure in Canada and of how helping professionals can learn about this and so alter their service values and modalities to complement, not contradict, ethnic-group culture and its practices. Here she turns from the applications of cultural forms and change for human services to individuals, families, and groups, to provide an exposition of the ethnic-group adaptation with particular emphasis on alterations in the nature and practice of the group culture. Her theory is remarkable not just because she formulates the adaptation process as beginning before immigration to Canada, but also because of her careful analysis of the focus and form of group cultural change over multiple stages in the immigrant and later generational experiences in Canada. Unfortunately, her theory stretches far beyond the capability of research on ethnic groups and their members' experiences to provide information about these stages. This is also true about the capability of the ethnic-group cohesion analyses here to verify the particulars of Herberg's model, despite the time-trend focuses of the data.

Notwithstanding, the final chapter does proffer innovative insights about the differing paces, emphases, and outcomes of the group-cultural transition from yesteryear to 1981. This part of the investigation has a dual focus, the first concentrating on the within- or between-group comparisons on the several ethnic-group cohesion mechanisms described in Part 2. The second focus is on the rates of change over the decades in the levels of ethnic-group cohesion. Finally all of this is summarized and interpreted, and future transitions in ethnic-group cohesion are projected.

## CHAPTER 10

Theories of Ethnic-Group Adaptation

INTRODUCTION: GENERAL THEORIES OF ETHNIC-GROUP ADAPTATION

For all the attention given in recent years to Canada's changing ethnic communities, there have been remarkably few theories developed to characterize or predict the process of ethnic-group adaptation. Perhaps because of this, the empirical explorations of such adaptation have been exceptionally rare, even when the focus was on only one group. Quite literally, the number of research works comparing multiple groups on the nature or outcomes-in-process in cultural adaptation in this country can be counted on the fingers of one hand. It was, of course, this dearth that prompted the present book.

Recent theories about ethnocultural adaptation can be divided into two categories, those that explicitly or implicitly describe a two-stage process of the immigrant and post-immigrant stages and those models that include a more elaborated adaptive process.

TWO-STAGE ADAPTATION

All of the two-stage models deal with the beginnings of the ethnic community as developed by the first sizeable number of immigrants to arrive here and settle close to each other (Stage 1). They then address the post-immigrant phase (Stage 2) considered all of a piece, with no differentiations made within that later period.

Of recent Canadian two-stage models of ethnic-group adaptation, probably the best-known is Breton's (1964; 1978b) that includes his ground-breaking analysis of ethnic-group institutional completeness. In this, he examined the conditions necessary for the establishment of the immigrant community (1978b), requiring first the development of ethnic group "enclosure," or what Kallen (1982: 90–92) termed "ethnic closure." Both terms refer to the initiation and maintenance of social boundaries surrounding the ethnic community, supplemented by internal networks of social association and interaction. The second requirement for ethnic-group maintainance is the formation in Canada of both its traditional and new-in-Canada institutions. This Breton called ethnic group "segmentation," and Kallen included this as a component of a group's "expressive strengths," and the entirety of her "organizational strengths." The "segmentation" and/or the "expressive" and "organizational" strengths comprise Breton's (1964) institutional completeness dimension of ethnic-group cohesion analyzed here in Chapter 9.

In his 1964 (p. 205) article, Breton indicated his belief (prediction?) that ethnic-group enclosure and its institutional completeness, as he had studied them in 1958–1959 Montreal, would wither away along with the dominance of the immigrants on the earliest phase of the ethnic community and that by the time the second-generation members of the ethnicity became pre-eminent in the group, the enclosure and institutional mechanisms might well have

disappeared.... Ethnic communities are formed, grow, and disappear; they go through a life cycle.... With time—and it may be quite long—the ethnic organizations will themselves disappear or lose their ethnic identity, completing the life cycle of the community.

A decade later, however, Breton as discussed in Reitz (1980: 127) appeared to have altered this conclusion somewhat when he stated that ethnic-group cultures are adaptable, since they do not depend utterly on pre-industrial social components, and that all ethnic community cultures, eventually, must adapt in response to their experiences in Canada (and especially in its cities). Some of his most recent works (1981; 1984), in fact, implicitly accept the adaptation of values and structures in Canadian ethnic groups as a more-or-less permanent dynamic of ethnic communities as they continue to be maintained by those of the second and later generations.

In two works, Driedger (1977a; 1977b) articulated a very different and more articulated theory of ethnic-group adaptation involving, first, the immigrant stage, and then an undifferentiated post-immigrant period within the urban environment. The first stage ensued when the initial wave of immigrants in an ethnicity either settled immediately in a city or moved to it from rural places and attempted to establish the group's structures and processes within an ethnic enclave, separate from those of other ethnocultural groups. This initial stage of community development Driedger called "enclavic pluralism"—the effort by multiple groups in the city to establish their own distinctive communities, together representing ethnocultural pluralism. In this enclavic stage, the immigrants attempted to establish a territorial concentration, including, especially, residential proximity and institutional development. In addition, the immigrants sought to establish their ethnocultural identity in the city through language retention, endogamy, networks of ethnic friendship and voluntary organizations, participation in the ethnic religion and parochial education, and the establishment of social distance from other ethnicities in the city. These immigrant urban villagers in the Canadian cities were/are, therefore, characterized by extensive boundary maintenance enclosing the enclavic community and very much controlling the links with outsiders as the strategy to attain a high level of ethnic-group cohesion.

There were/are two factors that impinge on urban villagers, however. First, concentration in absolute and relative numbers in the ethnicity along with the linguistic and other cultural characteristics of non-charter groups have varied greatly by locale. Second, in urban centres, enclavic pluralism may be difficult to preserve with respect to boundary enclosure.

Thus, enclavic pluralism was/is an important foothold the immigrant urban ethnic villagers must gain if their culture and the demographic integrity of their group was/is to survive in Canada. It was, moreover, by no means assured that every ethno-racial-religious group new to the city would be able to secure or develop the security of enclavic pluralism. But each ethnicity that did successfully establish a cultural enclave in a city needed to shift into a post-enclavic, post-immigrant community-development dynamic to continue the ethnic-group culture into the next generation. As

Canada changed into a more industrial and urban, a more culturally, racially, and religiously diverse society, then additional mechanisms or forces were needed by ethnic communities either as
unintended consequences of ethnic-group existence in the Canadian urban milieu, or through a purposeful engineering of the
ethnic-group character beyond the mere maintenance of the immigrant cultures as a community fetish in the post-immigrant period.

This post-enclavic phenomenon Driedger labelled a "regenerat-
ing pluralism" community, for which there are five essential "self-
identification factors." The first is the possession or development
of an *ideological mythology* for the group, centring on a religious or
political ideology to rally community members to a goal epitomiz-
ing the group's cultural or institutional values. The second factor is
historical symbols: knowledge about the group's (and the community's) origins and the stimulation of pride in both its heritage and
its contemporary manifestations. The third factor is *charismatic
leadership*, either in the community or of the ethnic society of
origin—leadership of a contemporary or historical nature sufficiently strong to secure the loyalty and service of group members to
its charisma.

Driedger's fourth factor is *social status symbols*. This means that, if
an ethnicity in the city can maintain its enclavic foothold long
enough to educate, train, and otherwise groom enough of its
members, then the socio-economic status in following generations
will have been raised to a level enabling them to compete successfully with other groups in the city. This socio-economic power and
the resources on which it is based permit the group to compete
culturally with the "dominant" and other groups on an equal basis
and to ensure thereby the survival of, and continuing pride in, the
ethnic culture (albeit an adapted one). The fifth of Driedger's
factors is support for the *ethnic language*, to the extent required to
access the ethnic culture and the community's system of values.

Post-enclavic ethnic communities, Driedger suggested, would
take on different regenerational structures and combinations of
ethnic-identification factors. For the French, he thought, and had
demonstrated through his earlier research, culture and values
centred on the French-Canadian (Franco-Manitoban/Ontarian,
Acadian?) culture and language. In contrast, Jewish community
culture and values in the post-enclavic, regenerative period
revolved around symbolic history and ideology, and their religion.

The multigenerational integrity of each ethnic community, then, depended initially on the nature of the cultural attributes in the immigrants' country(ies) of origin and on the character of the culture and the effort to maintain it in their new setting. But for Canadian-born members of the group, more than the successful carrying-over of the national character of the culture and people was/is required for group cultural continuation. Active and proactive industry by the membership is the *sine qua non*, for building beyond the enclavic existence (if it was attained!) to assure vitality in the later Canadian-born culture and collectivity of the ethnicity.

The next two theories on Canadian ethnic-group adaptation are doubly different from those of either Breton or Driedger. Both Breton and Driedger postulated a two-stage—immigrant versus post-immigrant—process. Looking at the formulations of Kallen (1982) and Berry (1987), though, we find only an implicitly developmental process of adaptation in ethnic groups or communities after the immigrants' settling-in phase. In her analysis, Kallen postulated differential outcomes sometime after the immigrants' settling in Canada (1982: 154–155). Which of the four arrangements that she discussed would eventuate "in any empirical instance is a variable influenced by the relative strength of push-and-pull forces impacting upon each of the interacting ethnic collectivities" (1982: 155).

Among ethnic communities involved in a contest for ethnic cultural survival in which each of the ethnic collectivities are relatively equal in cultural strength (what Kallen called a "two-way'" process), the outcome could take one of two forms. The first is the *fusion* of the original ethnic collectivities and the creation of a new, ethnically homogeneous society (the "melting pot" or "amalgamation" outcome, in Kallen's terms). The other possibility is the *retention and federation* of the different ethnic collectivities and the creation of an ethnically heterogeneous society ("cultural pluralism" or a "mosaic" of ethnic communities). She did not, however, suggest which conditions lead to which of the two outcomes.

In a situation in which the contesting ethnic groups are very unequal in the relative strengths of their cultural forces (a "one-way" process), then two other outcomes result. In one, the *absorption* of the weaker ethnic group by the stronger one creates an ethnically homogeneous society modelled upon the characteristics of the (original) stronger ethnicity; Kallen termed this "dominant conformity" or "absorption." The second eventuality was the institutionalized and/or coerced *suppression* of the weaker ethnic collectivity by the stronger one and the "creation of a caste-like society dominated and controlled by the stronger" ethnicity(ies)— this, for Kallen, is "paternalism" or "colonialism." Again Kallen failed to specify exactly the circumstances that distinguish one kind of adaptation from the other.

As is readily apparent, no precise connection is made to any point in development or time or generation following the immigrants' arrival in the host society, but only that, at some time, one of the four forms of adaptation will take place. Indeed, it is not always that the immigrating ethnicity(ies) is the one that will be surpressed or absorbed: the colonization of Canada's Native Peoples by the immigrant charter group was pointed to by Kallen as an exemplar of her Paternalism typology (1982: 174–178).

Berry (1987), like Kallen, took the establishment of the immigrant community as a given, and outlined four alternative outcomes of "acculturation." That is, in "culturally plural societies... individuals and groups in contact will influence each other, including some degree of change in each other's way of life...." In culturally plural societies such as Canada, Berry explained, there are two essential questions ethnic communities must answer, and, depending on their answers to each, they will experience different forms of community (and individual) adaptation. The first question was whether a group's members perceived value in maintaining their cultural identity and characteristics; there could be either an affirmative or negative answer to this. Likewise, the ethnic community members could affirm or deny that there was value in maintaining relationships with other ethnic, racial or religious groups in the city—the other side of life in a mosaic society. Depending on the particular responses to each of these questions, the ethnic community could adapt to one of four forms, as indicated in Table 10.1.

If it was determined that there was value both in retaining the group's cultural identity and characteristics *and* in maintaining relationships with other groups in the city, then the form of outcome from these decisions would be what Berry identified as *Integration*. This involves the maintenance of the cultural security of the ethnic community, as well as movement by the ethnicity to become an integral part of the larger societal framework. This leads to a condition of many distinguishable ethnic groups, all cooperating within the larger city, province, state. Kallen called this situation a "mosaic" or culturally plural structure, and Gordon (1975) called it "liberal pluralism."

Table 10.1
Model of Alternative Forms of Ethnic-Group Adaptation

		Value in Maintaining Cultural Identity and Characteristics?	
		YES	NO
Value in maintaining Relationships with Other Groups	YES	Integration	Assimilation
	NO	Separation	Marginalization

Source: Adapted from J.W. Berry. "Finding identity. . . ." In *Ethnic Canada*,
   edited by L. Driedger. (Toronto: Copp Clark Pitman, 1987), pp. 223–
   239.

Assimilation occurs when there is no desire or ability to maintain the ethnic group's uniqueness, but relationships with other groups are sought. In this, Berry noted, the group relinquishes its cultural identity and moves out into the larger society. Assimilation can take the form of absorption into an established or dominant ethnic group, or it can take the form of multiple groups amalgamating to form a new society and national people, as in the "melting pot."

Those ethnicities which seek no interaction with other groups, but do maintain their cultural integrity (or wish only to be left alone to do this), Berry characterized as following a path of *Separation*. In this, the ethnic community maintains its traditional pattern of life as best it can, outside full participation in the larger society. The group's desire to lead an independent existence, Berry observed, will be characterized by segregation or separation, depending on which group or groups have the power to determine the outcome—the ethnic collectivity seeking self-isolation (separation), or one or more of the other ethnic groups (segregation).

Finally, there are groups who lose or forsake their culture, but are unable to maintain an alliance with or become part of another ethnicity, or are rejected by the other group(s); this adaptation outcome is *Marginalization*. When this condition which Kovacs and Cropley analyzed in 1971 is one imposed by the larger society, Berry equates it with eventual ethnocide.

Thus, according to Berry's logic, the adaptive process can have several possible outcomes. It should be noted, moreover, that each of these outcomes can result as much from the unplanned "unfold-ing" of a group's existence in a city as from following a planned strategy. Finally, even if the group conscientiously followed its strategy, the result of a different strategy by another group, or the unplanned sequence of social evolution in intergroup relations could lead to an outcome different from that initially sought. Neither of these alternatives was included in Berry's consideration of the adaptation process.

THREE-OR-MORE-STAGE ADAPTATION

In comparison to the four models of ethnic group adaptation involving two phases (explicitly or not), there are at least five theories of group adaptation that specify or suggest at least three stages.

Probably one of the earliest of these was Hansen's (1938: 9–10) formulation of the "principle of third-generation interest." Hansen suggested that "what the son wishes to forget" about the ethnic culture and practices, "the grandson wishes to remember." That is, the second-generation members of an ethnic group, shy away from indoctrination in the immigrant ethno-religious culture as a way of overtly expressing identification with the adopted society. But, Hansen went on, their children, the third generation, take a some-what opposite path of cultural adaptation by evidencing an interest in and return to an altered form and practice of the immigrants' culture. Hansen characterized this phenomenon as being "almost universal" (1938: 495).

The cultural rebirth pattern of ethnic-group adaptation was enlarged upon by Will Herberg (1955), in his classic documentation of religious patterns in America, *Catholic-Protestant-Jew*. Herberg observed that, even in the American absorptive system, the pres-sure for religious assimilation could scarcely be said to exist, at least in part because of American constitutional guarantees of freedom in religious practice and the prohibition of state interference in or sponsorship of any religion. Thus, Herberg stated, immigrants to the United States were not expected to change their religion because, from the very beginning of the republic, religious diver-sity and substantial equality among religions were presupposed.

However, the assimilative ideology that comprised the official policy and practice of all levels of American government until about 1970 had its effect. First to be lost or consciously discarded was the ethnic language and, soon thereafter, went the culture associated with it—forced, at least in part, by official pressure, combined with voluntary zeal to become fully "American." Religion, too, was affected in that the second generation, Herberg found, developed an uneasy relation to the faith of their ancestors. Sometimes this meant indifference, though for a relatively few others, a shift was made to denominations perceived as "more American." In most cases, however, ties with the old religion were apparently never completely severed.

Herberg presented data showing that the third generation, pondering the quality of their Americanness in the aftermath of the Second World War, sought a more potent source of personal and social identity than could be provided by being "American." With the old-line ethnic group with its foreign (even "Un-American") culture and language being literally and figuratively alien to these third-generation people, family religion—the religion of their immigrant grandparents—was accorded a place in the American social scheme that made religious adherence at once genuinely American and a familiar principle of group cultural identity (Herberg, 1955: 34, 40–49).

On this same theme of intergenerational adaptation, Isajiw (1975) also characterized the process of ethnic-group identity maintenance in Canada as having three phases. The first of these was/is the *Transplantation* of the Old World culture via immigration to Canada. Similar to Hansen's theory of the second generation, Isajiw described a rebellious *Rejection* of the Old World culture by the immigrants' children, attended by movement beyond the ethnic community into the wider city. In contrast, the grandchildren of the immigrant settlers, Isajiw said, experienced *Rediscovery* of their ethno-racial-religious roots. This renewed concern with their ethnic identity leads to the emergence of an adapted ethnic culture and the development of some institutions different from those existing (or those which existed) in either the country of origin or the ethnic community. All community institutions would be crafted to make them more compatible with the third,+ generation's urban technological lifestyle and still serve the members in ethnoculturally significant ways.

While these three phases of ethnic-group adaptation (Transplantation, Rejection, Rediscovery) can be applied to the transition process experienced over time in succeeding generations, the cycle can also apply with equal facility to the shift in emphases and

interests of ethnic groups during the social change and development in the cities of Canada, or perhaps even in its rural parts. For
instance, the Transplantation phase could describe on a wider plane
the great wave of nation building through immigration that
occurred in Canada from the late 1800s until the Great Depression.
The following Rejection emphasis could then be applied to the era
from 1929 through the Second World War until about the mid-
1960s when the primary concern of the members of Canada's
constituent ethnic groups was the redefinition of the parameters of
Canadian and ethnic-group life during an era of constant social
turmoil and shift. Similarly, the Rediscovery pattern can readily
and acceptably characterize the past twenty-or-more years, with its
resurgence of all things ethnic, from the ethnic emphasis in the
celebration of the nation's centenary, to the legitimation of ethnic
pluralism in the Constitution Act of 1982 (our new Constitution),
and beyond that to the rapid maturation of probably dozens more
ethnic communities following the changed streams of immigration
since the later 1970s.

Relatedly, it need only be noted that the transplantation-rejec-
tion-rediscovery sequence could further apply to the immigrant
generation's change in attitude over the years toward their own
ethnic identity and cultural practices. In any case, the process of
ethnic-identity differentiation can be experienced by those identified with the original immigrant tradition, that of either the pre-
Depression or post-1960s waves of massive movement to Canada.
Contrasted to these are the rediscoverers in all generations, whose
recommitment to their culture and whose refashioning of ethnic-
community institutions is more symbolic and less of a fetish than in
the immigrant phase. Those returning to their ethnic heritage in
the recent past represent an entirely different accommodation to
life in Canada than that of the immigrants and their descendants
right up to the current era, an adaptation newly epitomized in
official multiculturalism at all levels of government.

From an entirely different perspective, Reitz (1980: 124–130)
used the concept of "life-cycle" to describe ethnic groups' transfor-
mations from the immigrant transplantation onward. For Reitz
(1980: 125) life-cycle referred to

> an aggregate of individual experiences, to the process of immigrant
> adaptation over time and to the transition from the first or immigrant
> generation to the second generation and to subsequent genera-

tions. . . . To an as yet unknown extent, differences in group cohesion may represent not differences in the life-cycle and the immigration histories, but differences in the nature of the life-cycle of a particular group. That is, there may be differences between groups, in their. . . culture or other characteristics, which produce lasting differences in the historical experiences of those groups in Canadian society.

Thus, what Reitz pointed to here was the confluence of two very different theoretical streams concerning the nature of the life of Canadian ethnic groups. First, each ethnic group has a life-cycle beginning with the first arrival of large numbers of immigrants from a particular group to the same location in Canada—what Isajiw termed the Transplantation phase. Second, what Reitz later referred to (i.e., the unlabelled, multi-staged, post-immigrant sequences in community life) is what in this book has been termed the "ethnic relativity" precept, that each ethno-racial-religious group not only is more different than one imagines, but it is more different than one *can* imagine. Ethnic groups, we have maintained, differ in values, structures, processes, and contents in ways that are obscure to non-group members, and the differences we can "objectively" distinguish cannot readily be traced to "objective" causal characteristics of ethnicity.

The last theory of ethnic-group adaptation in Canada, that of Dorothy Herberg, differs from the others in several ways. First, she emphasizes that the understanding of ethnic groups' experiences in this country begins with appreciation of the phenomena of the pre-immigration period in the country of origin. None of the other models have dealt with this facet in anything but a perfunctory way. Next, Herberg "unpacks" the immigrant transplantation phase into multiple constituent elements, again something few other workers in the field of ethnicity have done. Third, she links the nature of ethnic-group process and transition in Canada to the degree to which cultural practices and structures are based in "high" or "low" contexts of group life. High context denotes communal living. Low context denotes a more independent style of living, based on immediate perceptions and needs and ignoring, for the most part, the shared community meanings. Finally, Herberg identifies the principal parts of the ethnic culture and its group-cohesion mechanisms that adapt during the second, and the third,+ generations. Herberg's schema, providing such an innovative basis for thinking about and studying ethnic-group adaptation, appears here as Chapter 11.

SUMMARY

There are many and varied ways to conceptualize ethnic-community adaptation. All necessarily focus (either explicitly or implicitly) on the immigrant generation's first arrival in large numbers. The differences between the theories, therefore, are mostly in the degree of differentiation made within and between the Canadian-born generations. The two-stage theories cover the post-immigrant phase all of a piece, without attempting to sort out specifics or stressing separate elements within this long period of ethnic groups' lives. The three-or-more-stage theories differ in that they point to particular differences in attitude and practice between the generations. This involves the falling away by the second generation from practice and belief in the immigrant, Old-World culture, but a renewal among the third,+ generations in identifying with their ancestors' culture. In this quest for their ethnic, racial, and/or religious heritage, they redesign the symbols and institutions to complement the changed nature of their ethnicity and of Canada itself. Among these different models of ethnic-group transitions, Dorothy Herberg's is unique in its consideration of the pre-immigrant phase, the immigrant, and at least two of the post-immigrant generations and their ethnic practices.

CHAPTER 11

An Adaptation Framework of Ethnic Communities

Dorothy Chave Herberg

INTRODUCTION: MODELS OF TRANSITION

This chapter analyzes Canadian society as an everflowing, changing entity, and the process of ethnic-group cultural adaptation is
dealt with as one aspect of this changing society. Americans are
typically portrayed as understanding what their society was and
should be like, Canadians seem to be less sure about their country.
Although the national differences in this regard are probably more
apparent than real, nevertheless, the tendency of Americans to
focus on their assimilationist policy has given them a surer sense of
where they are going and how to get there. Canadians, with a long-
standing bilingual and multicultural foundation, have been less
able or less willing to deny their pluralistic base and more aware of
ethnicity as an integral part of Canadian social life. Grasping the
nature of Canadian society, then, means understanding the ongoing change and flow of many groups as well as that of the integrated

whole. Being able to appreciate and comprehend this complexity is an important part of Canadians' becoming surer of who they are.

Two models, the Adaptation Framework and Contexting, are used here to conceptualize the flow and transitions that highlight the ethnocultural structure of social life. Three precepts prevail: (1) one must know the origins of ethnoculture in order to understand the forms and functions of these in the present and discern those of the future; (2) common structures are present for all groups; and (3) family and other social forms are so valued by immigrants that there is the desire to keep what is familiar and reconstitute it in the new land.

ADAPTATION EXPERIENCE

Canadian societal diversity must be understood in a historical perspective, and concepts used to understand this diversity must have at least some temporal flow. The Adaptation Framework is a paradigm for organizing components of culture change and, by definition, includes explicitly the longitudinal perspective of ethnic-group cultural adaptation. Two aspects of Canadian social life can be conceptualized as the "ethnic-group" aspect and the "mainstream" aspect. In actual fact, these merge and interweave and are often indistinguishable. It is possible, in fact, to deliberately not distinguish them if the underlying ethnic model used is that of assimilation. Under those circumstances, the ethnic aspect, conceptually and "really," appears to be obscured, either not noticed or defined as socially inferior. For investigative purposes and because it is more "Canadian" to do so, the ethnic and the mainstream aspects are here drawn apart and described separately.

This separation is handled by first designating ethnic groups as immigrants (or the reverse) and then considering the Canadian-born second, third and later generations. This is not entirely accurate because, on the one hand, active ethnic-group membership and culture has been demonstrated to continue from generation to generation and, on the other, because some newcomers merge into the mainstream very quickly. The image emerges of Canadian society as a vast and broad river overflowing and constantly replenished by tributaries and streams from new and old sources since ancient times. The process starts with the initial contact between Europeans and the aboriginal peoples.

This image also connects to one of the most basic themes of

human life—death and rebirth. Campbell (1949: 30) explained this theme as the "standard path of mythological adventure...represented in the 'rites of passage': separation–initiation–return." In Campbell's work, these points on the mythological path are placed in a circle. However, for ease of analysis the Adaptation Framework lays these points out, in modified form, in a straight line.

This archetypal form permits consideration of ethnic-group culture change on many levels. At one level, when viewed close up, we see many "death-rebirth" phenomena as groups' members go through the archetypal steps: the separation from homeland; settlement initiated in Canada; and, eventually, a rebirth or return to life in a new community (D. Herberg, 1982). At another level, this enduring archetypal form can show our country as having been constantly transformed by the infusion of immigrants.

The Adaptation Framework is expressed in words that are as abstract and simple as the archetypal process described by Campbell. Thus, the schema can be used to characterize the cultural adaptation of individuals and families or it can, on another level, be used to understand waves of immigration of people from the same country of origin that came to comprise Canadian ethno-racial-religious communities. In short, this schema can be used to understand the cultural identity of any Canadian person or ethnocultural group. Thus, the framework is elaborated to include different generations. In every case, the "rebirth" or end-phase results in a new identity that combines the historical process of the change as well as the new life/community to which one is adapting.

The Adaptation Framework consists of a time-line going across the page. An arrow indicates that this is not a reversible process, although people may leave at any time and re-enter. The line ⟶ symbolizes time in the way those using a Western philosophy are taught to perceive it (i.e., as linear). In Eastern philosophy, time may be seen in a more cyclical, circular or qualitative way (Conze, 1951: 19); Westerners tend to see time as a linear, progressive, and quantitative phenomenon. Hence it makes sense to reflect these qualities in a symbolic representation of time.

In addition to the time-line, there are five basic points or Benchmarks. In the case of migration, a person, family or group of families "dies" in one culture and is "reborn" in another. Benchmark A is a place where life and the "death" take place. Benchmark D is the new place, the place of "rebirth." In between are Benchmarks B and C which, in the simplest way, refer to the cause of

Table 11.1
The Adaptation Framework

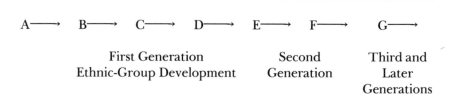

A⟶	B⟶	C⟶	D⟶	E⟶	F⟶	G⟶
	First Generation Ethnic-Group Development			Second Generation		Third and Later Generations

"death" (culture change) and the process of "rebirth" (settlement period). Finally, Benchmark E recognizes the new identity, a product of the foregoing processes. Later, Benchmarks F and G reflect identity differences with each succeeding generation's residence in Canada. The time-line with its Benchmarks is shown in Table 11.1 and is considered in detal in following sections.

The Framework can compare and differentiate between various statuses—immigrant, refugee, illegal resident or Native Person, for instance. Immigrant Canadians who retain a significant consciousness of their ethnicity as well as Canadians who have rejected or forgotten their ethnic roots are also recognized. Other dimensions of status can be understood from the Framework. There are elements in Canadian identity that have to do with a sense of belonging (to Canada) along with a sense of privilege. If the process of the transformation of Canadian society is likened to a gigantic river, then everyone is in a boat on this river. In Table 11.1, the time-line is conceptualized as just such a slowly-moving river. Some have just got on (new immigrants) and others have been on all their lives (the Canadian-born). Some have parents who were born on the river, and others have parents who were born elsewhere and became parents after they got on.

Many factors affect the adaptation process, but the *time* of the original immigration matters a great deal to your identity as a Canadian, on the one hand, and to your identity as a member of an ethnocultural community, on the other. Your identity is qualified by such comments as: "I am an immigrant to Canada." "I came as a child to Canada." "My family goes back several generations in Canada," and so on. In each case there is a recognition of origin and a sense of where and who one is in relation to those origins. A sense of status distinction, perforce, can be made on the basis of how long one has been in Canada. Those who have charter-group ancestry

(British or French) tend to see themselves as being especially privileged and may have difficulty adjusting to an erosion of those privileges as the dominance of other groups increases.

Not all life changes result in happy outcomes, however. In some cases, the end result will be worse than the circumstance promoting the change. Affecting the outcome are the type of change involved and the reason for the move. In the case of immigration, people voluntarily submit to the trauma of expatriation in order to gain a better life for themselves and their families. For refugees, however, expatriation is forced and unwanted. But, for immigrants and refugees both, one outcome may be that the loss of homeland is never fully accepted. The many ways in which the transition takes place and the transitions' varied outcomes for ethnic-group culture are the subjects treated in the Adaptation Framework.

A particular use of the Framework is to understand how the cultural dimension of a present event or problem can stem from a previous life or societal origin, to use the archetypal image. "Ethnic root behaviour patterns," dealt with in an earlier study (D. Herberg, 1982), refers to repeated behaviour patterns, whose origins, it is suggested, can be traced to powerful group-cultural values passed along from generation to generation. These patterns are seen as the remnants of more complete cultural structures that existed in a functional form in another societal context.

CONTEXTING

Another conceptual scheme that permeates discussion in the pages ahead is that of "contexting." This schema outlines changes in values and structure that may occur during adaptive acculturation. This idea was originally formulated by Edward T. Hall (1976) and was used to differentiate a modern industrial country like the United States from countries that were still organized, for the most part, in traditional cultural ways. "Third world" countries, developing countries, countries with a strong recent, colonial past are descriptives currently used to characterize countries "high" in context. What is being referred to is the high degree of kinship structures and values that govern everyday life. The traditional extended family is the centre of this high context and includes the network of relationships beyond the family within which individuals are imbedded.

Table 11.2
Continua of High- and Low-Context Cultures

Continuum	High-context Cultures	Low-context Cultures
Basic unit of society	Family or clan	Individual
Social structure	Hierarchical	Egalitarian
Gender relations	Gender segregation	Gender integration
Orientation to social world	Holistic	Fragmentary
Social referent	Religious	Secular
Medium of communicating the culture	Oral	Written
Validity of cultural beliefs	Unquestioned	Questioned
Form of social interaction	Interdependence	Independence
Time reference	Polychronic	Monochronic

Source: Adapted from D. Herberg. "Issues in multicultural child welfare:...*Social Work Papers* (Summer, 1983).

Low-context cultures or societies are those in which the traditional family and community bonds have been greatly weakened or eroded completely and replaced by nuclear-family values, structure, and process. The context is "low" because the old network is low or gone. Instead, low-context people must build up a relationship context in each new situation; the skill to accomplish this is part of this life's requirements, and newcomers must learn it. To quite an extent, the post-industrial middle-class lifestyle is coterminous with the low-context one.

Contexting is a process; dimensions of high and low contexts are shown on Table 11.2 and are described in detail later on.

Applying these dimensions to Canadian society can be done at the family level or at the level of ethnic organization or even entire ethnic communities.

The basic unit in a high-context community in Canada is the family, often the extended family. The members of a high-context family are related in a hierarchical and gender-segregated manner. The rules governing these relationships are expected to remain unquestioned. Out of this rigid but secure structure can come a high degree of interdependence, a sense of purpose, togetherness, and belonging. The rigidity on the one hand is offset by stability on the other.

As families of ethnic groups begin to adapt to the low-context culture of the Canadian mainstream, some questioning of rules must come about, and a more flexible structure emerges along with adapted cultural content. For some, adaptation is very difficult. The rigid structure does not yield. Families and even entire ethnic communities can become quite unstable and become the focus of concern for schools, employment agencies, and mental health institutions or other government and private social-planning agencies.

High-context attributes also apply to families *qua* families. Since families act to ensure their own good reputation and to promote their own place in a community, they strive to rise socially. Material achievement is a high priority as they seek to achieve a higher and more secure status. This competitiveness leads to a hierarchy of families based on prestige and income.

Gender segregation remains in families and, consequently, in ethnic communities because a sense of what is proper, especially for women, is part of a family's good reputation. However, the school system starts to change views about gender roles, as does labour-force participation, and a move towards greater gender integration leads to more egalitarianism—first in the family and, later, throughout the ethnic-group membership in a city.

The remainder of this chapter analyzes themes and institutions common to every group. The discussion begins with Benchmark A, origins, (Table 11.1) and highlights issues needed to understand the nature of ethnic-group adaptation later.

BENCHMARK A: PLACE OF ORIGIN

The nature of the family in high-context societies is hierarchical, gender-segregated, and highly interdependent. Relatives tend to live near each other, and the whole group is rooted in a "place"; the hamlet, village or farm will have been "home" for generations; and high residential concentration may exist in Canada. The continuity of the family and its good reputation and well-being is a high priority. In adversity, it is the larger family to whom people turn. There are several issues relevant to later adjustment levels in Canada. One of these is the basic motivation for leaving the homeland. Here, differences between immigrant and refugee statuses are very important. Whether the family has urban or rural experience, whether the English language was known before moving, and whether the group was a minority, and especially a racially visible minority, in their place of origin, will all have a major effect on the nature of the group adaptation in Canada. Finally, if there was recent experience of colonial rule, then the effects of this will be transferred to all the group's institutions: e.g., education, religion, culture/arts, government, and economics. In this way some of the changes to low context may have begun in the country of origin.

The *educational* system of the place of origin will affect the chances of adult immigrants in the Canadian economy and influence their expectations of the schools their children attend in Canada. Some will have the inheritance of a British educational system; Hong Kong Chinese, Indo-Canadians, West Indians and immigrants from other Commonwealth countries will have this familiar base. People from Mediterranean and Middle-Eastern countries and those from many parts of Southeast Asia will have other experiences. Role learning, stern discipline, and authoritarian teachers with high status and power are some elements in the educational systems of countries of origin; expecting these from Canadian schooling can make adaptation to Canada more difficult.

Religion for high-context people is highly integrated into every aspect of daily life. Among groups whose religion includes animism and spiritualism, these elements will be carried along in any migration. Generally, there is a holistic approach to the maintenance of health and the understanding of illness. Health practitioners are often closely associated with religion in such groups and are often very close in life experience and socio-economic status to the people they serve (Eisenberg and Kleinman, 1980). Among ethnic groups for whom colonialism included Christian missionary activity, the changes toward low-context culture will have begun decades before immigration to Canada.

Several aspects of the experience of *government* in the homeland will affect adaptation. The first is the degree of government involvement in the lives of citizens. If, for example, there has been the experience of a high degree of involvement, then there may be an expectation for a high degree of awareness and help from governmental agencies in finding housing, jobs, social and health needs, and the like. When such expectations continue to exist, the "free-market" approach to these basic needs that exists in Canada can produce great disappointment and confusion about what to do (Marcus, 1979). The relevant life experience is absent, and adjustment may be slow. A different pre-emigration experience with government is that of overarching surveillance and domination of citizens. In this case, government may be viewed with suspicion, and Canadian civil servants in any position will be distrusted. People who have fled from such regimes, often will have come to Canada with refugee status, and in immediate terms, the reason for emigration lies with a government that was inimical to them.

There can also be extreme differences in the *economy* between the country or culture of origin and that of Canada. Some groups came to Canada originally to farm the Prairies and western lands, and the shift to urban residence and participation in an industrial/post-industrial labour force was made by their descendants. Recently, however, two other kinds of people have come to Canada. The first are refugees or escapees from Communist states who, once here, seek to become the free entrepreneurs or employees they could not be in their country of origin: the Polish, Russians, Hungarians, Czechs, and others come to mind. The second kind are emigrants or refugees from underdeveloped nations in which the economy is based in agriculture, local market production, and cottage industries. For both sets of people, the part of their ethnic culture that relates to economic norms and roles is dysfunctional with respect to mainstream Canadian norms and roles, and this will cause economic dislocation during the settlement phase or slow adaptation later on. But then, even people who came from countries similar to Canada often experienced difficulties in adapting to the particular nature and needs of our economy.

BENCHMARK B: A SIGNIFICANT CULTURAL SHIFT

A Significant Cultural Shift is the part of the process whereby the break with the original culture is initiated, takes place, and affects later adjustment. For most people this will have begun with first consideration of emigration to Canada and ends with arrival here. Immigrants go through a planned legal process. Refugees may be hustled into the country in disorganized panic, fleeing from persecution or exploitation. Illegal immigrants also experience a cultural shift, but it is done in precarious circumstances that prejudice future adjustment (Robinson, 1983). Finally, Native Peoples have undergone a different, but equally significant, change; it was to include them in the Framework that this Benchmark was called "cultural shift" and not "emigration." Obviously, Native Peoples have not left one country for another; in a more realistic sense, the country left them and made them foreigners in their own land. The invasion of their lands over many generations eroded their cultural ways, and their way of life has been under attack for almost 400 years.

In the earliest period of immigration people arrived from Europe after months of perilous passage under sail. Later the journey became swifter and safer as ocean vessels became larger and more technically sound. Today, most immigrants arrive by plane, and the shift is accomplished in a few hours. The transition of leaving one's place of origin and arriving in Canada often physically involves a matter of mere hours, but, culturally, there can be a gap of decades and, perhaps centuries, between immigrants' and refugees' original culture and the way of life in Canada.

BENCHMARK C: SETTLEMENT PHASE

This point follows the emigration process and initiates the phase of developing ethnocultural communities in Canada. This process is different for each ethnicity and for each era in which it occurs. Immigrants today are granted "landed" status. Refugees, often processed by special teams of immigration officials organized for emergency conditions, also become "landed immigrants." Illegal immigrants go through no such legitimizing ritual and usually live in continual fear of detection. For Native Peoples, the analogous period in their history might be considered the early years of involvement with the English and French when they still maintained much of their traditional life (Krauter and Davis, 1978: 7–25).

It is only from this stage (and into the next stages as well) that people can be analyzed as "ethnics" in Canada, and it is in this stage that ethnic communities develop. Language difficulties, marked accents, and different cultural practices identify most people at this stage as newcomers. With some exceptions, notably those who are "transilients" (Richmond, 1969: 23)—sophisticated sojourners—immigrants' ethnic culture and practices are usually not obvious to the group's members. It is often hard for the immigrants, early in their presence here, to understand programs provided for language and cultural retention or better communication between ethnic groups or whatever the "mainstream" reasons are for promoting ethnicity. Their main concerns, initially, are the basic ones of human survival: jobs, housing, food, and clothing—later comes maintenance of their culture.

During the early years of this century, immigrants received little assistance from either government or private mainstream agencies. Gradually, self-help groups developed within the ethnic community to offer support. Benevolent societies, workers' groups and mutual-aid societies emerged as the big cities became magnets drawing new settlers. With the big waves of immigration from Southern Europe from the 1950s to the 1970s immigrant-aid societies in different ethnicities developed, expanded, and persisted in altered or smaller ways through to today, along with the expansion of other institutions. English-as-a-second-language and life-skills classes became more common and standardized.

The 1970s and 1980s have seen the Settlement Phase move predominantly into refugee sponsorship and assistance, one of the predominant aspects of immigration services. Broader involvement by the public in refugee work has resulted from media attention to political crises around the globe. Immigration policy regarding refugees has become more salient and of general concern to Canadians. Churches, which before focused primarily on missionary work, now direct their attention to a wider humanitarian concern for people caught in apparently unresolvable political struggles in their own lands.

In recent years, refugee detention camps in various parts of the world have confined large numbers of people in crowded, squalid conditions. Prior even to such detention, there often was persecution, torture, and grief from family break up. These, taken singly or together, can leave little energy for dealing with their primary adaptation to Canada.

The Settlement Phase is an uncomfortable time because it is then that the pain of loss of homeland and identity may be felt most keenly by members of the ethnicity. If this painful process can be kept in view as "normal" to the aforementioned archetypal process of "death-rebirth," then the last phase will gradually emerge. An adapted group-cultural identity emerged in ethnic communities in Canada, as responses to questions like "Who are we?" or "Why are we here?" Perceptions of alienation and of being in limbo often lead ethnic-group members to begin the development of ethnic institutions in Canada and to alter their group culture to a form more consonant with life in Canada.

BENCHMARKS D → E: ETHNIC COMMUNITIES AND IDENTITY

Since the earliest days of European settlement in Canada, as waves of immigrants moved in, ethnic-group communities have grown, expanded, and evolved. At one and the same time, the collectivity evolved as a place of opportunity or bleak prospect, and from this its particular character developed.

Settling into Canadian communities, immigrants and their Canadian-born descendants help to lay down the structure of their group's cultural life in those locales. They develop ethnic community institutions that adapt the cultural ideas brought with them from their place of origin to their situation in Canada. Some of these institutions are beloved, familiar, and sources of great comfort and security. Religious institutions—churches, synagogues, temples, and mosques—were built. Food and dry-goods stores carry familiar and prized goods. The residences of the group's members may be developed close together, making language retention easier. Job opportunities within the ethnic community or an ethnic sub-economy keep many members of the group together; whereas, for others, geographic mobility is required, and people are split away from the community. Adaptive responses to changing community conditions are largely predicated on level of education, English/French-language ability, and urban/rural background of the group's members. To address new problems arising from settlement and community development in the Canadian milieu, new institutions, such as immigrant-aid societies, are formed.

In any one locale, myriad forces affect the development of ethnic groups. Particular ethnic groups appear to have assimilated quickly and easily. The high-context groups of northern Europe, such as the Scandinavians, Germans and Dutch, were, a century or so ago, largely agriculturalists with strong religious connections. Canadian society presented relatively few surprises in terms of climate, language, social and family structure. Consequently, these groups adapted quickly and possessed few mechanisms of ethnic-group cohesion. Members of such groups will have developed moderate to low ethnic-group identities, especially as they and Canada changed to being of a low-context nature. Another set of ethnic groups, upon immigration to Canada in large numbers a century ago or less, became urban ethnic peoples. The Jewish and Italians settled in the cities and immediately developed their traditional ethnic institutions—religious and cultural—and soon after initiated organizations to enable urban cultural survival: ethnic education, social-service agencies, social and recreational organizations, and the like. These enable the maintenance of a high-context culture in the midst of the low-context urban centre.

Other ethnic groups, however, come from lands very different from Canada then or now, Asians and West Indians, for example. For such groups, skin colour, language and/or culture act as substantial barriers to settlement. Stores and restaurants specializing in familiar products and the cuisine of the ethnicity have done double duty as sources of customary food and also as bases for entrepreneurial activity. Schools and churches using the ethnic language grow, and ethnic newspapers increase in number and readership. This degree of proliferation of ethnic-group institutions depends on support from the people in the respective ethnicities in an area bounded by the limits of transportation; the distance from stores, schools, and churches must be a reasonable one.

As the various ethnic communities blossom and thrive, they become centres of attraction, drawing other members of the ethnicities from other parts of Canada who miss the language and culture of home. The very factors of density and richness of institutions reflecting a group's culture intensifies the observance of ethnic-group norms, values, and practices, thereby also influencing the pattern of cultural adaptation of the group.

Where immigrants in these large ethnic communities are of high-context origin, the strong values of hierarchy, gender segregation, and interdependence will emerge as ethnic-community norms and relationships, now seen as "ethnic" by non-group members. Normally, the man will be seen as undisputed family head, and the woman will be expected to maintain the home. Children are expected to be submissive to parental authority. Strong communal ties and mutual awareness by members of the ethnic community reinforce these values and practices, and members of the group are as cognizant of community attention to their maintenance of "proper" behaviour as they are of each other's behaving correctly. Where the correct behaviour of females is concerned, there is enormous concern, and often it is as important that women *appear* to be chaste as to actually be so.

The social control exerted on an ethnic group's members by the ethnic community grows out of the mandates of high-context cultures and gives each ethnic community its particular ethnic flavour. There usually is strong pressure in such communities for members to marry within the group, and various sanctions, from disapproval to expulsion, can be placed on those marrying outside.

One of the first forces to "crack" the united front of high-context culture is the employment of women outside the home, even if it is employment within the ethnic community. Although many high-context-culture women attempt to be both wage earners and traditional housewives (i.e., continuing to conduct all the home maintenance tasks ascriptively assigned to them), many start to question their gender-subordinate position and to demand a greater part in family and even community decision making. These changes, along with different values learned by their children in the school system, constantly force cultural changes, first on families but, inevitably, on the ethnic community as a whole.

As communities adapt both to forces from the larger society and to the needs of their own members, the nature of community institutions changes. Families move away from the "ethnic" areas of high residential concentration and either develop new ethnic communities or merge into very ethnically-mixed residential areas. The identity of community members also gradually changes. Even if they continue to be highly identified with their ethnoculture, their involvement in the community may be reduced. Ties with the ethnic church may be broken. Domestic routines become less dominated by the need for products from the homeland. Language retention declines.

Before leaving this topic, another dimension of community should be outlined. In the previous paragraphs "ethnic community" is spoken of as if it were a homogeneous, unified entity. In actual fact, there are many schisms in communities, the sources of which often lie in the past history of the homeland. Differences can be traced back to religion, social class, urban/rural culture, politics, and origins in different regions of the homeland. Where there is one main religion, the situation can be termed a Religious Monopoly. Generally, however, all of these dimensions can produce splits along which subgroups form. Even where there is high Religious Monopoly, there can be divisions based on the degree of orthodoxy or some other idiosyncratic issue which may be of local interest only. It is the impact of a multitude of these factors that makes each ethnic community unique.

So many varying conditions from within and from without combine to create the largely unpredictable events known as "ethnic communities." For Canada, they are the contents of the ever-changing society.

BENCHMARK F: THE SECOND GENERATION

The second generation were people born into immigrant homes. Their identity was laid down in the context of often-conflicting loyalties. On the one hand, the immigrants tried to instil the group cultural values that originated in the home country while at the same time the school system and other mainstream influences like media impressed different, often individualistic, values of the host society. In ethnic groups still predominantly high-context in culture, there was at least some conflict, sometimes marked and severe conflict, leaving parents, children, and youth in the ethnicity deeply stressed and divided. Schools and mainstream social agencies caught up in these problems often found resolution beyond their capability. Eventually, these second-generation members of the group matured and, through their adult participation in the community, influenced alterations in the ethnic values, structures, and practices. As ethnic communities evolve, expectations are modified, and the second generation experiences less community censure and exclusion. Of course, in immigrant homes where connection to high-context culture became reduced more quickly after settlement, there was greater and readier acceptance of the mainstream norms that affected the second generation and, therefore, less conflict from marked value differences.

This second generation provides another layer of schism in communities, but they also provide overlapping membership in the wider city outside the ethnic community. Thus, they connect the earlier generation to the larger society as well, even if in an indirect fashion.

BENCHMARK G: THE THIRD GENERATION AND BEYOND

In some ethnic groups, strong and pervasive ethnocultural links were rare at this stage of adaptation. Ethnic-group membership was usually of minor interest, and lifeways and cultural identity were often described simply as "Canadian." Looked at from the perspective of the third generation, many ethnic communities seemed "old fashioned," quaint or simply "ethnic," even though the third generation's roots are technically "ethnic" as well. The farther away one gets from the original migrating family, the more strange and alien "ethnicity" may seem.

However, among other ethnic communities, an opposite reaction occurred: a return to ethnic roots. Often the fully-acculturated third generation has made a conscious decision to renew its acquaintance with the old culture. These people sometimes sought language lessons for their children, manifested an interest in the old cuisine or even revived interest in the ethnic religion. These activities and connections gave a new vigour to community life, and members from the third, + generation found cultural meanings where there were none before. The pumping of interest back into the ethnic group from this rediscovered source is another tributary or stream that feeds the everflowing entity of ethnic life that comprises Canadian society.

## CHAPTER 12

Transitions: The Adaptations of Canadian Ethnic-Group Cohesion

INTRODUCTION: THEORETICAL APPROACHES

This chapter synthesizes the nature, direction, and magnitudes of adaptation Canadian ethnic groups have experienced in cultural cohesion. In this, some of the shifts already documented will be summarized. But, much of the empirical analysis and its interpretation will focus on indices chosen specifically to point directly to alterations and adaptations in ethnic-group culture.

In his discussion of ethnic communities' life cycles, Reitz (1980: 125) suggests two lines of analysis by which one can measure the degree of ethnic-group cultural adaptation: (1) the immigrant generation over time and (2) "the transition from the first or immigrant generation to the second generation and to subsequent generations." Unfortunately, the 1981 census did not contain questions about the birthplace of the respondents' parents, so the intergenerational distinctions cannot be made with the most recent data. Where the data for 1971 seemed essential to answering a particularly vital question on some aspect of ethnic cohesion, this was taken up in the chapter covering that cohesion index and will, therefore, be only summarized in this chapter. However, Reitz's notion of adaptation by the immigrants over time is more useful for the objectives of this part of the analysis of ethnic-community cohesion, but not in its existing form. What we do here is to expand Reitz's central precept of change to immigrants (i.e., change in cultural practices, structures) into the concept of *Longitudinal Change* in eth-nic-group cohesion. What this means in practice is comparing the level of cultural cohesion in the past to its most recent level—1981. This is done by calculating a ratio of longitudinal change: dividing the 1981 degree of cohesion by that found for an earlier date (× 100). To the extent the ratio exceeds 100, there has been an increase in the degree of ethnic-group cohesion, but to the degree the ratio is below 100, there has been a loss of cohesion in the ethnicity.

The Ratio of Longitudinal Change in ethnic-group cohesion obviously does not (cannot) also include specification of the many social factors within or external to the ethnicity that may have influenced its cultural transition, for example, the level of immigra-tion over the years, the nature of the cultural foundations in the group, the newness of the group to Canada in any large numbers, the ways in which the group varied from the charter ethnicities (especially in skin colour, religion, and so on), and the level of cultural cohesion in the group during its transplantation-immi-grant phase. More detailed statistics from the Canadian Censuses and original data will eventually shed some light on these social aspects, but for now, we will have to be content with the bare outline of the cohesion transition in the ethnic groups afforded by the longitudinal ratio.

A second focus of synthesizing the alterations in ethnic-group cohesion is the different forms that adaptation has taken within each of the various groups, as well as in general tendencies, if any can be validly traced. The "different forms" of adaptations men-tioned just above refer specifically to (1) groups that have in one or more indices of group cohesion apparently assimilated to the majority/another culture; and (2) the different structures of ethnic cohesion and change in cohesion as of a recent date. These analyses will be based on an inspection of graphs that indicate the relative positions of ethnic groups on a particular measure of ethnic-group cohesion and through graphs comparing the relative strength of different cohesion components within each ethnicity.

The final line of adaptation analysis followed here is to assess the extent to which the existing level of ethnic-group cohesion was dependent upon the degree to which immigrants made up the ethnic-group membership. Once more, this is conducted via the calculation of a ratio: the level (in percent) of ethnic-group cohesion divided by the percentage of the group then comprised of immigrants (× 100). The degree to which the ratio exceeds 100 would indicate ethnic-group cohesion extending into the Canadian-born generations, but ratios below 100 would point to cultural loss, even within the immigrant generation.

1981 OR 1971 INTERGROUP ETHNIC-COHESION RATES

At the outset, it must be assumed that in most of the Canadian ethnic-cohesion measures—language, residential proximity, endogamy, interaction networks, and so on—all groups must once have had cohesion rates close to 100%. Only in religious affiliation was it likely that cohesion rates could not have been very high in Canada in certain groups for whom there was religious diversity in the country of origin, for example, Britian and Germany. Thus, the positions of the ethnic groups in Canada at the time of the 1981 census (or the 1971 census for items on which there is not complete 1981 data) reflect the degree of adaptation here from a condition that existed during the immigrant-transplantation phase. The rates of ethnic cohesion for the various indices are contained in Figure 12.1, depicting the position of each ethnic group according to the particular cohesion mechanism. The "data" in this figure are in the form of symbols for each group (identified in the legend at the end of the figure) marked against the level of cohesion recorded on the margins of the figure(s).

Inspecting the seven central cohesion variables (the two language-retention factors, residential proximity, religion, the two media indices, and endogamy), certain regularities can be perceived: there are a collection of ethnic groups which exhibited high cohesion in all, or almost all, of the factors mentioned or which were at least not in the lower range of many indices: Asians, Jewish, Italians, French, Greeks, and Portuguese. Conspicuously absent

Figure 12.1

Ethnic Cohesion, Family and Other Social Indices among Canadian Ethno-Racial-Religious Groups

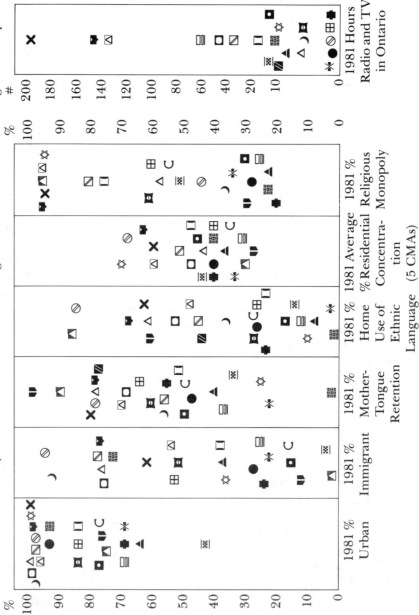

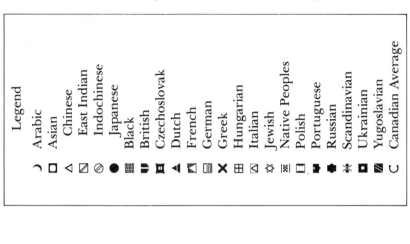

Figure 12.1 continued

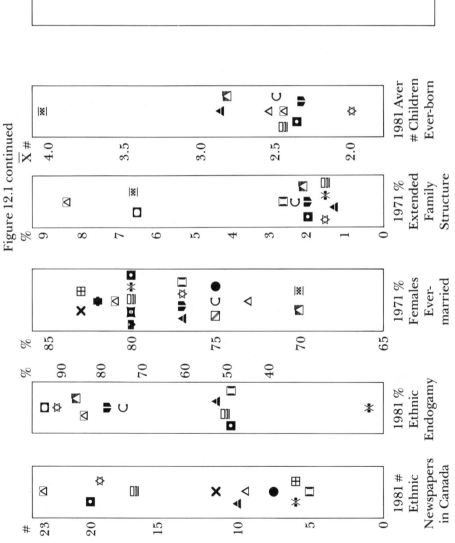

from this high-cohesion category are three visible-minority groups, the Japanese, Native Peoples, and Blacks (all of whom tend to have either intermediate or low levels of cohesion), and the British, who are generally low except in the language measures. At the lower reaches of ethnic-group cohesion are the British, plus Germans, Dutch, Scandinavians, Poles, and Ukrainians. Between these extremes are the remaining white ethnicities and Native Peoples. Thus, there seems to be some initial evidence here for a proposition that there indeed is mutual benefit between the different ethnic-cohesion mechanisms: i.e., a high cohesion level in one factor is associated with elevated rates on most, if not all the others. The reverse seems also to be true; i.e., a low cohesion level in one factor is accompanied by reduced rates in the other variables.

On the one hand, this empirically verifies that many Canadian groups fit into the Cultural Pluralism-Mosaic model of ethnic-group adaptation mentioned by Kallen (1982:155). Moreover, such outcomes of consistently high ethnic-cohesion mechanisms in multiple groups would be unlikely in a nation characterized by another form of adaptation. On the other hand, these data also suggest that there is a core of ethnic groups in Canada who have become either assimilated or marginalized, to use Berry's (1987) terms, or absorbed, in Kallen's nomenclature.

Regarding the family cohesion factors other than endogamy, the pattern is quite different. Some of the ethnicities like the Jewish, French and Chinese are not at the top, having either an intermediate or low level. Native Peoples, however, moderate to low in the previous measures, are high here in fertility and in the percent with an extended family structure. The Italians, otherwise high in cohesion, continue that in two of the family indices, but not in fertility. Other groups maintain their intermediate levels of ethnic-group cohesion in the family factors also.

Figure 12.2 approaches the intergroup comparison of ethnic-cohesion synthesis from the opposite direction; i.e., the figure(s) illustrates the hierarchy of ethnic-cohesion mechanisms within each group separately. From this, we gain a kind of topographic map of ethnic cohesion within each ethnicity and also the ability to compare interethnic variation in the structures of group-cultural mechanisms. In Figure 12.2, each of the variables of cohesion is denoted by a letter (definitions for these are given in the legend at the end of the figure). There is one category of ethnic groups with all, or almost all, of the cohesion influences registered in the top half of the figure's range, especially the central mechanisms of language (signified by "L" for Mother-Tongue Retention and "H" for Home-Language Use), Residential Concentration ("C"), Religious Monopoly ("R"), and Female Ethnic Endogamy ("M"). This category, having a high-range topography of ethnic cohesion, includes: East Indians, Indochinese and perhaps the Chinese among the Asian ethnicities; Greeks, Italians, Portuguese and probably the Spanish peoples. One could also add to this very cohesive aggregate the French (lower than others in Residential Concentration) and the Jewish (with very depressed language retention/use).

There is also the opposite set of ethnicities, those whose group-cohesion topography is characterized by most of the important cohesion factors being spread from middle to low rates: Japanese, Blacks, Czechoslovaks, Dutch, Germans, Hungarians, Native Peoples, Poles, Scandinavians and Ukrainians. The British form a separate category; because of the official status of their ethnic language they registered high in that factor, but in the other crucial cohesion influences they went from the high-middle to much lower ranges. Only the Portuguese (with the data available on them) conform to a nearly ideal typology, every group-cohesion index being in the top half of the range. The nearest examples of the opposite type are the Dutch or perhaps the Scandinavians.

In any case, what Figure 12.2 vividly depicts is that, even among groups with quite high overall ethnic-group cohesion, there are quite different structures of ethnic cohesion. If one accepts the Jewish as a group with an admirable degree of ethnic cohesion, then that group provides evidence that ethnic-community cohesion can be attained in Canada and maintained in this post-industrial era without the benefit of ethnic language maintenance—something that was in question. The French and Chinese show that today one can maintain high group cohesion with only moderate residential proximity, while the situation of the Blacks, Japanese, Arabs and Native Peoples demonstrates that simply being a visible minority these days is insufficient to lead to high group cohesion. Obviously, then, ethnic-group cohesion in the 1980s is founded upon the voluntary interactions developed within the ethno-racial-religious community, and is not forced onto the group as a protective reaction to blatant and widespread discrimination and segregation. If the latter were the case, then all the visible minorities would tend to have high cohesion levels, especially in residence, and this is hardly the case.

Figure 12.2

Indices of Ethnic Cohesion, Family and Other Social Factors within Canadian Ethno-Racial-Religious Groups

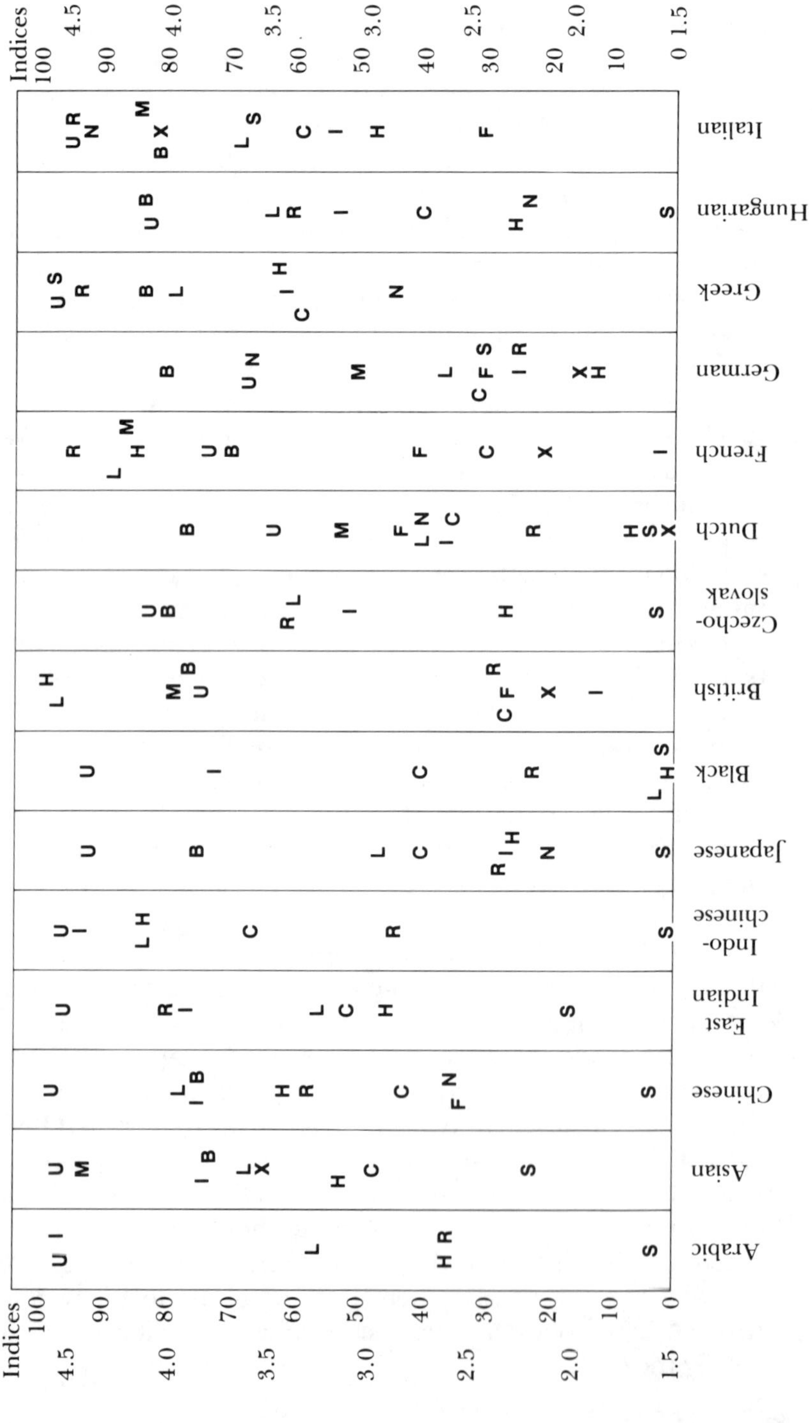

Legend

U	1981 % Urban
I	1981 % Immigrant
L	1981 % Mother-Tongue Retention
H	1981 M-T Used as Home Language
C	1981 Average % Residental Concentration
R	1981 % Religious Monopoly
M	1981 % Female Ethnic Endogamy
S	1981 # Radio & RV Hours Broadcast in Ontario (/2)
N	1981 # Ethnic Newspapers in Canada (× 4)
B	1971 % Females Ever-Married
X	1971 % Extended Family Structure
F	1981 Average # Children Ever-Born (outer index)

Indices: 100 4.5 · 90 · 80 4.0 · 70 · 60 3.5 · 50 3.0 · 40 · 30 2.5 · 20 2.0 · 10 · 0 1.5

Groups: Ukrainian, Spanish, Scandi-navian, Russian, Portu-guese, Polish, Native Peoples, Jewish

LONGITUDINAL SHIFTS IN ETHNIC-GROUP COHESION

A very common way to conceptualize shifts in ethnic-group cohesion is to ascertain differences over time. The "time" variable, however, covers more than just alterations over a period of years. Because the demographic and structural composition of the ethnic communities also are changing over "time," what may also be caught in the measuring of time shifts in cohesion are the effects of both the assimilative tendencies from duration in Canada as well as more low-context values and processes in the ethnicities. This will be so especially if the communities in question have experienced a change from the immigrant-transplantation stage to a community controlled more by Canadian-born members. With the kind of data at hand, it is impossible to sort out the varying influences from time-flow alone versus those exclusively from community structural and other social changes. Even so, measuring the extent of alteration in the ethnic-cohesion mechanisms will provide an indication of where the ethnic group was as of a certain date and, thereby, in what direction and with what rapidity ethnic-group cohesion was headed.

Table 12.1 reports longitudinal cohesion ratios of change; ratios below 100 indicate a decline in that particular mechanism of group cohesion within the ethnicity over the period cited. Five facets of ethnic-group cohesion are followed: Mother-Tongue Retention, Home Use of the ethnic language, Religious Monopoly, Residential Concentration, and the Male Endogamy Rate. The dates of comparison are not the same across all variables, either because data was not available from 1931 in the home-language and residential aspects (1951 data are also missing for home language), or the absence of complete 1981 data on gender endogamy. Still, over most ethnicities included in this table, a rough comparison across different group-cohesion mechanisms is possible to derive a sense of the shifts that have taken place.

It is obvious that decline in group cohesion has been greatest in retention of the ethnic language. At the other extreme, the methods used to measure residence patterns reveal that there have been broad increases in the concentration of residence by members of most ethnic communities between 1951 and 1981. Figures too lengthy to have been included here affirm that of five cities compared (Halifax, Montreal, Toronto, Winnipeg, and Vancouver),

Toronto had by far the greatest average increment in Residential Concentration during this period: Ratio of 174, compared to 109 for Halifax, 128 for Montreal, 153 for Winnipeg, and 119 for Vancouver. Since the data sources and definitions for Residential Concentration differed only slightly over the dates included, there is every likelihood of these changes being real.

The impact of the post-1951 immigration to Canada is evidenced in all ethnicities by the much lower rate of cultural decrement or by even higher cohesion rates in the more recent (1971–1981) comparison period than in the older (1951–1981) one. Excepting the two charter ethnicities, Asians generally have suffered less cultural loss than other groups, especially over the half-century before 1981. In addition, several of the ethnicities which, in 1951, were well on their way to cultural extinction appear, by 1971–1981, either to have greatly improved group cohesion, or else to have achieved a marked slowdown of deterioration in group cohesion, these include: the Dutch, Germans, Polish, Scandinavians, and Ukrainians. Finally, those groups that in 1931 or 1951 had very high rates of cultural cohesion generally maintained those rates: the French, Greeks (although there is only partial data available), Italians, and Jewish. The major loser in ethnic-group cohesion and the main exception to the patterns just pointed to are the Native Peoples, whose language cohesion has eroded disasterously and whose level of endogamy is probably continuing to decline.

One further bit of information on longitudinal alterations in ethnic-group cohesion can be commented upon: "ethnic" newspapers, which, in the definitions of the genre, excluded newspapers printed by or for the British or French groups in Canada and the large dailies or weeklies published for everyone throughout Canada. Figures on Table 12.2 give the change ratios over three periods and lead to several conclusions. First, the Scandinavians have experienced a decrease through this century in their group's newspapers, more so than any other of the ten ethnicities compared. Second, from 1965 to 1981, there was a smaller increase in the number of these papers than in the two longer periods (1921 and 1951–1981). Indeed, from 1965 to 1981, Hungarians, Poles, and Ukrainians lost many newspapers, where in comparison to the earlier dates, 1981 represented more papers than before. Third, in six of the ethnicities and in the average over all the groups, there was at least a modest increase in the number of newspapers during the years from

Table 12.1

Longitudinal Cohesion Ratios in Ethnic-Group Cohesion Mechanisms for Canadian Ethno-Racial-Religious Groups, 1951–1981, 1971–1981

Ethnic-Group Cohesion Mechanism and Years of Comparison

Ethnicity	Mother-Tongue Retention		Home Use of Language	Religious Monopoly		Residential Concentration		Endogamy Rate##	
	1981/1931	1981/1951	1981/1971	1981/1931	1981/1951	1981/1951	1981/1971	1981/1931	1981/1951
Asian	69	92	96	*	*	98	115	*	116
Chinese**	79	87	98	79	*	*	*	*	*
East Indian	*	69	102	*	*	*	*	*	*
Japanese**	47	59	108	43	*	*	*	*	*
Black	*	*	*	53	*	*	*	*	*
British	99	99	100	88	83	104	84	*	93
Czechoslovak	73	98	93	76	97	*	*	*	*
Dutch	114	93	80	69	81	103	92	95	121
French	94	97	100	98	98	143	130	*	96
German	65	90	86	69	89	100	100	63	96
Greek	91	136	89	145	*	*	*	*	*
Hungarian	66	87	79	82	97	*	75	*	*

Italian	79	115	83	102	106	151	118	100	106#
Jewish	26	44	77	95	96	105	110	97	96
Native Peoples	35	40	56	98	96	*	*	83####	84####
Polish	55	72	100	88	107	90	112	64	86
Russian**	61	83	100	71	91	98	89	*	*
Scandinavian	32	61	100	55	72	136	100	36	45
Ukrainian	52	67	74	*	214	100	122	55	67
All Groups	62***	88**	100***	95	82	135	109	*	94

Notes: The higher the ratio, the greater has been the maintenance of ethnic-group cohesion. To the extent the ratio is below 100, ethnic assimilation has occurred between the dates cited. Ratios above 100 indicate that ethnic-group cohesion was greater at the time of the later date than in the earlier year.

    *   No Data.

  **   Religious category with the largest % of the group in 1981 was "No Religion."

***   Figure is for unofficial languages.

    #   1981/1961 ratio.

  ##   Joint gender rates used.

1971 rates used instead of 1981 rates.

Sources: Tables 5.1, 5.2, 6.2, 7.2, 8.1 (above).

Table 12.2
Longitudinal Cohesion Ratios for the Number of Ethnic
Newpapers in Canadian Ethno-Racial-Religious Groups

Ethnicity	1981/ 1921	1981/ 1951	1981/ 1965
Chinese	900	450	150
German	425	340	142
Greek	*	*	220
Hungarian	600	600	67
Italian	460	383#	209
Japanese	250	250#	167
Jewish	633	158	127
Polish	250	167	83
Scandinavian	67	100	75
Ukrainian	333	250	62
All groups	738	583	162

Notes: The higher the Ratio value, the greater was the 1981 number of newspapers. To the extent a Ratio was below 100, a decline in the number of
newspapers in 1981 had been experienced by the group over the period
specified.
* No data.
# Conservative estimate.
Source: Table 9.6 (above)

1965 to 1981—up to more than twice the number. Thus, overall,
the newsprint medium seems to be on a good footing in most of the
ethnicities, and the expectations are for at least a modicum of stability within most groups at the very worst or continued expansion at
best.

COHESION RATIOS BASED ON
PERCENT IMMIGRANT

It will be recalled that Breton (1964) had suggested that the many
bonds of ethnic-community cohesion might well be a product of the
immigrant phase of a group, when few of the community members
were Canadian-born and the culture of the group in Canada was
essentially an Old-World culture brought here by the immigrants.
Breton believed that, as the members of the ethnic community
became more integrated into the wider city activities and as the
second generation grew more numerous, the ethnic group's cul-

ture and cohesion would wither away, and cultural assimilation would replace cultural cohesion. To test that hypothesis, one must be able to ascertain the degree to which elements of ethnic-group cohesion are dependent upon the immigrant portion of the ethnic community.

This can be roughly ascertained using the census data presented earlier, by dividing the level of cultural maintenance for each of the major cohesion mechanisms by the percent of the group that was immigrants (× 100). This measure is here called the *Cohesion Ratio* based on an immigrant presence. The Ratio can be calculated as far back as there is data on each particular cohesion index. For Mother Tongue this is 1921; for Home Language, 1971; Religious Monopoly, 1871 for three ethnicities and 1931 for most others; Residential Concentration, 1881; Ethnic Endogamy, 1921 for three groups and 1931 for almost all others. So there is a long period of ethnic community existence that can be surveyed to ascertain the degree of group cohesion dependent upon immigrants in the group. To the extent that a ratio is above 100, the degree of cultural cohesion in the group was being maintained by the Canadian-born generations—was *not* dependent solely upon the immigrant portion of the group's membership for cultural cohesion. When a Ratio is below 100, the implication is that there has been decay of cultural cohesion even among the immigrants in the ethnicity (Tables 12.3 to 12.7).

Mother-Tongue Retention

Although previous figures have shown that the deficit in cultural cohesion has been great for maintenance of the ethnic language, Table 12.3 provides evidence that, even in 1981, the group's heritage language was being maintained in most groups above the level that would suggest immigrants as the primary or sole language protectors. Prominent among these groups in which Canadian-born members must be language maintainers (in addition, of course, to the group's immigrants) were the Japanese, Czechoslovaks, Germans, Greeks, Hungarians, Italians, Poles, Portuguese, Russians, and Ukrainians. To these ten ethnicities can also be added the two official charter groups (whose language-maintenance levels are exceptionally high because of their legal status, no doubt) and the unofficial charter ethnicity, the Native Peoples.

At the other end of the cohesion continuum there is a small

Table 12.3

Ratio of Mother-Tongue Retention Level to Percent Immigrant in Canadian Ethno-Racial-Religious Groups, 1921–1981

Ethno-Racial-Religious Group

Year	Arabic	Asian	Chinese	East Indian	Indo-chinese	Japa-nese	British	Czecho-slovak	Dutch	Filipino	French	German	Greek
1921	*	114	106	*	*	137	385	159	165	*	3330	193	129
1931	*	127	112	*	*	190	396	114	85	*	3167	190	144
1941	*	164	121	*	*	249	495	130	144	*	4700	221	146
1951	*	*	128	*	*	296	619	111	124	*	4600	191	95
1961	*	*	136	*	*	273	707	80	106	*	4500	144	107
1971	*	131	127	*	*	187	817	110	109	*	4450	148	132
1981	117	92	104	73	88	174	817	118	108	59	4450	148	130

Year	Hungarian	Italian	Jewish	Native Peoples	Polish	Portu-guese	Russian	Scandi-navian	Spanish	Ukrainian	Yugo-slavian	Non-British, Non-French
1921	190	165	167	9400	196	*	100	132	*	215	74	205
1931	118	191	171	9300	140	*	115	134	*	219	71	186
1941	134	182	155	9999	169	*	145	130	*	263	85	206
1951	123	124	123	8300	125	*	112	106	*	243	53	264
1961	107	125	89	*	115	*	111	107	*	278	57	152
1971	123	131	73	2750	142	115	161	100	*	283	95	139
1981	121	130	69	825	134	109	239	100	100	327	*	147

Note: Ratio = (% M-T Retention/% Immigrant) × 100.
Source: Tables 3.4, 5.1 (above)

number of ethnicities whose level of cultural maintenance was just at to far below the level that they possessed as immigrants, indicating a failure in the group to sustain ethnic-language cohesion: East Indians, Indochinese, Filipinos, Jewish, Scandinavians, and Spanish peoples. The Jewish in Canada have had a rapidly-falling cohesion situation in language since 1931, when there was still a large number of immigrants in their community, so it would appear there was/is an endemic tendency among the Jewish toward linguistic absorption. This must also be the case in the two other ethnicities with Ratios well under 100—both heavily dominated by immigrants in their respective populations, but unable or unwilling to sustain their ethnic languages.

Some of the ethnic groups, however, are characterized by higher Cohesion Ratios earlier in the century when the fraction of immigrants in the groups was greater. For these groups—Japanese, Germans, Italians, Jewish, Poles, and Scandinavians—the decline in the size of the immigrant fraction seemed directly related to the fall from ethnic linguistic grace. Yet, there are other ethnicities in which the trend has generally been toward an increase in the Cohesion Ratio over the decades: the British, French, Russians, Ukrainians, and, perhaps, the Greeks. The British and French (through the Official Languages Act) have been able to institutionalize their languages with corporate status so that, as their immigrant fraction decreased, the Cohesion Ratio increased because language maintenance was virtually at 100% throughout the entire period covered. Russians and Ukrainians, who do not have the same structural supports for their languages, have experienced regular declines in the importance of immigrants for their populations, yet they still realized higher Cohesion Ratios as the decades passed, so much so that their 1981 Ratios were the highest recorded in this century. Since there are no apparent external forces, it must be that the rates of language retention have been falling more slowly than the percent of immigrants.

One might have predicted the Native Peoples to have a continuously high linguistic Cohesion Ratio, and it is very high, at a level any non-charter group dreams of. Yet, the level of cohesion reflected here is one of precipitous decay, despite the low portion of immigrants in the group. If it continues at the same pace, linguistic assimilation can be predicted. The causes for this may turn out to be the capture of Native Peoples in the towns and cities of Canada and their subsequent social and economic integration. The only other major surprise in Table 12.3 is the small margin of cultural maintenance exhibited by the Portuguese. The trend since 1971 is also one of linguistic loss—so great that the Portuguese may find it impossible to sustain their language as a major element of their urban-Canadian culture, especially as the number of Portuguese immigrants has been declining sharply in the 1980s.

Home Use of the Ethnic Language

The prospect for cultural cohesion through use of the heritage language in the home is much bleaker than for Mother-Tongue Retention (Table 12.4). In a very real way, home use of the language is even more critical, partially for definitional reasons, but also for reasons involving ethnic-cohesion dynamics. Mother-Tongue Retention is based on the census definition of continued "knowl-edge" and understanding" of the language first learned or learned jointly with another. However, neither knowledge nor understand-ing of a heritage tongue necessarily implies its use. No doubt many, perhaps even most, of those who recorded an unofficial language as their Mother Tongue do actually use it in their daily lives, at least sometimes. But the "Home-Use" measure refers not to knowledge or understanding but to routine use of the ethnic tongue as the usual medium of communication at home—a very utilitarian refer-ent, pointing not to cognition, but to behaviour. Thus, the Home-Use Cohesion Ratio touches much closer to home in the mainte-nance of the group's culture and, therefore, is probably a much better indicator of the degree of linguistic survival and use of the language than Mother-Tongue Retention.

Thus, the figures in Table 12.4 bode ill for continuation of the ethnic language as a viable vehicle for community cultural cohesion in most groups other than the charter ethnicities. Even for Natives, there is considerable reason to worry, given the stunning decline in their ratios. Only the Ukrainians and Russians were still able in 1981 to maintain their language as the home medium at a level above the theoretical minimum of immigrant usage. Especially destructive to ethnic culture were the disastrously low levels of Cohesion Ratios 50% or more below the percent of immigrants in the ethnicities in 1981: Dutch, Filipinos, Germans, Hungarians, Jewish, and Scandinavians. In contrast to the figures for Mother-Tongue Retention, no ethnicity showed an upturn or even stability in the Home-Use Cohesion Ratio between 1971 and 1981. The

Table 12.4
Ratio of Home Use of the Ethnic Language to the
Percent Immigrant in Canadian Ethno-Racial-
Religious Groups, 1971–1981

Ethnicity	1971	1981
Arabic	*	75
Asian	89	70
Chinese	100	81
East Indian	*	58
Indochinese	*	88
Japanese	100	96
Korean	*	58
British	542	500
Czechoslovak	59	53
Dutch	29	22
Filipino	*	36
French	4250	4250
German	56	48
Greek	111	102
Hungarian	69	50
Italian	107	91
Jewish	35	28
Native Peoples	2150	600
Polish	70	61
Portuguese	100	88
Russian	100	100
Scandinavian	14	14
Ukrainian	128	113
Yugoslavian	33	*

Notes: Ratio =(% using ethnic language at home/% immigrant in the
group) × 100.
* No data.
Sources: Tables 3.4, 5.2 (above).

picture that emerges from these statistics, then, is somberly pessi-
mistic with respect to both the existing linguistic support of ethnic-
community culture and to any hope that there will soon be a
levelling off at an only slightly lower plateau. If, as some suggest,
absence of linguistic vitality leads to an ethnic community's becoming dissociated from its cultural resources and practices, then the
future looks bleak for most of Canada's ethnic groups. There may
be hope, however, in the possibility—exemplified by the Jewish—
that an ethnic community can remain vibrant and forceful, even

improving its group cohesion without functional utilization of the heritage language.

Religious Monopoly

The story is quite different for religious cohesion in ethnic communities. One has to keep in mind that, in some of the ethnic groups, there is great religious diversity, so that only if there were relatively few immigrants in that ethnicity could the Cohesion Ratio be above 100. A good comparative example of this is that between the British and the Blacks. Each has a low Religious-Monopoly Rate indicative of the divisions within the groups between two or three major religions. Thus, when the proportion of Black Canadians who were immigrants was lower than the immigrant fraction within the British (i.e., 1931), the Blacks had a much higher Religious-Cohesion Ratio. Today, though, the situation is very much reversed with respect both to immigrant presence and, thereby, the Religious-Cohesion Ratio. Because of the issue of religious differentiation within certain ethnicities, the reader may wish to refer back to Chapter 7 to review the degree of Religious Monopoly in each group.

Overall, since 1931 the Religious-Cohesion Ratio has been variable, highest in the 1951 to 1971 period and lowest in 1931. Almost all ethnicities that are comparable (Table 12.5) have a long history of Cohesion Ratios in religious affiliation well above 100; the few exceptions to this, or to having an above-100 Ratio in recent decades (when there were no earlier figures) are Arabs, Chinese, Indochinese, Blacks, Dutch, Filipinos, and Russians. The French and Native Peoples' Ratios are so high, of course, because of the infinitesimal proportion of their memberships that were/are immigrants, although the Native Ratios are still worrisome because of their persistent declines. Other groups with elevated Religious-Cohesion Ratios are the British, Greeks, Italians, Polish, Ukrainians, and, especially, the Jewish.

Notwithstanding the above, certain groups are characterized by a mildly to greatly increasing Ratio over the decades: British, French (from 1931), Greeks, Jewish, Russians, Scandinavians, and Ukrainians (since 1951). There were fewer ethnicities who experienced a generally decreasing Ratio for Religious cohesion: Blacks, Germans, Italians (from 1941) and Native Peoples. And another five ethnic communities have shown a curvilinear pattern of

Table 12.5
Cohesion Ratio of the Rate of Religious Monopoly
to the Percent Immigrant in Canadian
Ethno-Racial-Religious Groups, 1871, 1931–1981

Ethnicity	1871	1931	1941	1951	1961	1971	1981
Arabic	*	*	*	*	*	*	75
Asian	*	86	86	*	*	44	47
Chinese	*	82	82	*	64#	87	76
East Indian	*	*	*	*	*	*	104
Indochinese	*	*	*	*	*	*	47
Japanese	*	125	*	*	*	142	104
Black	*	205	*	*	*	53	31
British	109	132	170	219	257	258	242
Czechoslovak	*	111	123	115	128	122	120
Dutch	*	160	194	108	67	94	59
Filipino	*	*	*	*	*	*	91
French	9999*	3233	4850	4850	4800	4700	4750
German	238	120	133	133	104	104	100
Greek	*	114	*	*	*	143	154
Hungarian	*	101	121	119	107	127	115
Italian	*	198	233	220	158	174	179
Jewish	*	177	202	228	255	251	261
Native Peoples	*	5200	9999*	5300	3667#	1425	1275
Polish	*	160	193	159	162	215	197
Portuguese	*	*	*	*	*	128	126
Russian	*	61	58	65	74	87	87
Scandinavian	*	111	137	138	141	150	155
Spanish	*	*	*	*	*	*	103
Ukrainian	*	160	177	140	143	178	200
All Groups	359	259	317	440	350	373	331

Notes: To the extent Ratio exceeds 100, Religious Monopoly was higher than the
    level of immigrants in the group.
    * No data.
    # Estimated.
    9999* = Ratio above 10000.
Sources: Tables 3.4, 7.2 (above)

change: up, then down and maybe up again, or the reverse (Chinese, Japanese, Dutch, Polish, and Ukrainians). Finally, there are the Czechs and Hungarians whose patterns were more ones of stability than anything else.

Residential Concentration

The measure of residential proximity within ethnicities (averaged over five Census Metropolitan Areas—CMAs) is a more linear measurement, like language retention/use and endogamy and unlike religious affiliation. Thus, the interpretation of the Cohesion Ratio is more straightforward, as long as one recalls the patterns of immigration within a particular ethnicity.

In outcome, the Cohesion Ratio for residence is more like Mother Tongue than religion, in that just over one-half of the groups, rather than most of them, have recent Ratios well above 100. Highest (above the average of 219) in 1981, were the charter groups, Native Peoples and Ukrainians, all with small immigrant fractions. There is a second category of ethnic groups whose Cohesion Ratio was above 100 but below the very elevated levels of the four above groups. In this category were the Japanese, German, Italian, Jewish, Polish, Russian, and Scandinavian communities, most of which also incorporate a low percent of immigrants. There are two ethnic collectivities—the Dutch and Greeks—who had Cohesion Ratios of 97, probably not significantly below parity.

Then there are the seven other ethnicities that had 1981 Ratios well under 100. Lowest were the Spanish, Blacks, Chinese, East Indians, and Indochinese, all characterized both by a high percent of immigrants in their populations and the fact of being a visible minority. That such visible minorities should have such low residential Cohesion Ratios is excellent evidence that residential patterns in Canada's cities today are no longer determined by so-called dominant white ethnicities wishing to segregate the ethnicities, but instead by dynamics internal to the ethnic community. These groups, along with the other white ethnicities (Hungarians and Portuguese), signify that exceedingly high residential proximity is not mandatory in all groups to sustain an ethnic community. True, some of the low Cohesion Ratios are exaggerated (or technically so) because of the high "denominator" factor of the percent immigrant in the ethnicity. At least two of these seven groups, the Indochinese and the Portuguese, were characterized by very high 1981 rates of residential density. Moreover, not all of the visible minorities were high in residential concentration, as was emphasized in Chapter 6, and that relationship is continued here in their Cohesion Ratios. So, what will have to be done eventually is a detailed analysis, by generation-in-Canada, of differences in the

Table 12.6
Cohesion Ratio of the Average Residential Concentration (over 5 CMAs)
to the Percent Immigrant in Canadian Ethno-Racial-Religious Groups,
1881, 1901, 1911, 1951–1981

Ethnicity	1881	1901	1911	1951	1961	1971	1981
Asian	84	48	39	100	89	67	64
Chinese	*	*	*	*	*	*	57
East Indian	*	*	*	*	*	*	66
Indochinese	*	*	*	*	*	*	71
Japanese	*	*	*	*	*	*	152
Black	*	1250	*	*	*	*	56
British	117	208	130	162	186	267	225
Dutch	*	4100	457	140	97	111	97
French	8250	4000	3600	1050	1100	1150	1500
German	230	444	2800	147	119	124	124
Greek	*	*	70	*	*	*	97
Hungarian	*	*	*	*	*	110	77
Italian	85	84	66	95	81	93	111
Jewish	*	*	*	153	165	170	192
Native Peoples	*	*	5600#	*	*	*	1075
Polish	79	*	*	118	95	127	124
Portuguese	*	*	*	*	*	*	80
Russian	79	*	49	121	141	196	174
Scandinavian	82	66	44	100	115	159	155
Spanish	*	*	*	*	*	*	52
Ukrainian	*	*	*	150	170	211	300
All Groups	200	246	145	193	181	213	219

Notes: To the extent a Ratio exceeds 100, the level of Residential Concentration
    (as measured) was higher than the percent immigrants that comprised the
    group.
    *No data.
    # Estimated.
Sources: Tables 3.4, 6.2 (above).

levels of residential concentration and a formal assessment of the
ratio of immigrant-to-third, + generational residence tendencies.
    Between 1881 and 1981, there was a moderate degree of fluctua-
tion in the Cohesion Ratio for residential density, highest at the
beginning and at the end of the hundred years portrayed, lowest
during the period of highest immigration to Canada. This pattern,
however, characterizes only four or five of the eight ethnicities for
which a good time-series exists: Asians, Italians, Russians, Scandi-

296 / The Adaptations of Ethnic Groups in Canada

navians, and probably the British. A more downward trend fits the Dutch and, perhaps also, the Blacks, the Native Peoples, and even the French. But, based on available data, an incremental degree of residential cohesion beyond the immigrant maintenance was experienced among the Greeks, Jewish, and Ukrainians. Were figures for the full time series available on these last ethnicities, their patterns might be found more similar to the "U-shaped" time pattern. Interestingly, there seem to have been no ethnicities that had a stable residential Cohesion Ratio, even in the years following the Second World War.

Ethnic Endogamy

The final factor in assessing ethnic-group cohesion beyond the immigrant generation is that of gender endogamy (Table 12.7). Unfortunately, 1981 figures existed only for the charter groups and the Jewish. For the other groups in 1981, joint male-female rates were used from Table 8.1. Because endogamy, in most groups, tended to be so high (or moderate in groups with few immigrants), only one ethnic category in 1981 had an endogamy Cohesion Ratio below 100, the Scandinavians. The hierarchy in this Cohesion-Ratio set is rather similar to the others. At the top in 1981 were the French and the British by far; followed by Ukrainians, Jewish and Germans, all having a Ratio above 200. Based on the 1971 data, Native Peoples probably also had a very high 1981 Ratio, similar to that of the charter groups. At the bottom, were the Scandinavian, Polish, Asian, Dutch, and Italian categories—in that order.

In time sequence, the relative standings that existed in 1981 were not much different from those of 1931 or 1941; the major change since those earlier decades has been the much-improved Cohesion Ratio for endogamy among Jewish, Italians, Polish, and Ukrainians (1971 or 1981 compared to 1931 or 1941). At the other extreme were the Dutch, Germans, Native Peoples, and Scandinavians, whose recent Ratios were very much diminished from those of 1931 or 1941; the first two groups had fewer immigrants relatively than the Italians and Jewish, but more than the charter groups, Natives and Scandinavians. What this suggests is that in the Canadian-born generations, endogamy continues to be observed and valued, almost to the point of assuring ethnic group separation from others.

Table 12.7

Ratio of Ethnic Endogamy Rate to Percent Immigrant among Canadian Ethno-Racial-Religious Groups, by Gender, 1921–1981

Ethnicity	1921		1931		1941		1951		1961		1971		1981#	
	Male	Fem.	Male	Fem.	Male	Fem.	Male	Fem.	Male	Fem.	Male	Fem.	Male	Fem.
Asian	*	*	*	*	120	*	129	311	157	215	131	141	126	
British	*	*	*	*	281	*	531	537	579	547	675	615	666	651
Czechoslovak	*	*	100	133	94	*	*	*	*	*	*	*	*	
Dutch	*	*	241	311	312	*	172	179	149	160	144	165	141	
French	*	*	*	*	4650	*	4500	4400	4400	4300	4300	4200	4365	4280
German	237	*	218	250	223	*	236	260	186	189	204	204	200	
Greek	*	*	114	210	*	*	*	*	*	*	*	*	*	
Hungarian	*	*	117	137	88	*	*	*	*	*	*	*	*	
Italian	122	*	145	233	104	*	*	*	128	144	138	146	158	
Jewish	*	*	173	162	170	*	216	223	246	238	246	247	249	257
Native Peoples	*	*	9500	9000	9500	*	9400	8900	*	*	3950	3500	*	
Polish	*	*	136	159	88	*	119	142	117	143	123	124	129	
Russian	*	*	142	195	112	*	*	*	171	185	*	*	*	
Scandinavian	86	*	74	98	*	*	97	134	103	137	112	145	77	
Ukrainian	173	*	194	221	170	*	220	263	238	290	270	318	327	
All Groups	*		*		*		533		481		507		469	

Note: Ratio = (Endogamy %/% Immigrant for each group) × 100. To the extent a Ratio exceeds 100, endogamy is maintained by the Canadian-born members of that group. To the extent a Ratio is below 100, endogamy is below even the extent that immigrants are represented in the group.

*No data.

#Joint male-female endogamy rates used for most groups.

Sources: Tables 3.4, 8.1 (above).

ETHNIC-GROUP COHESION IN THE 1980s
AND BEYOND

Reitz (1980: 239) has raised an interesting "political" question: "Should ethnicity survive?" By this, I understand him to mean: Should there be in Canada a political will or decision to permit ethnicity to survive? In contrast, he also addressed the "sociological" questions of the extent to which ethnic-group cohesion existed and why it did so in this country. By asking the "sociological" question, I believe, Reitz made the "political" question irrelevant and rhetorical. The only real issue here is the degree to which ethnic communities can continue to survive, or increase their potential to do so. This is because, in Canada, there is absolutely no realistic social or political alternative to permitting the very many, different ethnic-group cultures to exist. Official multiculturalism has been the stance of the federal government since 1971 and of all provincial and most municipal governments within a few years thereafter. Moreover, section 23 of the Canadian Charter of Rights and Freedoms—Part 1 of the Constitution Act, 1982—explicitly recognizes the multicultural nature of Canada and its peoples with respect to language. And, section 15 of the Charter specifically prohibits discrimination based on "race, national or ethnic origin, colour, religion," or the like. With such prohibitions, the Charter says, essentially, that there are no legal "minority groups" in Canada (with the possible exception of the Native Peoples); linked to the fact that no individual ethnicity in Canada comprises a numerical majority, all groups are, demographically, "minorities." With such conditions, it can be reiterated that, unless the values and structure governing the nation are drastically altered, there is no democratic alternative to "permitting" all ethnic, racial and religious communities both to exist and to be self-maintaining within the bounds of the collectivity.

The only physically possible alternatives to permitting ethnic communities to continue are unthinkable in terms of the kind of democratic society we now comprise. The three means to prevent the continued survival of ethnic cultures in this country would have to be: (1) deportation of those unwilling or unable to be absorbed/amalgamated; (2) forced segregation of the culturally and racially distinctive within cultural and racial "homelands" outside the cities of Canada or in special ghettos inside them; or (3) extirpation of those who will not or cannot eliminate their cultural/racial difference from the homogenous majority.

But if the first strategy were to be followed, where could the new Canadian authorities send the nearly two million Jewish, Eastern Orthodox, Hutterite-Mennonites, non-Judaeo-Christians, Italians, Dutch, Polish, Ukrainians, and others who are Canadian-born, yet very likely to persist in retention of their ethnic and/or religions cultures? And, to where could such a government deport the nearly 330 000 members of visible minorities whose roots, among Blacks and Asians, go back at least two generations in Canada? Also, even granting that many of these Canadian-born ethnics could be classified as having a "country of origin" to which they could be banished, where could the 500 000 Native Peoples be shipped?

The third "solution" listed is, of course, altogether inconceivable in a Canada that had not fallen into moral ruin. If the first and the final solutions to achieving assimilation/absorption of culturally, racially and/or religiously divergent peoples are morally vile or impossible to implement, then the erection of segregated "homelands" or ghettos for racial or cultural minorities in Canada would be too impractical. Would—could—Quebec be made into the homeland for all French Canadians who refused to subscribe to complete cultural abandonment, forcibly separated from what would undoubtedly become an Anglo-dominant Canada? Even the racist, militarily-buttressed South African regime seems now— following the election of a more rightist, more racist parliament in early 1987—to doubt whether economic segregation of cultural or racial minorities is reconcilable with the dependence upon many of these same minorities being economically integrated.

So too would it be in a Canada newly turned to achieving assimilation or dominant conformity. To eliminate ethnic-group cultural survival or to end cultural pluralism as state policy, which Lupul (1983) and Peter (1981), for instance, seem to be suggesting, the Canadian government would have to be transformed into a machine, not just for cultural-racial-religious oppression and repression, but also for very crude economic exploitation. Such treatment of the classified minorities would, sooner or later, make the segregated places into the homelands of resistance. Inevitably, a cycle would arise of counter-resistance by military and police actions following each new act against repression. Indeed, any of the three solutions for ending ethnic-group survival would ultimately be self-defeating. The maintenance of Canada's existing post-industrial society, and especially its economy, requires an absolutely unrestrained integration of workers in the society and economy, based on individual merit and potential for productive contribution. This kind of essential egalitarianism is absolutely incompatible with any kind of legal or geographic constraints on either free movement or the rights of all ethnic peoples and communities to participate voluntarily.

No, deviation from Canada's constitutionally-guaranteed "mosaic" form of respecting and promoting ethnic, racial, and religious differences would destroy not only the economic labour force, but, derivatively, our entire society as well. Just as time cannot run backwards, neither is it feasible to return to a pre-pluralistic mode, or move to a post-pluralistic system negating our existing nearly-absolute guarantees of cultural, religious, and racial rights. Indeed, Prime Minister Trudeau, more than 17 years ago, recognized not only the principle of justice behind an official multicultural policy on the part of the federal government, but also the benefit from making a virtue out of the necessity for such a policy, a policy now espoused also by the junior levels of government. With that step, Canada was, it seems, inevitably set on the road to the present existence of constitutional specifications for ethno-racial-religious freedom of individuals and ethnic communities. These rights are irrevocable. It is inconceivable that the immense shift backwards to cultural-racial totalitariansm could take place; there is no turning back, barring an extreme national catastrophe, such as a nuclear Armageddon. Accepting the logic of all this, then the only other questions worthy of study and debate are those dealing with the extent to which ethnic culture has survived and how it manages to do so.

In addressing the issues of ethnic-group cohesion and the mechanisms involved in this, it becomes readily evident that the very diverse and relatively new sources for immigration since the 1960s have combined (not coincidentally) with the official cultural pluralism to create an environment in which the cultural survival of every ethnic, racial, religious community is feasible, given the will of the members to develop and sustain it. But equally clear, I think, is the fact that without major, planned and sustained intervention by ethnic community leaders in joint enterprise with both senior and junior levels of government, only some of the mechanisms of ethnic-group cohesion can survive. From the pattern of findings presented in this book and their interpretations, eight patterns can be seen emerging in the life of Canada's ethnic communities in the 1980s and beyond, outcomes entirely different from the patterns of the past.

Ethnic-Language Retention and Use ✍

First, heritage-language retention and use seem to have been utterly ravaged in some ethnicities and almost non-functional in many (most?) others as a means of ethnic-group cohesion. It is so diminished in so many groups, I believe, that it exists merely as a cultural fetish for the Celts, Germans, Japanese, Jewish, Native Peoples, Polish, Scandinavians, and Ukrainians, among others, in a nation now dominated by official bilingualism. Given that even largely-immigrant urban ethnic communities are today imbedded in an Anglo-Francophone milieu, allophonic groups have increasingly smaller chances of maintaining their languages' utility, unless major alterations in the survival methodology are adopted.

If plans were mounted by the respective ethnic communities for massive efforts to revive the language within their communities, and if such plans received the socio-political and financial support of all levels of government, it might just be possible for Canada's ethnic groups to revive the unofficial languages as a fully-functioning device of group cohesion. Even so, what probably is essential to achieving such a linguistic resurrection is the transformation of official bilingualism into official multilingualism "where sufficient numbers warrant," as the Royal Commission on Bilingualism and Biculturalism investigated, seriously considered, but eventually rejected. In places where there are sizeable ethnic groups and perhaps territorial concentration as well, making these now unofficial languages legal media of communication in the schools, courts, legislatures, and so on would probably enable the revitalization of ethnic languages—at least in those locales and perhaps throughout Canada. Total linguistic legitimation in every venue of social activity is not being suggested here; it is assumed that the economy, most schooling, court cases, and parliamentary activity would be conducted in English or French, but it would be legitimate to utilize other, specially designated newly-official, languages in the legal and institutional lives of people in the region. Lest it be feared as too radical, this change would not be precedent-setting, since Switzerland and Sweden have long permitted legal multilingualism for state operations.

Even so, it is doubtful that, even with collectively-planned ventures by ethnic communities and governments and even if appropriate changes were made in the Official Languages Act, that these can be effected soon enough to halt the demise of so many of the ethnic languages. This pessimism exists despite the apparent plateau of language maintenance reached in most ethnic groups in 1981, and even the minor increments in a few others. In large part, my doubts about soon or sufficient change derive from the recalcitrance of provincial governments to accept official bilingualism in their spheres, let alone official multilingualism.

Increased Role of Ethnic Organizations

What seems to be emerging as a substitute for ethnic language in the cultural communities, especially within Canada's cities, is ethnic-group cohesion being well maintained by the increased influence and combination of other mechanisms. What I conclude from the statistical and other data is that Canada's ethnic communities have gone through a transition from survival based in the heritage tongue during the immigrant transplantation phase (as Isajiw called it) or the immigrant-urban enclave (as Driedger perceived it), to enter the post-immigrant, post-enclavic period in which ethnic-group survival is founded in the development and expansion of a very elaborated set of formal ethnic institutions—in short, communities based on institutional completeness.

Other group-cohesion forces that have become the principal community supports today—residential concentration, religious monopoly, and endogamy—are very closely tied to the increasing importance and sophistication of ethnic organizations. The most recent ethnic groups to arrive with large numbers in Canada, the Latin Americans, Filipinos, and the Southeast Asian groups of Vietnamese, Laotians, and Cambodians (during the late 1970s and early 1980s) plus the Chinese, East Indians, Koreans, Portuguese, and West Indians (a decade before) are demographically dominated by the immigrant generation, as would be expected. Even so, rather than depending primarily on linguistic integrity as their community mainstay, these peoples have been building formal organizations to meet their group-cohesion needs: religious, economic and financial, cultural, recreational, governance, media, and especially social and health agencies. In many of these sectors, governments at all levels have become advisors and financial partners in constructing and maintaining the institutional infra-structure of the ethnic communities.

This is a far different situation from that which existed in the immigrant enclaves prior to the Second World War; more likely than not, governments back then were indifferent at best and active opponents at worst to organizational development specifi-cally, and to the sustaining of ethnic communities' cultural cohesion generally. There are so many ready examples of regular adversarial government relations with ethnic communities then in terms of restrictions on the expansion of ethnic-community territory, immi-gration prohibitions, withholding of the franchise, and other hos-tile treatment of non-charter ethnicities, that the present mutual friendliness and respect between governments and ethnic groups are nothing short of representing a stunningly welcome reversal. And, if current (mid-1988) media reports become reality, there is to be an expansion of the multicultural programmatic assistance to ethnic communities and many more specific government policies to implement the constitutional provisions for cultural pluralism and against discrimination.

In any case, the institutional development in our urban ethnic communities is a readily-understood outcome from even a brief period of living in a post-industrial society. The ethnic organiza-tional elaborations parallel and complement those of the wider society, where goods and services are institutionalized. This elabo-ration of ethnic institutions compares to the residual nature of meeting ethnic community members' social wants and needs pri-marily through individual or kinship efforts. With the emergence of institutional completeness as a (or *the*) main buttress of ethnic-group cohesion, there has been a corollary transition to residential proximity, religious affiliations, and endogamy in cultural mainte-nance instead of reliance on maintaining and using the ethnic language as the community's major vehicle of communication, information exchange, and social interaction.

Residential Concentration

The degree of residential proximity in most of the ethnic groups studied has been increasing since 1951 and exists within the Cana-dian-born generations to a significant extent in about one-half of the ethnicities. Concentration of residence, of course, has been both cause and effect of ethnic communities' organizational development. From the statistical findings, the residential factor is closely linked to the post-enclavic maturation of ethnic communities, although the origins for this lie within the closeness of residence during the immigrant/transplantation phase of ethnic-group adaptation.

What is remarkable today is the almost immediate transition from the use of residential concentration to isolate ethnic-group members from extra-ethnic influences, and to help develop traditional institutions like the ethnic church, to its use as a basis for convincing governments and other mainstream funders in the city to help develop organizations useful to the membership mass. The reason for these funders' complying with at least some of the requests for support is that the services being developed are not traditional ones, but new ones arising from the ethnic community's being imbedded in a developed society. The function of most of these new organizations and services is to enable greater integration of the group members into the city and its majority institutions, rather than enforcing a self-isolating enclosure around the group and its separation from the extra-ethnicity structures. For instance, in one of the major new kinds of ethnic organizations, social- and health-service agencies, co-operation with mainstream funders as well as mainstream agencies seems to be emerging as the desired form for development and operation of services to meet new needs in the residentially concentrated ethnic community (Herberg and Herberg, 1987), instead of relying on the traditional immigrant agencies of problem resolution, the church and the kin network.

Religious Monopoly

Religious Monopoly in most of the ethnicities dealt with has remained stable and has even increased recently in some groups. The connection between the ethno-religious enclosure of group cohesion and the formal organizational network in the ethnic community is both intimate and obvious. Religion, as practised by members of Canada's ethnic communities, exists as a manifestation of churches—formal organizations of religious belief and practice. Thus, as ethnic-group cohesion has become increasingly reliant on the diversity and number of its formal institutions, the formally-organized religious observance has grown in its contribution to the community's retention of membership and its loyalty. And, it should not be forgotten that ethnic churches often overlap into the provision of educational, cultural, recreational, and social services by dint of their formal structures' having the human, material, and financial resources essential for meeting community needs. In this way, too, the other formal organizations that share the same functions, acting collectively with the ethnic churches, legitimize the expansive role of the religious institution, in turn encouraging continued loyalty to the ethnic religion and its places of worship.

Ethnic Endogamy

Marriage within the ethnic community continues, for the most part, to be a powerful contributor to ethnic cohesion. In a way different from other factors, Canada's post-industrial policy of multiculturalism has permitted the maintenance of ethnic endogamy. Since endogamy is a conservative reflection of ethnic cohesion, being based in events that occur only once or twice in most people's lifetimes, the greater valuation of ethnic cultures and community cohesion has validated the concept of marriage within the group as a means by which individuals can simultaneously follow traditional norms while also implementing the post-industrial value of maintaining ethnic cohesion. Moreover, the existence of multiple formal ethnic organizations—the joint product of modernity and multiculturalism—can be perceived to comprise additional arenas for the social and personal associations between prospective intra-ethnicity marital partners. In view of endogamy's so effectively fitting in as a still-prominent source of ethnic-group cohesion in Canada today, it is not surprising that there is a synergistic exchange benefit with other cohesion mechanisms. This interaction effect is so widespread and influential that ethnic endogamy is among the strongest ethnic-group cohesion forces affecting the Canadian-born generations in most ethnic communities. Given this situation, little change in the importance of endogamy to ethnic community maintenance is likely.

The Adaptations of Ethnic Groups in Canada

Most of the ethnicities in Canada have taken on a post-industrial, urban, ethnic-community form, dependent primarily on the development of new, particularly relevant, formal organizations. This transition from traditional institutions to ones more compatible with life in the urban milieu has begun to benefit even the mostly-assimilated ethnic groups in Canada—Japanese, German, Celtic, Scandinavian, and some others. Readers in virtually any Canadian urban locale, if they ask the right questions of the right informants and conduct even informal, but conscientious and constant, observation, will come up with ample evidence that groups that were almost completely *de facto* assimilated have, nevertheless, begun to develop new types of cultural organizations. These may include those needed to obtain mainstream financing for cultural revival, for instance, or for establishing a new umbrella organization to represent the ethnicity regionally or nationally. It is a matter of question, though, exactly how far such last-resort efforts can reverse the ebbing tide of community cohesion, however farseeing and well-thought-out such ventures may be.

For other ethnic communities that successfully established their transplantation-enclavic stage, it would appear that Driedger was, in large measure, accurate when he suggested that forthright, carefully-planned actions were the only means to assure the community's transition to a post-enclavic form by means of a more compatible, revitalized, urbanized structure and process. The data in this book and external information on institutional development lead me to conclude that the post-enclavic, post-industrial system for group cultural cohesion is now characteristic of the older Jewish, Italian, Chinese, Black, French, Hungarian, Polish and Ukrainian communities, as well as of the more recently founded Latin-American, Muslim-Arab, Vietnamese-Lao-Cambodian, and Filipino group establishments. What all of these and, probably, some other ethnic communities manifest are cultures that do not reflect immigrant or traditional ethic values, expectations, and processes so much as all of these adapted over the past 15 or so years so as to inculcate and exhibit the beliefs and social forms dominant in the urban centres of the country. It is these transitions that hallmark present forms and methods of ethnic-group cohesion. In a strange way, ethnic communities today are developing group enclosure mechanisms and their formal organizations not to maintain separation from the rest of Canadians, as was the case before the Second World War, but, actually to enable individual and collective integration of group members into the extra-group society. Thus, the enclosure and compartmentalization processes today operate not to achieve exclusivity, but accommodation.

Ethnic Relativity

The data evaluated in this book consistently pointed to regularities over time and ethnicities in ethnic-cohesion patterns, and there do seem to be some overarching principles governing the nature of ethnic-group cohesion in Canada and its adaptation over the decades. But there was also a substructural set of findings throughout this work that is almost contradictory: the differences that persist between groups in the levels of ethnic cohesion, the diversity in cohesion processes between groups, and the varying patterns of transition from one kind of cohesion structure to another. In short, there is ample documentation of underlying differences between ethnic groups in their values, structures, processes, and contents that have led to entirely distinct ethnic-group lives. Each different pattern is sociologically legitimate and should be appreciated as being an expression of the organic process unfolding in each of the ethnic collectivities.

Even quite exaggerated values, structures, and directions of adaptations must be acknowledged as arising from the ongoing order in interactions and institutions within ethnic communities possessing different histories of settlement and cultural transplantation. They also have different patterns of success or failure in establishing what Dreidger termed the urban ethnic enclave and the transition from that to developing new ethnic-group processes and institutions of ethnic-group cohesion in the post-industrial era. It is in this sense that the term "ethnic relativity" characterstizes the uniqueness of each ethnic group. In terms of the ethnic-relativity process, different conditions and characteristics of the various ethnic communities gave rise to distinctiveness of pattern and purpose in the social phenomena of group cohesion. While the rationale, if there was/is one, and the particular paradigm of foresight held by the group can only be understood and appreciated from within the group and from participation in these collective journeys through time and culture, the data—in an "objective" sense—project a shadow of this ethnically relativistic experience that can be perceived by everyone in a unidimensional way. In another forum (E. Herberg, 1987) I emphasized that the kind of analysis conducted here must be balanced with other research and interpretations originating from inside each ethnic community, so that the subjective distinctiveness of the group's culture can be better appreciated in a fashion something like the way in which the members of each group understand and live it.

The Cultural Demise of Canada's Native Peoples

There is one ethnic collectivity in Canada that, from the analyses presented in this work, seems destined for cultural disintegration: the Native Peoples. Shockingly, their cultural cohesion over recent decades, as charted here, has become progressively more moribund. I cannot but associate this precipitous decline with the equally-swift urbanization of Native Peoples in this country. It appears that more than one-third of the Native Peoples migrated to the cities where they became culturally absorbed (E. Herberg, 1986)—despite the excellent work being done in Native friendship centres and other Native urban organizations in most cities to prevent, halt or reserve such cultural loss.

I believe that such cultural injury occurred because so much of Native culture is bound up with the reserve-wilderness ideology, which mandates that the Native values of being part of and cousins to the other parts of nature should be manifest in daily activities— something impossible in the city, where one can only talk or sentimentalize about it. Without a reserve-wilderness existence, it seems, Native cultural cohesion deteriorates.

Currently there is controversy as to whether an adapted Native urban culture can be created that reflects a more compatible relationship to city life (Redbird, 1980; Weinfield, 1985). Many Native People believe that the only possible source for their community culture today and tomorrow is one that reflects the reserve ideology and pan-Native values (Anderson and Frideres, 1981: 268, 308), and that crafting an urban Native culture that still contains true Native values and perspectives is not feasible. Others insist that this can be done and, more importantly, that it must be done—that the development of such a cultural identification compatible with city structure and process represents the sole means of permitting the almost 250 000 urban Native persons to develop a sound foundation for the survival of Native communities in urban locales.

The root of the Native Peoples' cultural vulnerability is their lack of control over their community life, something no other Canadian ethnicity has experienced to the same degree. The Indian Act and the federal and provincial departments designated to oversee Indians, Inuit, and other Native Peoples have conducted their offices for the benefit of the government and non-Natives who have a centuries-old exploitative interest in Native Peoples' lands and monies. Most Native Peoples today are based in government-established and supervised reserves or other segregated places, often involuntarily and/or without total (or sometimes any) legal control of territory. They are unable to conduct their collective lives as they see fit. The preservation of that small fraction of their culture remaining from the pre-European era has been made even more problematic by the intrusive, paternalistic supervision of governments over almost all aspects of their existence. It is no wonder that Native People, with little experience permitted them in shaping their culture and its adaptation on the reserves, have fared even worse in the cities. Native leaders sometimes refer to their people as constituting the "Fourth World": lacking a sound economy and suffering social, health and other deficiencies that limit their ability to compete with others, they are governed by non-Natives as a colony within Canada.

It may be that the achievement of Native self-government and settlement of their land claims offer the sole remedies for the revitalization of Native cultural cohesion. Autonomy and control over their territory would, or at least, could, constitute the foundations for crafting the values and structures of an adapted culture, appropriate to social independence. This sort of cultural set would be more appropriate for the transition to the city which seems to be occurring continuously.

However, if the attainment of socio-political control over their lands and governance is the answer to the Native Peoples' cultural insufficiencies, then the outlook for the future is cruelly foreboding indeed, in view of the devastating failure of the First Ministers' Conference on Aboriginal Self-government in early 1987. The federal government's utter refusal to even consider a date to re-examine this issue, despite the pleadings of Native leaders, gives painfully clear evidence that the fundamental structural problems disabling Native community life will not soon be resolved. The consequences for both reserve and urban cultural cohesion of the Native Peoples will continue to be brutally deleterious.

Notwithstanding, even if land and government autonomy were won by the Native Peoples tomorrow, it is unclear how these would apply to the large minority of Native Peoples who reside perma-nently in urban locales. How could Natives in the city, for instance, exhibit any significant measure of the self-government that reserve

Natives would enjoy? What implications from settlement of Native land claims would there be for urban Native Peoples? How would the values and structures of the new reserve culture(s) transfer to urban Native communities as a basis for culture there? Would the self-government and land entitlement possessed by reserve-wilderness Native Peoples function as a cultural talisman only for them and not their urban cousins?

It is a tragic irony that as Native Peoples cultural cohesion continues to collapse, especially in the cities, many other urban ethnic communities situated on once-Native lands are thriving. The benefits to ethnic-group cohesion from changed law and policy now enjoyed by so many non-Native ethnicities in this nation clearly elude the Native Peoples. The cultural transitions of the non-Natives mark a pilgrimage that Native Peoples have barely begun, a quest for community that few Natives will ever conclude. The experiences of the Jewish, Italians, Chinese, Blacks, and many other group, especially the newly-resident peoples whose arrival in Canada ended their refugee odyssey, however horrific, now appear to have created quite satisfying ethnic community lives in Canada's cities. But unless there is radical change in the constitutional provisions for Canada's first peoples, we may be witnessing the physical dispersion of Natives, split between reserves-wilderness and the cities, with the consequent demise of their culture.

Bibliography/ References

Abu-Laban, B. 1980. *An Olive Branch on the Family Tree: The Arabs in Canada*. Toronto: McClelland and Stewart.

Adachi, K. 1976. *The Enemy That Never Was*. Toronto: McClelland and Stewart.

Anderson, A. B. and J. S. Frideres. 1981. *Ethnicity in Canada: Theoretical Perspectives*. Toronto: Butterworths.

Anderson, G. M. and D. Higgs. 1976. *A Future To Inherit: The Portuguese Communities in Canada*, Toronto: McClelland and Stewart.

Balakrishnan, T. R. 1976. "Ethnic residential segregation in the metropolitan areas of Canada." *Canadian Journal of Sociology* 1, 4 (Winter) : 481– 498.

———— 1978. "Changing patterns of ethnic residential segregation in the metropolitan areas of Canada." Paper presented at the annual meeting of the Canadian Sociology and Anthropology Association. London, Ontario.

Balakrishnan, T. R. and J. Kralt. 1987. "Segregation of visible minorities in Montreal, Toronto and Vancouver." In *Ethnic Canada*, edited by L. Driedger, pp. 138–157. Toronto: Copp Clark Pitman.

Berry, J. W. 1987. "Finding identity: separation, integration, assimilation or marginality?" In *Ethnic Canada*, edited by L. Driedger, pp. 223–239. Toronto: Copp Clark Pitman.

Binns, M. A. 1971. *Cultural Pluralism in Canada: An Exploratory Study of the Italians and the Ukrainians in London Ontario*. M.A. thesis, University of Western Ontario.

Boldt, M. and J. A. Long, eds. 1985. *The Quest for Justice*. Toronto: University of Toronto Press.

Brazeau, J. 1958. "Language differences and occupational experience." *Canadian Journal of Economics and Political Science* 24, 4 (Nov.): 532–540.

Brebner, J. B. 1970. *Canada: A Modern History*. Revised and enlarged by D.C. Masters. Don Mills, Ontario: Longmans.

Breton, R. 1964. "Institutional completeness of ethnic communities and the personal relations of immigrants." *American Journal of Sociology* 70, 2 (Sept.): 193–205.

―――― 1978a. "Stratification and conflict between ethnolinguistic communities with different social structures." *Canadian Review of Sociology and Anthropology* 15, 2: 148–157.

―――― 1978b. "The structure of relationships between ethnic collectivities.' In *The Canadian Ethnic Mosaic*, edited by L. Driedger, pp. 55–73. Toronto: McClelland and Stewart.

―――― 1978c. "The assimilation of immigrants. . . ." *The English Quarterly* 9, 2 (Summer): 29–38.

―――― 1981. *The Ethnic Community as a Resource in Relation to Group Problems*. Toronto: University of Toronto Centre for Urban and Community Studies.

―――― 1984. "The production and allocation of symbolic resources: an analysis of the linguistic and ethnocultural fields in Canada." *Canadian Review of Sociology and Anthropology* 21, 2 (May): 123–144.

Breton, R. and P. Savard, eds. 1982. *The Quebec and Acadian Diaspora in North America*. Toronto: Multicultural History Society of Ontario.

Burgess, E. W. 1925. "The growth of the city: an introduction to a research project." In *The City*, edited by R. E. Park, E. W. Burgess and R. E. McKenzie, pp. 25–62. Chicago: University of Chicago Press.

Burnet, J. 1975. "Multiculturalism, immigration and racism: a comment on the Canadian Immigration and Population Study." *Canadian Ethnic Studies* 7, 1: 35–39.

Campbell, J. 1949. *Hero With A Thousand Faces*. Bollinger Series XVII. New York: Pantheon Books.

Canada. 1890. *House of Commons Debates*, 1: 623.

Cardinal, H. 1969. *The Unjust Society*, Edmonton: Hurtig.

Chan, A. B. 1983. *Gold Mountain*. Vancouver: New Star Books.

Christiansen, J. M., A. Thornley-Brown, and J. A. Robinson. 1983. *West Indians in Toronto*. Toronto: Family Service Association of Metro Toronto.

Clark, S. D. 1962. "The Canadian Community and the American Continental System." In *The Developing Canadian Community*, by S. D. Clark, pp. 185–198. Toronto: University of Toronto Press.

Coats, R. H. and E. S. McPhail. 1924. "Introduction" Volume 2 of the *1921 Census of Canada*. Ottawa: Government of Canada.

Conze, E. 1959. *Buddhist Scriptures*. Baltimore: Penguin Books.

Creighton, D. 1961. *Dominion of the North*. Toronto: Macmillan.

Dahlie, J. 1983. "The future of ethnicity." *Canadian Ethnic Studies* 10, 1 (Spring): 4–5.

Danesi, M. 1983. "Early second language learning: the heritage language educational experience in Canada." *Multiculturalism* 7, 1: 8–12.

Darkovich, W. ed. 1980. *A Statistical Compendium on the Ukrainians in Canada, 1881–1976*. Ottawa: University of Ottawa Press.

Darroch, A. G. and W. G. Marston. 1971. "The social class bias of ethnic residential segregation: the Canadian case." *American Journal of Sociology* 77 (Nov.): 491–510.

———— 1987. "Patterns of urban ethnicity." In *Ethnic Canada*, edited by L. Driedger, pp. 111–137. Toronto: Copp Clark Pitman.

Darroch, G. and M. Ornstein. 1980. "Ethnicity and occupational structure in Canada in 1871. . . . "*Canadian Historical Review* 61, 3: 305–333.

Delos, J. T. 1944. *La Nation*. Volume 1. Montreal: Sociologie de la Nation.

DeVos, G. 1975. "Ethnic pluralism: conflict and accommodation." In *Ethnic Identity*, edited by G. DeVos and Ross L. Romanucci, pp. 5–41. Palo Alto, Cal.: Mayfield.

deVries, J. and F. G. Valee. 1980. *Language Use in Canada*. Ottawa: Statistics Canada.

Driedger, L. 1975. "In search of cultural identity factors: a comparison of ethnic students." *Canadian Review of Sociology and Anthropology* 12, 2 (May): 150–162.

———— 1976. "Ethnic self-identity: a comparison of ingroup evaluations." *Sociometry* 39, 2 (June): 131–141.

———— 1977a. "Structural, social and individual factors in language maintenance in Canada." In *The Individual, Language, and Society in Canada*, edited by W. H. Coons, pp. 211–241. Ottawa: The Canada Council.

———— 1977b. "Toward a perspective on Canadian pluralism: ethnic identity in Winnipeg." *Canadian Journal of Sociology* 2, 1 (Winter): 77–95.

———— 1978. "Ethnic boundaries: a comparison of two urban neighbourhoods." *Sociology and Social Research* 62, 2 (Jan.): 193–211.

Driedger, L. and G. Church. 1974. "Residential segregation and institutional completeness: a comparison of ethnic minorities." *Canadian Review of Sociology and Anthropology* 11, 1 (Feb.): 30–52.

Driedger, L., C. Thaker, and R. Currie. 1982. "Ethnic identification: variations in regional and national preferences." *Canadian Ethnic Studies* 14, 3: 57–68.

Eisenberg, L. and A. Kleinman. 1980. "Clinical Social Science." In *The Relevance of Social Science for Medicine*, edited by L. Eisenberg and A. Kleinman, pp. 1–26. Hingham, Mass.: D. Reidel Publishing.

Elkas, K. 1987. "Arabs in Canada." University of Toronto, course research paper.

England, R. 1929. *The Central European Immigrant in Canada*. Toronto: Macmillan.

———— 1976. "Ethnic settlers in Western Canada: reminiscences of a pioneer." *Canadian Ethnic Studies* 8, 2: 18–33.

Estabrook, B. 1982. "Bone age man." *Equinox* 1, 2 (March–April): 84–96.

Francis, E. K. 1947. "The nature of the ethnic group." *American Journal of Sociology* 52, 5 (March): 393–400.

———— 1976. *Interethnic Relations*. New York: Elsevier.

Frideres, J. S. 1983. *Native People in Canada*. Scarborough, Ont.: Prentice-Hall.

Glazer, N. and D. P. Moynihan. 1963. *Beyond the Melting Pot*. Cambridge, Mass.: MIT Press.

———— 1975. "Introduction." In *Ethnicity: Theory and Experience*, edited by N. Glazer and D. P. Moynihan, pp. 1–26. Cambridge, Mass.: Harvard University Press.

Gordon, M. M. 1978. *Human Nature, Class and Ethnicity*, New York: Oxford University Press.

Greenglass, E. R. 1972. "A comparison of maternal communication style between Italian and second-generation Italian women living in Canada." In *Social Pyschology: The Canadian Context*, edited by J. W. Berry and G. J. S. Wilde, pp. 335–344. Toronto: McClelland and Stewart.

Hall, E. T. 1976. *Beyond Culture*. New York: Doubleday.

Hansen, M. 1938. *The Problem of the Third Generation Immigrant*. Rock Island, Ill.: Augustana Historical Society.

Harney, R. F. 1978. "Religion and ethnocultural communities." *Polyphoney* 1, 2 (Summer): 3–10.

———— 1979. "Introduction" and "Records of the mutual benefit society." *Polyphoney* 2, 1: 1–3, 5–18.

Haug, M. R. 1968. "Social and cultural pluralism as a concept in social system analysis." *American Journal of Sociology* 73, 3 (Nov.): 294–304.

Hawkins, F. 1972. *Canada and Immigration*. Montreal: McGill-Queens University Press.

Helewa, C. 1982. "The Lebanese Palestinian Community in Canada." University of Toronto, course research paper.

Henripin, J. S. 1968. *Tendences et Facteurs de la Fécundité au Canada*, 1961 Census of Canada monograph. Ottawa: Statistics Canada.

Henry, F. 1973. *Forgotten Canadians: The Blacks of Nova Scotia*. Don Mills, Ont.: Longman.

Herberg, D. C. 1982. "Discovering ethnic root behaviour patterns." *International Journal of Intercultural Relations* 6: 153–168.

———— 1983. "Issues in multicultural child welfare: working with families originating in traditional societies." *Social Work Papers* 17 (Summer): 45–57.

Herberg, D. C. and E. N. Herberg. 1987. *Agency Needs and Problems in the Mental Health Issues Affecting Immigrants and Refugees*, brief to the Canadian Task Force on Issues Affecting Immigrants and Refugees (May).

Herberg, E. N. 1980. *Education Through the Ethnic Looking-Glass: Ethnicity and Education in Five Canadian Cities*. University of Toronto Ph. D. thesis.

_____ 1986. *Rural Residence and Ethnic Group Cohesion: Three Hypotheses Tested*, paper presented at the annual meeting of the Canadian Sociology and Anthropology Association. Winnipeg: University of Manitoba (June).

_____ 1987. *Ethnicity and Religious Affiliation in Canada, 1871, 1931– 1981*. Paper presented at the annual meeting of the Canadian Sociology and Anthropology Association. Hamilton, Ont.: McMaster University. (June).

Herberg, W. 1955. *Protestant-Catholic-Jew*, New York: Doubleday.

Higgs, D. 1982. *The Portuguese in Canada*. Ottawa: Canadian Historical Society.

Hill, D. G. 1981. *The Freedom Seekers*. Agincourt, Ont.: Book Society of Canada.

Hughes, E. C. 1948. "The study of ethnic relations." *Dalhousie Review* 27, 4 (Dec.): 477–482.

Humber, C. A. 1983. "The Loyalists" (letter to the editor), *Canadian Heritage* (Aug.–Sept.): 3.

Hurd, W. B. 1942. *Racial Origins and Nativity of the Canadian People*, 1931 Census of Canada monographs, Vol 13: 535–828. Ottawa: King's Printer.

Irving, W. H. 1987. "New date from old bones." *Natural History* 96, 2 (Feb.): 8, ff.

Isajiw, W. W. 1975. "The process of maintenance of ethnic identity: the Canadian context." In *Sounds Canadian*, edited by P.M. Migus, pp. 129– 138. Toronto: Peter Martin Associates.

_____ 1978. "Olga in Wonderland: ethnicity in a technological society." In *The Canadian Ethnic Mosaic*, edited by L. Driedger, pp. 29–38. Toronto: McClelland and Stewart.

_____ 1979. *Definitions of Ethnicity*, occasional paper #6. Toronto: Multicultural History Society of Ontario.

_____ 1980. "How to understand today's ethnic group." *Canadian Ethnic Studies* 12, 2: v–ix.

_____ 1981. *Ethnic Identity Retention*. Toronto: University of Toronto Centre for Urban and Community Studies.

Isajiw, W. W. and T. Makabe. 1982. *Socialization as a Factor in Ethnic Identity Retention*. Toronto: University of Toronto Centre for Urban and Community Studies.

Jansen, C. J. and L. R. LaCavera. 1981. *Fact Books on Italians in Canada*. Downsview, Ont.: York University.

Japanese Canadian Cultural Centre Newsletter 11, 7 (September, 1984): 4.

Jeness, D. 1976. "Canadian Indian religion," In *Religion in Canadian Society*, edited by S. Crysdale and L. Wheatcroft, pp. 71–78. Toronto: Macmillan.

———— 1977. *Indians of Canada*. Toronto: University of Toronto Press.

Jenness, R. A. 1971. "Canadian migration and immigration patterns and government policy." *International Migration Review* 8, 1 (Spring): 5–22.

Jopling, A. V., W. N. Irving, and B. F. Beebe. 1981. "Stratigraphic, sedimentological and faunal evidence for the occurence of pre-Sangamonian artifacts in Northern Yukon." *Arctic* 34, 1: 3–33.

Joy, R. J. 1972. *Languages in Conflict*. Toronto: McClelland and Stewart.

Kalbach, W. E. 1980. *Historical and Generational Perspectives of Ethnic Residential Segregation in Toronto, Canada, 1851–1971*. Toronto: University of Toronto Centre for Urban and Community Studies.

———— 1981. *Ethnic Residential Segregation and its Significance for the Individual in an Urban Setting*. Toronto: University of Toronto Centre for Urban and Community Studies.

Kalbach, W. E. and W. W. McVey. 1979. *The Demographic Bases of Canadian Society*. 2d ed. Toronto: McGraw-Hill Ryerson.

Kallen, E. 1982. *Ethnicity and Human Rights in Canada*, Toronto: Gage.

Kallen, H. M. 1924. *Culture and Democracy in the United States*, New York: Boni and Liveright.

Keyser, R. and J. Brown. 1981. *Heritage Language Survey Results*. Toronto Metropolitan Toronto School Board.

Kovacs, M. L. and A. J. Cropley. 1971. "Assimilation and alienation in ethnic groups." *Canadian Ethnic Studies* 4, 1–2: 13–24.

Krauter, J. F. and M. Davis. 1978. *Minority Canadians: Ethnic Groups*. Toronto: Methuen.

Kurelek, W. 1977. "Development of ethnic consciousness in a Canadian painter." In *Identities: The Impact of Ethnicity on Canadian Society*, edited by W. W. Isajiw, pp. 46–56. Toronto: Peter Martin Associates.

Lamarand, R. 1977. "Language and culture—role of the school." In *Multiculturalism in Education*, Conference Report, edited by S. V. C. Dubois, pp. 63–80.

Lieberson, S. 1961. "A societal theory of race and ethnic relations." *American Sociological Review* 26, 6 (Dec.): 902–910.

Lupul, M. R., ed. 1978. *Ukrainian Canadians, Multiculturalism and Separatism: An Assessment*. Edmonton: Canadian Institute of Ukrainian Studies.

———— 1983. "Multiculturalism and Canada's white ethnics." *Multiculturalism* 6, 3: 14–18.

Lyman, S. M. 1968. "Contrasts in the community organization of Chinese and Japanese in North America." *Canadian Review of Sociology and Anthropology*, 5, 2 (May): 51–57.

MacLean, H. 1982. *Indians, Inuit and Métis of Canada*. Toronto: Gage.

Marcus, R. L. 1979. *Adaptation: A Case Study of Soviet Jewish Immigrant Children in Toronto, 1970–1978*. Toronto: Permanent Press.

Marques, D. and J. Madeiros. 1980. *Portuguese Immigrants: 25 Years in Canada*. Toronto: West End YMCA.

Marston, W. G. 1969. "Social class segregation within ethnic groups in Toronto." *Canadian Review of Sociology and Anthropology* 6, 2 (May): 65–79.

Maxwell, T. R. 1977. *The Invisible French*. Waterloo, Ont.: Wilfrid Laurier University Press.

Maykovich, M. K. 1971. "The Japanese family in tradition and change." In *The Canadian Family*, edited by K. Ishwaran, pp. 111–125. Toronto: Holt, Rinehart and Winston.

McLean, J. 1970 [1889]. *The Indians, Their Manners and Customs*. Toronto: Wm. Briggs. (Reprint, Coles Canadiana. Toronto: Coles, 1970).

Montero, G. 1977. *The Immigrants*, Toronto: James Lorimer.

Morton, W. L. 1981. "The historical phenomenon of minorities: the Canadian experience." *Canadian Ethnic Studies* 13, 3: 1–39.

Multicultural Programme, Ethnocultural Data Base. 1982. *Mother Tongue Atlas of Metropolitan Toronto*. Toronto: Ontario Ministry of Citizenship and Culture.

Nagata, J. A. 1970. *English Language Training for Women with Preschool Children*. Downsview, Ont.: York University Institute for Behavioural Research, Ethnic Research Programme.

———— 1971. "Adaptation and integration of Greek working class immigrants in Toronto: a situational approach." In *Canada: A Sociological Profile*, edited by W. E. Mann, pp. 58–72. Toronto: Copp Clark. pp. 58–72.

Ng, W. 1982. "Immigrant women: silent partners of the women's movement," In *Still Ain't Satisfied*, edited by M. Fitzgerald et al., pp. 249–256, Toronto: The Women's Press.

Nixon, R. 1984. "The Indians...," *The Toronto Star*, July 14: M1, 10.

Palmer, H. 1977. "History and present state of ethnic studies in Canada." In *Identities: The Impact of Ethnicity on Canadian Society*, edited by W. W. Isajiw, pp. 167–183. Toronto: Peter Martin Associates.

Parsons, T. 1975. "Some theoretical considerations on the nature and trends of change in ethnicity." In *Ethnicity: Theory and Experience*, edited by N. Glazer and D. P. Moynihan, pp. 53–83. Cambridge, Mass.: Harvard University Press.

Peter, K. 1981. "The myth of multiculturalism and other political fables." In *Ethnicity, Power and Politics in Canada*, edited by J. Dahlie and T. Fernando, pp. 56–57. Toronto: Methuen.

Petryshyn, W. R., ed. 1980. *Changing Realties: Social Trends Among Ukrainian Canadians*. Edmonton: Canadian Institute of Ukrainian Studies.

Ponting, J. R. and R. Gibbins. 1980. *Out of Irrelevance*. Toronto: Butterworths.

Porter, J. 1965. *The Vertical Mosaic*. Toronto: University of Toronto Press.

———— 1975. "Ethnic pluralism in Canada," In *Ethnicity: Theory and Experience*, edited by N. Glazer and O. P. Moynihan, pp. 267–304. Cambridge, Mass.: Harvard University Press.

Price, J. A. 1987. "Indian cultural diversity." In *Ethnic Canada*, edited by L. Driedger, pp. 181–197. Toronto: Copp Clark Pitman.

Rayfield, J. R. 1976. "Maria in Markham Street: Italian immigrants and language-learning in Toronto." *Ethnic Groups* 1, 2: 133–150.

Redbird, D. 1980. *We Are Metis*. Toronto: Ontario Métis and Non-Status Indian Association.

Reid, W. S., ed. 1976. *The Scottish Tradition in Canada*. Toronto: McClelland and Stewart.

Reitz, J. G. 1974. "Language and ethnic community survival." *Aspects of Canadian Society, Canadian Review of Sociology and Anthropology* (Special Issue): 104–122.

———— 1980. *Survival of Ethnic Groups*. Toronto: McGraw-Hill Ryerson.

Reitz, J. G., L. Calzavera, and D. Dasko. 1981. *Ethnic Inequality and Segregation in Jobs*, Toronto: University of Toronto Centre for Urban and Community Studies.

Richard, M. 1980. *The Portuguese and West Indians in the Toronto CMA, 1971: A Cultural Profile*. Toronto: University of Toronto course paper.

Richmond, A. H. 1969. "Immigration and pluralism in Canada." *International Migration Review* 5, 4 (Fall): 5–23.

———— 1972. *Ethnic Residential Segregation in Metropolitan Toronto*. Downsview, Ont.: York University Institute for Behavioural Studies, Ethnic Research Programme.

Richmond, A. H. and W. E. Kalbach. 1980 *Factors In The Adjustment of Immigrants and Their Descendants*. Ottawa: Statistics Canada.

Robinson, W. G. 1983. *Illegal Migrants to Canada*. Ottawa: Ministry of Supply and Services Canada.

Rosenberg, S. E. 1971. *The Jewish Community in Canada, Volume 2: In the Midst of Freedom*. Toronto: McClelland and Stewart.

Royal Commission on Bilingualism and Biculturalism. 1970. *Report: Book 4: The Cultural Contribution of the Other Ethnic Groups*. Ottawa: Information Canada.

Rubin, I. 1975. "Ethnicity and cultural pluralism." *Phylon* 36, 2 (June): 140–148.

Sapir, E. 1933. "Language." In *Encyclopedia of the Social Sciences*, Vol. 9, pp. 155–168. New York: Macmillan.

Schermerhorn, R. A. 1970. *Comparative Ethnic Relations*. New York: Random House.

Sturino, F. and J. Zucchi, eds. 1985. *Italians in Ontario*. Theme Issue of *Polyphony* 7, 2 (Fall-Winter).

Swyripa, F. 1978. *Ukrainian Canadians*. Edmonton: Canadian Institute of Ukrainian Studies.

Takata, T. 1983. *Nikkei Legacy*, Toronto: NC Press.

Toronto Planning Board. 1972. *Ethnic Origin Maps of the City of Toronto*. Toronto: Toronto Planning Board.

Tracey, W. R. 1942. *Fertility of the Population of Canada*. 1931 Census of Canada monograph, Vol. 12, Pt. 2.

Troper, H. 1976. "Multiculturalism in the classroom: pitfalls and options." *History and Social Science Teacher* 12, 1 (Fall): 3–7.

Trovato, F. and T. K. Burch. 1980. "Minority group status and fertility in Canada." *Canadian Ethnic Studies* 12, 3: 1–18.

Vallee, F. G., M. Schwartz, and F. Darknell. 1957. "Ethnic assimilation and differentiation in Canada." *Canadian Journal of Economics and Political Science* 27, 4 (Nov.): 540–549.

Van den Berghe, P. L. 1981. *The Ethnic Phenomenon*, New York: Elsevier.

Ward, W. P. 1982. *The Japanese in Canada*. Ottawa: Canadian Historical Society.

Wardhaugh, R. 1983. *Language and Nationhood: The Canadian Experience*. Vancouver: New Star Books.

Weinfeld, M. 1985. "An urban option for Native People." *Policy Options* (March): 10–12.

Weinfeld, M., W. Saffir, and I. Cotler, eds. 1981. *The Canadian Jewish Mosaic*, Toronto: John Wiley.

Winks, R. 1971. *Blacks in Canada: A History*. Montreal: McGill-Queen's University Press.

Woodcock, G. 1970. *Canada and the Canadians*. Toronto: Macmillan.

Ziegler, S. 1977. "The family and international migration: the perceptions of Italian immigrant children." *International Migration Review* 11, 3 (Fall): 326–333.

Zybala, S. 1982. "Problems of survival of the ethnic press in Canada." *Polyphoney* 4, 1 (March): 15–29.

Index

and religious monopoly, 176-81
and segregation, 131-32
Urban societies, post-modern, 5

Vancouver, 46, 283
Vietnamese, immigration rates
    of, to Canada, 69
Visible minorities
  barriers to settlement, 269
  and ethnic-group separation, 8
  and immigration to Canada, 74
  language retention by, 289-90
  religious monopoly among,
      147-48
  urban residential
      concentration of, 137, 139

West Indians
  immigration rates of, to
      Canada, 69
  see also Blacks; Visible
      minorities
Winnipeg, 47, 283
Women
  appearance of chasteness of,
      269
  see also Gender

Ziegler, S., 102